Graphic
Design Basics

Fifth Edition

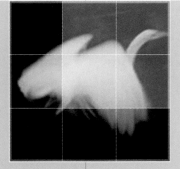

Graphic
Design Basics

Emerita

AMY E. ARNTSON

University of Wisconsin–Whitewater

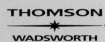

Australia • Brazil • Canada • Mexico • Singapore • Spain • United Kingdom • United States

THOMSON
WADSWORTH

Graphic Design Basics, **Fifth Edition**
Amy E. Arntson

Publisher: Clark Baxter
Acquisitions Editor: John R. Swanson
Assistant Editor: Anne Gittinger
Editorial Assistant: Allison Roper
Technology Project Manager: David Lionetti
Senior Marketing Manager: Mark Orr
Marketing Assistant: Alexandra Tran
Senior Marketing Communications Manager: Stacey Purviance
Senior Project Manager, Editorial Production: Kimberly Adams
Creative Director: Rob Hugel
Executive Art Director: Maria Epes

Print Buyer: Barbara Britton
Permissions Editor: Joohee Lee
Production Service: Lachina Publishing Services
Text Designer: Jerry Wilke
Photo Researcher: Linda Sykes
Copy Editor: Robert Green
Cover Designer: Denise Davidson
Cover Image: Amy E. Arntson and Seth VandeLeest
Cover Printer: C&C Offset Printing Co., Ltd.
Compositor: Lachina Publishing Services
Printer: C&C Offset Printing Co., Ltd.

Printed in China
2 3 4 5 6 7   10 09 08 07

Library of Congress Control Number: 2005938698

Student Edition: ISBN-13: 978-0-495-00693-0
ISBN-10: 0-495-00693-9

Thomson Higher Education
10 Davis Drive
Belmont, CA 94002-3098
USA

For more information about our products, contact us at:
Thomson Learning Academic Resource Center
1-800-423-0563

For permission to use material from this text or product, submit a request online at **http://www.thomsonrights.com**.

Any additional questions about permissions can be submitted by e-mail to **thomsonrights@thomson.com**.

To those special students, friends, and teachers
who make learning a joyful process.

Preface

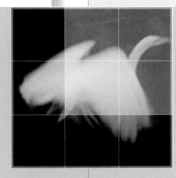

Graphic Design Basics introduces students to an exciting and demanding field. Design is linked tightly to society as it both reflects and helps to shape the world around us. Designers are part of this dynamic, important process. To enter this field requires discipline-specific information, hands-on practice, and an understanding of time-honored principles. The fifth edition of this text continues to weave a concern for design principles with specialized information about applications in the field of graphic design.

Following in the tradition of the previous editions of *Graphic Design Basics*, the fifth edition offers students a comprehensive introduction to the field of graphic design that stresses theory and creative development. This edition includes additional beautiful, full-color visuals that reflect many stylistic directions. The size of the text has been increased to allow for larger images, and the fifth edition offers an increased number of color images. The designs and illustrations are chosen from some of the best work in historical and contemporary design. Although graphic styles are constantly evolving, the structural underpinnings of good design remain constant. Their application leads to successful design solutions.

The tools of the graphic design field are changing quickly, offering opportunities for new complexities of creation and delivery of content. The fifth edition of *Graphic Design Basics* integrates background information about computer graphics throughout the text and provides a guide to generating successful files for electronic prepress. It also interweaves samples of successful Web design throughout the chapters. "Digital Focus" boxes have been added throughout the text to highlight the importance of the computer in graphic design.

The pedagogical features in *Graphic Design Basics* are useful for both students and instructors. Each chapter of the fifth edition begins with "Terminology" and "Key Points" to prepare students to get the most out of the material. The terminology and glossary introduce and explain theoretical and technical terms, while the bibliography opens the door to further discoveries and is helpfully arranged by chapter. The accompanying Web site (**http://art .wadsworth.com/arntson_gdb5e**) includes links for additional exploration as well as free clip art for practice.

Graphic Design Basics introduces both the form and the function of graphic design. It works well for courses in the field of design, as well as related courses dealing with visual communication and advertising. Updated projects and exercises challenge students to internalize the lessons in the text and to learn by doing. Goals and objectives for exercises as well as suggestions for critique help students get the most out of these exercises. Written and oral presentations are emphasized.

Major changes to the body of the text include enlarged sections on graphic design history, computer graphics, and the increased presence of Web design.

Color is introduced earlier in the text. Chapters 1 and 2 present an introduction to the design process and to the field of design history. Chapters 3, 4, and 5 discuss the vital principles of visual percep-

tion, dynamic balance, and gestalt, and how they relate to graphic design.

Chapters 6 and 7 focus on principles and practices of text and layout design in both print and Web applications. Traditional and electronic color are discussed in Chapter 8 with information about the application of color theory on and off the computer. Illustration and photography are presented in Chapter 9, with samples of a wide variety of digital and analog artwork. Chapter 10 gives an overview of the goals, media, and methods of advertising design.

Chapter 11 discusses the process of getting a design successfully into print, with a step-by-step guide for electronic prepress. Chapter 12 gives an overview of preparing files for the Web, and compares the similarities and differences between print and Web design.

Thank you to the following reviewers for their help in preparing this edition: Joyce Drewanz, Anne Arundel Community College; Lynn Damberger, North Central State College; Christopher W. Tompkins, Norfolk State University; Elizabeth Fomin, University of Michigan–Dearborn; Rosanne Gibel, Art Institute of Fort Lauderdale; and James R. Chisholm, North Shore Community College.

Thank you especially to the staff at Thomson Wadsworth and at Lachina Publishing Services for their excellent work.

ABOUT THE AUTHOR

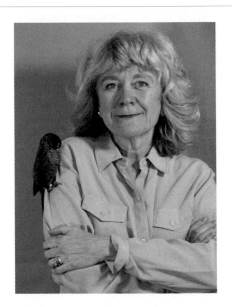

Amy E. Arntson is a Professor Emerita at the University of Wisconsin–Whitewater, where she taught art, design, and computer graphics for over twenty years. Her artwork is exhibited nationally and internationally. Her presentations on the nature of design and perception have been given in Europe, Scandinavia, Central and South America, China, and the United States. Currently a full-time artist, Professor Arntson is also the author of *Digital Design Basics*.

Brief Contents

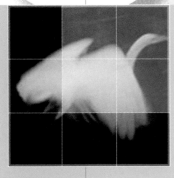

Contents

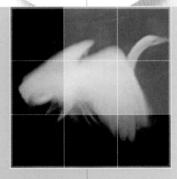

4 Toward a Dynamic Balance 60

5 Good Gestalt 78

XV

Contents

9 Illustration and Photography in Design

TERMINOLOGY

CHAPTER 1

See glossary
for
definitions.

Graphic Design	Web and Multimedia	Comprehensives
Age of Information	Design	Design Studios
Industrial Age	Research	In-House Design
Industrial Design	Thumbnails	Advertising
Environmental Design	Roughs	Agencies

Applying the Art of Design

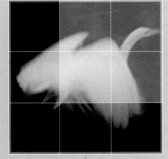

KEY POINTS This chapter defines the field of graphic design and describes its processes. It describes and illustrates the stages in the development of a finished design. Finally, it introduces potential career choices to help you understand the wide parameters of the challenging field you have chosen to study.

PRINCIPLES AND PRACTICES

This book is about applying the *principles* of visual perception to the *practice* of visual communication. The premise is that a course of study in graphic design should begin by applying the principles and theory of basic design. Interwoven with information about how we perceive and shape a two-dimensional surface will be its application to graphic design problems.

Information from one college class is still pertinent in the next. Although you will be learning special information and terminology in this text, you will discover how closely it ties in with the basic theory of design you already know.

Students often believe a class in graphic design or computer graphics is about the hardware and software. That's only a partial truth. The computer is a powerful, complex, exciting tool to be mastered, but the end product is no better than the concept that defines it. The computer is a tool and a partner that aids in the development of your original concept. You are responsible for the research, the concepts, and the visual development related to those concepts.

Problems in graphic design almost always relate to communication. There are methods of making a design hold together as a unit to communicate information. This text discusses them in simple and straightforward language and contains many fine illustrations throughout, from various periods of design history. You will discover how applying basic design theory and principles can enhance visual communication. You will also explore the nature of visual perception, the role of visual illusion, and the contrast between visual and verbal communication, as well as the full range of basic design skills. Each chapter includes a feature on related digital topics.

Visual arts in general, and two-dimensional disciplines in particular, share a common language. The study of shapes on a flat ground has yielded a great deal of information about how we see, understand, and interact with the image on the page. You will learn to apply this universal information to solve graphic design problems.

A designer is not in search of one solution, but of several. There is no one correct answer in graphic design, but a rich set of possibilities. This book presents principles like Gestalt unit-forming, balance, emphasis, and eye direction as tools, not as rules. Use them to increase your options and widen your vision. These methods may become intuitive after a while, but in the beginning you will need to study and consciously apply them. Later, you will learn to interpolate and experiment, combining formal study with a more personal, intuitive approach.

WHAT IS GRAPHIC DESIGN?

Graphic design is traditionally defined as problem solving on a flat, two-dimensional surface. New fields of Web design and multimedia expand the field into 3-D and time-based 4-D applications. New-media designers sometimes refer to themselves as "information architects," referring to the importance of organizational hierarchy. The design field's practitioners are searching for contemporary definitions that reflect and help clarify the field's importance.

The designer conceives, plans, and executes designs that communicate a specific message to a specific audience within given limitations—financial, physical, or psychological. A poster design, for example, may be restricted to two colors for financial reasons. It may be physically restricted in size by the press it will be run on or because of the mailing method. It may be restricted by the standard viewing distance for a poster in a hall or store window, by the size of a Web surfer's screen, or by the age and interests of the group for whom it is intended. Nevertheless, the designer must say something specific to a given audience about a given product or piece of information. Communication is the vital element in graphic design.

It is this element of communication that makes graphic design such an interesting and ever-evolving contemporary field. Designers must present current information to modern taste with up-to-date tools, staying informed about trends, issues, inventions, and developments.

Design education is a lifetime activity. Constant change requires constant renewal.

It is not a career for a slow-paced, nostalgic person. To keep up with this fast-changing field, you must approach the basic principles, new technologies, and practices with a flexible and curious mindset.

Values

Our current society is based on processing information more than producing goods. This is the Age of Information, not the Industrial Age. The Industrial Age was characterized by a population that was divided evenly between agricultural and manufacturing industries. The development of large-scale energy production and metallurgy were the technological innovations.

The Information Age is a term applied to the period where movement of information became faster than physical movement, during the late 20th century (**http://encyclopedia.laborlawtalk.com/20th_century**) and early 21st century. The product itself, the information disseminated, the point of view illustrated, and the mode of communication used, all contribute to shaping the world in this Age of Information.

It is a good idea to ask early in your career (now would not be too soon) how you feel about certain issues. As a designer you will be making career decisions that shape your life and contribute to shaping the character of our society. **Figure 1-1** is an example of design work that helps advertise and support a not-for-profit arts organization.

A successful designer vividly described one of his early career decisions. His first job out of college was as a junior designer at a small advertising firm, where he was put to work designing a hot dog package. After preparing several roughs, he presented them to the client, only to be sent back to the drawing board. Rejected time after time, the designer grew more familiar with hot dogs than he ever wanted to become. He persevered, learned the basics, and now has his own firm specializing in educational and service-oriented accounts. This allows him more creative freedom and work that is consistent with his personal values.

Kazumasa Nagai, a pioneer of contemporary Japanese design, created the design in **Figure 1-2** for the UCLA Asian Performing Arts Institute. His style is recognizable and different from the styles in the United States and other countries. As with the client for the illustration in Figure 1-1, however, the artistic nature of Nagai's client made for an unusual degree of creative options.

Most beginning design jobs do not offer many opportunities for the exercise of creative freedom. The field is a very applied, practical discipline. For the most part, we are designers working in a consumer society. Designers are integrally involved in the production and marketing of consumer goods. However, it is important that we consider our potential impact on society. The major artistic movements of the 20th century each had a theory of society that provided a structure and direction for their

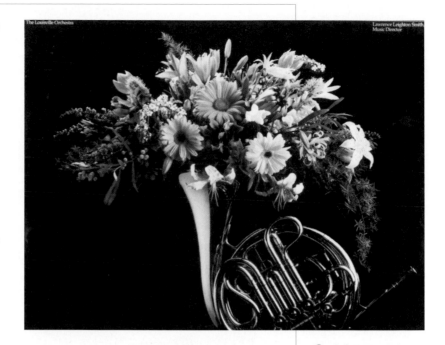

artwork. The futurists, constructivists, dadaists, and surrealists actively helped define their society and their role in relationship to it. As designers, we have a vital role that needs to be continually examined as it shifts and changes in this 21st century.

Creating a design that is appropriate for a given product and its audience may not always give you an opportunity to exercise your own sense of aesthetics. (Laying out a motorcycle products catalog may not provide much of an opportunity to experiment with visual effects.) In addition to directing the visual to a particular audience, the individual client's preferences often also need to be considered. In the face of all the compromises that must be made, keep sight of your own goals and do not become frustrated early in your career. There are many different kinds of jobs in this field, and as a beginning designer, plan on staying at your entry position only until you have mastered skills and gained experience.

Each of us must satisfy our own values in our career path, as well as learn to satisfy the requirements of the workplace. Try asking yourself these questions: Are there products or points of view you do not want to promote? Is there something

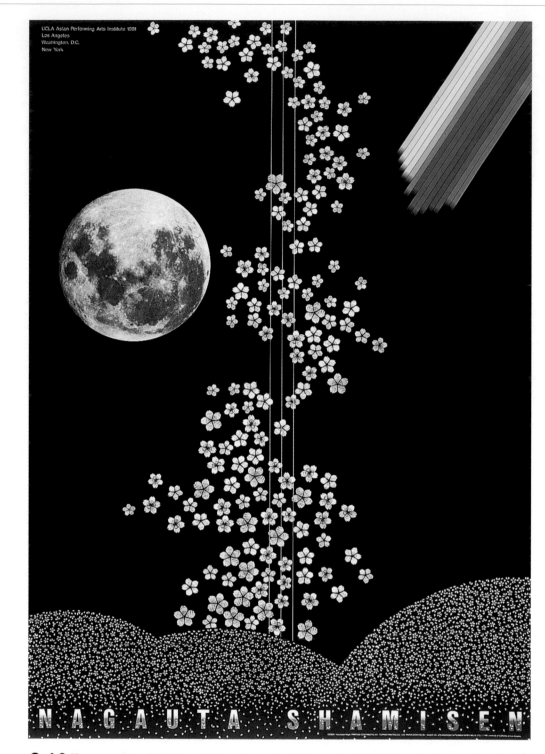

● **1-2** *Kazumasa Nagai. (Nippon Design Center, Inc.). Design for UCLA Asian Performing Arts Institute.*
Courtesy of the artist.

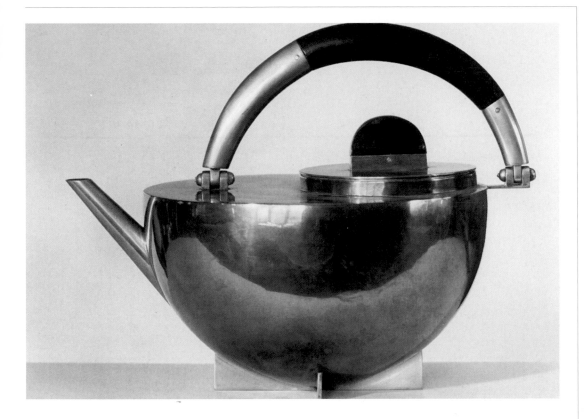

you do want to promote? How important is salary? What will make this career successful for you? What kind of lifestyle do you want for yourself? How hard are you willing to work for it? Where do you want to be in ten years? How will you work to achieve your goals?

Design Fields

The field of applied design includes industrial design, environmental design, graphic design, and Web and multimedia design. *Industrial design* is the design and development of three-dimensional functional objects. **Figure 1-3** shows a strikingly elegant teapot, considered an important landmark in the history of functional design. Machines, tools, kitchen implements, and other products are among the objects shaped by the industrial designer. Package design for these objects is often placed in the category of graphic design because it must be designed and printed flat before assembling. The industrial designer

attempts to simplify the use and manufacture of objects as well as increase their safety and efficiency.

Environmental design is a large general category that includes the design of buildings, landscapes, and interiors. Again, the designer attempts to fashion designs that are safe, efficient, and aesthetic. In the unified, flowing floor plan shown in **Figures 1-4** and **1-5,** curves and angles and varying levels are used as unifying elements.

Graphic design is the design of things people see and read. The field is constantly expanding. Posters, books, signs, billboards, advertisements, commercials, brochures, Web sites, and motion graphics are what graphic designers create. They attempt to maximize both communication and aesthetic quality.

Web and multimedia design are the design of interactive, often motion-based graphics. Multimedia design is information in more than one form. It may include the use of text, audio, graphics, animations, and full-motion video. Graphic designers are

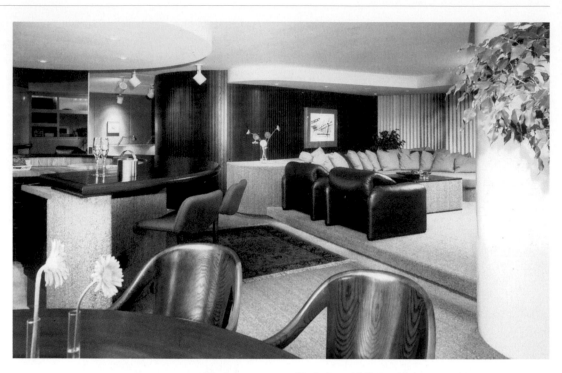

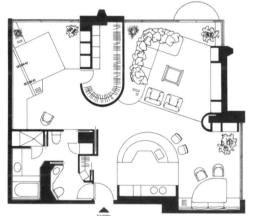

● **1-4** *and* **1-5** *David Saylor. (ASID). Interior and floor plan of the Cohen apartment, Milwaukee.* Photo by Jim Threadgill. 1983.

often expected to have skills in both print and Web design. **Figure 1-6** shows Website pages that use a full range of the visual design skills we will study in future chapters.

Buildings, environments, products, Web sites, and written communications will affect us whether they have been carefully and deliberately designed or not. Design cannot be eliminated. The printed piece will always communicate more than words alone, because it uses a visual language. It may, however, communicate exactly the

opposite of the intended message. It can damage the image of a company or cause. Learning to apply the *theory* of design and information processing to the *practice* of graphic design will help you achieve the intended communication. That is the underlying premise of this text. All information is structured to help with this goal.

Designers must interface with fields other than their own. They need to address the basic marketing concerns of the client, the concerns of colleagues, such as illustrators or photographers, and the requirements of the printing process.

Some graphic designers do a whole range of work—typography, illustration, photography, corporate identity, logo design, and advertising. Others specialize in only one of these areas. Whatever area of design or illustration you pursue, it is best to follow the design process.

Graphic Design Basics

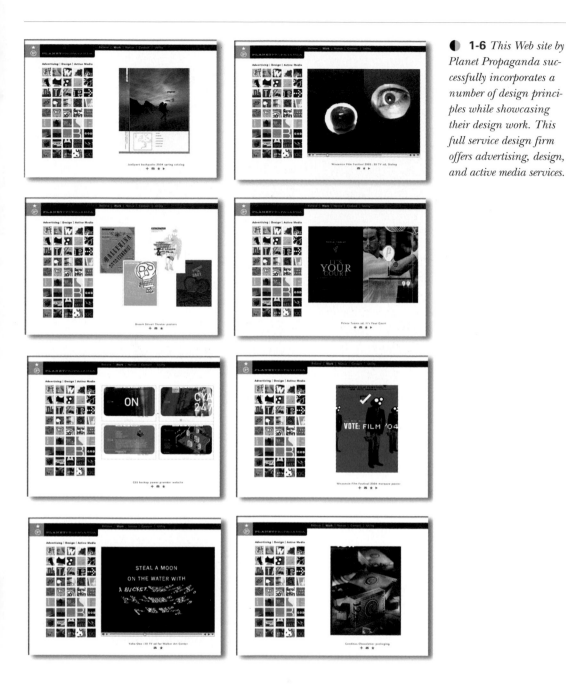

◗ **1-6** *This Web site by Planet Propaganda successfully incorporates a number of design principles while showcasing their design work. This full service design firm offers advertising, design, and active media services.*

THE DESIGN PROCESS

Research

The first step in preparing a design solution is research, determining the parameters of the problem. Who is the audience? What constraints are there in format, budget, and time? What is the goal of the project?

The next step is to gather and study all the related materials. Selling this design to a client (or an instructor) will be easier if it is backed with research and justified from a perspective the client will understand. In the future, you may work in a large firm or agency where most of the research and information gathering is done by marketing professionals. Visual research, however, both then and now, is the designer's area. It's important to know what has been done before and what is being created locally and nationally for this type of design situation. Develop a feeling for contemporary work by studying design annuals, periodicals, and Web sites.

Designers also keep a file of anything that is interesting or well done. A personal file of such samples can be useful to look through for ideas to build upon. Subscribe to graphic design magazines and plan to save all the back issues. Never simply lift another designer's solution; that is unethical. Lifting isolated parts from someone else's work will not give a unified design, and lifting the entire solution will be immediately recognizable as plagiarism. Looking at how someone else solved a particular problem, however, is part of your education. Designers are expected to build on the work of others. We do not create in a vacuum, but are influenced by the hundreds of samples of good and bad design we are all exposed to every day.

Expand your visual vocabulary and plan to use that vocabulary to build new designs. Doing this is similar to an author using a word vocabulary developed over time. An author does not have to create a new alphabet or a new language in order to create an original piece of literature. He or she needs to combine these elements in an original fashion.

As part of the research stage, search for a creative approach to your design problem in as many ways as possible. Build your visual and conceptual vocabulary. Try looking up a dictionary definition of your topic. Look in an encyclopedia for additional background. Search the Internet for information on the topic. Use a thesaurus. Make a word association list of everything you can think of that is associated with your topic. Save personally significant visuals and collectibles. *Approach a design as both prose and poetry.* Be both logical and intuitive.

Thumbnails

A designer needs to explore many alternative solutions. Thumbnails are the second step in the design process. They are idea sketches that provide visual evidence of the thinking, searching, and sorting process that leads to final solutions.

Exercising the mind with thumbnail sketches is like exercising any muscle. The more it is exercised, the more powerful it gets. The more you work to develop ideas through small, preliminary sketches, the richer will be the range of solutions available to choose from for the final design. Never short-cut this stage, because it determines the strength of the final solution. For a student, the thumbnails are more important than the final project, because they demonstrate thinking, experimentation, and growth. Keep these thumbnails. The ideas in them may be of use to you in other projects. Prospective employers may wish to see evidence of the flexibility and tenacity of your thinking (**Figure 1-7**). Tammy Roemer created the computer generated thumbnail experiments in Figure 1-7 for an ice drink logo to be placed in her student portfolio.

Thumbnails are usually small because they are meant to be fast and not detailed. They are around 2 × 3" (5 × 8 cm) and drawn in proportion to the dimensions of the finished piece. Fill a sheet of paper with ideas. The accompanying Web site for this chapter has a blank thumbnail page to fill with concepts. Never reject an idea; just sketch it in and go on. Work through the idea with your pencil or mouse from every perspective you can imagine. Then try taking one good idea and doing several variations on it. If you're using a pencil, tracing paper or lightweight bond is excellent for this purpose. You may also want to cut and paste and recombine existing images for new effects. It may be faster to work at a size determined by existing elements. In that case the thumbnails may become larger or smaller. The principle of "sketching" through ideas holds true no

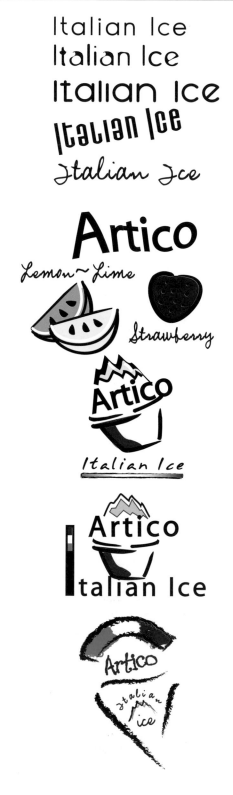

matter what the size or format of your preliminary investigation. Be as neat and precise as is necessary to show the relationship between elements and their general shapes. The stages of thumbnails, roughs, comps, and camera-ready art, however, often blend together when executed on a computer. The danger with this blending is that, although software may help provide quick, workable solutions, it can be tempting to short-cut the planning stages. Thumbnails are often best done by hand. They are vital to good design, in whatever size or stage of polish. They must exhibit flexible, tenacious *visual thinking*. **Figure 1-8** shows how the pen and ink thumbnails for the cover design of this text investigate a variety of approaches.

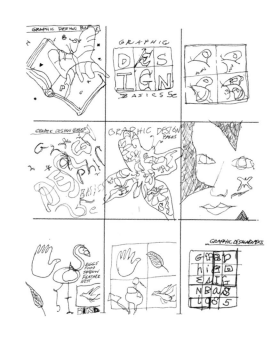

● **1-7** *A series of computer-generated thumbnails by Tammy Roemer investigate type and image combinations for an ice drink logo.*

● **1-8** *Pencil thumbnails created for the cover of this text.*
A. E. Arntson.

Roughs

Once the range of ideas has been fully explored, select the best thumbnails for refinement. You may want to talk this choice over with other designers and with the instructor. Later, as a professional designer, you will present the thumbnails to an art director or the roughs to a client for review. Or you may be the art director who is reviewing someone else's design. Often, considerable redefining and rethinking occur at these stages. The thumbnail process may begin all over again.

On a computer, you may want to do a full-size rough. The purpose is to test whether the original idea works on a larger scale. Take this opportunity to work out small problem areas that you could not deal with or foresee at the thumbnail stage. The type style, the other shapes, the relationship of these elements to the edge of the format, and the color and value distribution can all be refined at this stage. **Figure 1-9** shows the rough designs presented for the cover of this text. The butterfly-dominated proposals were rejected by the publisher because they seemed too close to the InDesign identity.

Comprehensives

The comprehensive, or *comp,* is the fourth step in the design process. It is the piece of art you present to the client for final approval. Although based on the rough, it is much more carefully done. Once again, consult with art directors, editors, or the instructor before choosing the rough idea to refine for your final solution.

The client can judge the design solution from the comp, because it looks much like the finished printed piece. There is no need to explain "what would go there" or how "this would be smoother." A comp is usually computer generated, with all components assembled and exactly positioned. It might include such diverse elements as photographs, computer-generated type, tight electronic illustrations, and a scanned pen-and-ink rendering.

In most projects from this text, the comp will be the final step. These comps will form the basis of your portfolio, which you will continue to develop in future classes (**Figures 1-10** and **1-11** show photographs of three-dimensional comprehensives). In the workplace, the final stage is the printed project. Compare the final printed cover for this text with its thumbnails and roughs, and consider what choices and changes you might have made.

Comps take different forms depending on the media for which they are intended. Television and film ideas are presented as storyboards, with key scenes drawn in simplified and stylized fashion, or as abbreviated animation. The three-dimensional comp for a package design may be presented in multiples in order to demonstrate the stacking display possibilities of the package. A publication such as an annual report or a newsletter is usually represented by the cover and certain key pages in the layout design. A Web site is presented to the client with a flow chart and key pages completed. A rough or a comp can be sent to a client for approval via CD, e-mail, or fax. This streamlines the process and makes the designer's and client's diverse locales a less important consideration.

Presentation

Practice selling the concept verbally before presenting it. Demonstrate that you understand the client's perspective and goals. Discuss your design enthusiastically in terms the client or art director can understand. Be prepared, however, to listen and to compromise. If revisions are called for, note them carefully. In this text, you will often be asked to write a brief presentation that will accompany your visual solution. Class critiques will give you an opportunity to practice your verbal presentation skills and your listening skills.

Ready for Press

Once accepted, the job is now ready for production. The comprehensive shown to

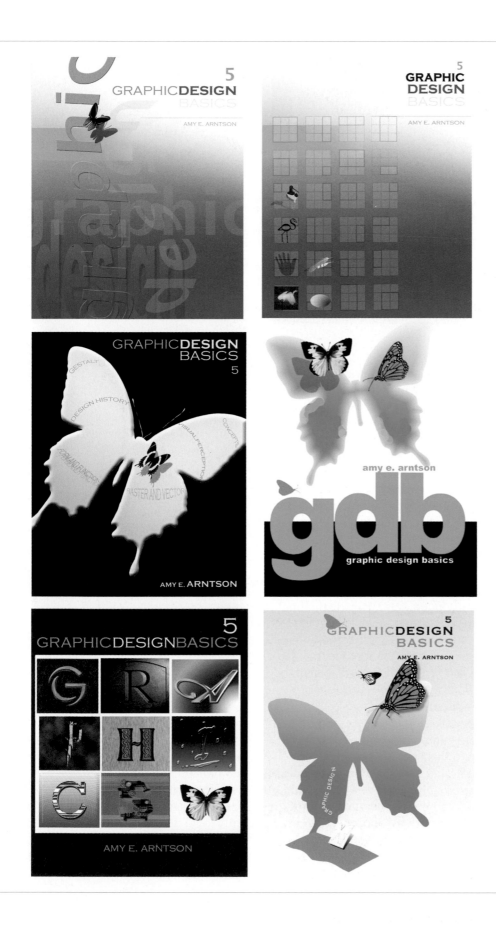

1-9 *Computer-generated rough designs for the cover of this text.* A. E. Arntson.

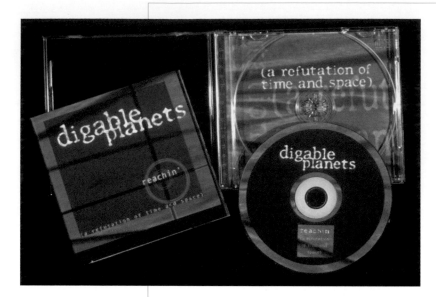

● **1-10** *Jennifer Freson. CD comprehensive. Inkjet prints with folding insert and plastic holder makes this student portfolio piece look very professional.*

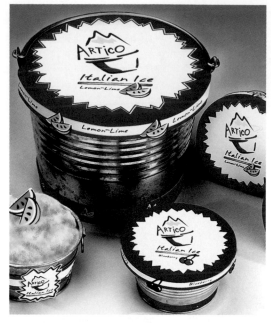

● **1-11** *Tammy Roemer. A three-dimensional comprehensive of the Artico product developed from the thumbnails shown in Figure 1-7.*

the client may look exactly like the finished piece, but it often cannot be used to produce the final printed product. Everything must be sent to the printer ready for press. Printer's inks must be indicated, as well as paper selection.

The file must be cleanly prepared, with all links and fonts included. Electronic files that print well inside a classroom may not "RIP" on an imagesetter (see Chapter 11). The disk or e-mail that contains the file must be carefully prepared.

Base the designs you create on a sound knowledge of the reproduction and printing process introduced later in this text. The first chapters focus on building concepts and understanding design structure, while later chapters discuss the reproduction process. You need to practice building a strong design before focusing on how to reproduce it. Begin your very first project with a respect for precision, accuracy, and cleanliness. There can be no compromise with perfection in this line of work.

Many designers are responsible for selecting and communicating with a printer. Often the work must be bid on by two or three printers, giving each an opportunity to estimate costs. Selecting printing firms to bid for the work is often based on prior experience with the firms. If you are unfamiliar

with a printing firm, ask to see samples of its work, especially samples with production problems similar to those of the new job. Quality in printers, like quality in designers, varies. Finding a good printer and establishing an easy working relationship is important. A good printer can be an excellent reference for answering tricky production questions and suggesting alternate solutions to an expensive design.

CAREERS

A variety of working environments occur in the design field, with varying advantages and limitations. What suits one person may feel like a limitation or undue pressure to another. You will want to have an idea of what the opportunities are before beginning your job search after college. As an entry-level designer, you may only be able to locate a job that gives you "experience." The following categories give an idea of the design positions available.

Design Studios

Clients with *various* needs and backgrounds may seek the assistance of a design studio.

The studio will have designers, production artists, account service representatives, and often illustrators and photographers on staff or on call. Design studios hire freelance creative help when their regular staff is too busy or lacks specific skills to handle a project. Designers working in a studio generally have other artists around to discuss and share ideas. The number of working hours spent on each assignment is logged and the time billed to a client's account or to the studio itself. A high value is placed on an ability to work quickly and with a clear understanding of the client's needs and preferences. Clients consist primarily of various advertising agencies and large and small companies or institutions. The graphic design work prepared for these clients includes brochures, mailers, illustration and photography, catalogs, display materials, Web sites, and promotional videos. Studios vary in size and in their client roster. Small studios with only a couple of designers who have good skills and equipment can provide full-service design. Larger studios can provide room for advancement and a stimulating creative environment.

In-House Design

Many institutions employ their own in-house design staffs. These in-house designers serve the particular needs of institutions ranging from hospitals, banks, newspapers, insurance companies, publishers, and colleges and universities to large and small manufacturing concerns. In-house design organizations vary greatly according to the type of product or service their institution provides.

Designers work on projects that relate to the parent institution's activities. Individual designers may keep track of their hours if the design department bills its time to other departments. Many in-house design operations offer services free to the other departments within the company. Individual designers may work closely with the client or receive all information and instructions funneled through an art director.

An in-house design organization may lack the variety of other artists and the challenge of interpreting and representing various clients that a design studio provides. However, an advantage to working in an in-house operation is the opportunity to get to know one company in depth by developing a relationship with it and its various departments. Oftentimes the deadline pressure is less and the job security better than in a studio. It is sometimes possible to develop a corporate career by moving up within the organization. The growth of computer software has caused a boom in in-house design as more and more companies find it possible to meet many of their publication needs themselves.

Printing Companies

Many positions for designers exist at local printing companies. These companies sometimes have their own in-house design departments or hire graduates to do prepress work. A printing company can be an excellent place to gain valuable experience in the technical aspects of reproduction.

The Advertising Agency

Ideas and sales are the cornerstones of the advertising agency. It is dominated by people who deal in words. Account executives bring in the jobs and develop the advertising concepts with the creative director. The creative director, designer, and copywriter execute the concepts, although the number of people involved and the exact tasks performed vary from agency to agency. Projects cover all forms of print and multimedia advertising, from film and video work to packaging, display, print ads, billboards, and Web sites. A good creative director is versatile. He or she is skilled at conceptualizing and presenting ideas verbally and visually as well as directing others and organizing assignments. More money is spent on advertising than on any other area of graphic design, which is reflected in the salary a designer can expect to earn in this field.

Freelance

Working as a freelance artist allows a maximum amount of freedom, but it calls for certain business-related skills. Personal promotion, networking, and a constant vigilance to find new customers will help establish a freelance career. Good organizational skills in billing and record keeping, along with talent and hard work, keep a freelance business going. Computers, modems, and fax machines make it possible to live outside a metropolitan area and still maintain client contact, once it is established. One of the drawbacks to a freelance career is the lack of company benefits. Health insurance and retirement benefits are not part of the package. It can also be comparatively lonely though creatively fulfilling work.

New Media

Web-site creation calls for design skills with page layout, logo design, scripting, illustration, typography, and animation. Many companies now use the Internet to communicate with prospective clients, and designers play an important part in facilitating this informational and persuasive communication. Motion graphics and interactive and multimedia design are also exciting and rewarding new career directions. Every situation is unique, and this chapter provides only a generalized description of the types of situations in which a designer can find employment. Many, many variations occur within the categories described.

THE CHALLENGE

The challenge of being a graphic designer involves working through the restrictions and demands of the design process. It involves visualizing the completed job, although the actual finished product will not be done by hand. It may be completed on a press with printer's paper and inks, with elements that may have been photographed or drawn by other artists, and with copy written by others. Or it may be shown on a Web site or via another electronic mode of presentation. It involves meeting *personal* design standards as well as the needs of the client and the audience. It calls for organization and self-discipline to meet the constant deadline pressure. In the classroom, students generally get one project at a time and a generous length of time to complete it. The emphasis in school is on learning. On the job, however, designers work on several projects at once and must uphold design standards while concentrating on time and money issues. A good education in design fundamentals that stresses theory and creative development as well as production techniques is important in this environment. Designers must constantly update their education and stay current with new technologies. Technology has made major changes in the design field in recent years, and greater changes are on the way (see Chapter 2).

Digital Focus

Graphic designers work at an array of jobs, using a variety of software to prepare their files. Opinions differ on how best to prepare a student for this field. Some academic programs separate their software instruction from their classes in graphic design concepts but teach them concurrently. Other programs begin the first classes with non-digital techniques, intending to build strong design skills through concentrating on principles before spending time on software rendering skills. Some programs integrate the two from the beginning, in all classes, believing they are best and most efficiently learned together. Whichever approach your program takes, by the time you graduate, you'll need a command of both graphic design principles and concepts and the related digital techniques.

Your final challenge is to take a responsible stance in the world. Traditionally, it has been the fine artist who has set new visual trends and opened fresh creative ways to see ourselves. The designer now also plays this role (see **Figure 1-12** by well-established designer McRay Magleby). One of the issues facing contemporary design is the impact of our printed product on the environment. Recycled paper products are part of an attempt to lessen the negative impact of printed materials on the environment. Online graphics are also helping. The aesthetic qualities of design affect our lives in many ways, but the total effect of a design solution has numerous varied and important impacts on our lives. As designers, we are continually in the process of redefining our field. We need to examine how our culture and others function, and how our perceptions and our values shape, and are shaped by, the world around us. **Figure 1-13**, by freelance illustrator Diane Fenster, examines our various perceptions.

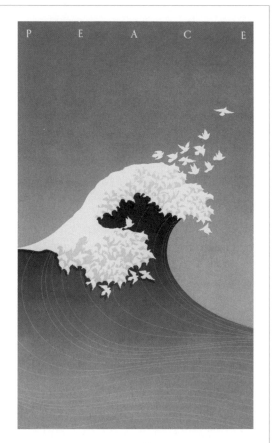

◗ **1-12** *McRay Magleby.* Wave of Peace *poster design.* Courtesy of the artist.

◗ **1-13** *Diane Fenster.* LookListen. *Fenster was the first artist to be inducted into the Adobe Photoshop Hall of Fame, in September 2001.* Courtesy of the artist.

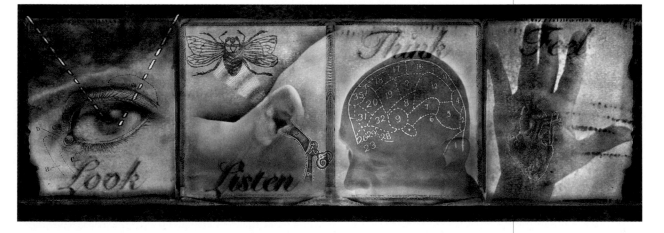

EXERCISE

Research the types of employment opportunities in your geographic area. Find samples of a design firm, an in-house facility, and an advertising agency. Arrange a field trip to one of each. If no such opportunities exist in your area, do the research on the Internet. Write a brief report, sharing the information with your classmates.

TERMINOLOGY

CHAPTER 2

See glossary
for
definitions.

Industrial Revolution	Futurism	Swiss Design
Art Nouveau	Dada	International
Arts and Crafts	Photomontage	Typographic Style
Movement	Suprematism	Art Deco
Cubism	Constructivism	Surrealism
Expressionism	de Stijl	Modernism
Fauvism	Bauhaus	Postmodernism
Gestalt	New Typography	Computer Graphics

Graphic Design History

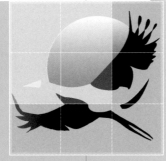

KEY POINTS For a graphic designer, the movement of ideas is as important as changes in style. In fact, they are closely related. Design is affected by the fine arts as well as by scientists, psychologists, and the development of new technologies. The study of design history is a relatively new discipline, but it can provide inspiration and insight into the future of design. This chapter's overview shows how design developed both as an art form and as a reflection of society. The history of art and design provides a great deal of inspiration to contemporary designers.

THE BEGINNING

The birth of graphic design can be traced back 30,000 years to cave painting or about 550 years to Gutenberg's invention of movable type. Whatever the origin, the explosive development during the last decade of the 19th century is a good beginning point for study. Fine art and design often inspire one another.

The Industrial Revolution brought about new attitudes and inventions, both of which contributed to the sudden growth of graphic design. It was a period of rapid industrial growth, when machines and large-scale production replaced hand tools. It began in the mid- to late 1700s in England and spread to other countries in the 1800s. During this period, lasting in the United States and Europe through most of the 1800s, nations shifted from an agricultural to a manufacturing base. A spirit of innovation and progress gave rise to a new interest in providing information to an entire culture rather than only to an affluent elite. The growth of population centers, industry, and a money-based economy all increased the need for the dissemination of information. Advertising flourished during this exciting time, and great strides were made in printing. The first photographic metal engraving was invented in 1824; the first halftone screen was made in 1852. A halftone screen is a pattern of dots of different sizes used to simulate and print a continuous-tone image in color or black and white. Color process work was first successfully printed in 1893. The first automated steam press for lithography was designed around 1868, and the first offset press in 1906.

Advancement in stone lithography color prints in the 1880s encouraged artists to work directly on the stone for multiple reproductions of large-scale posters. They were freed from the stiff, geometric confines of the letterpress. Stone lithography involves drawing the image on a stone by using a greasy black lithographic pencil. Plates are made for each color. The resulting burst of sensual and decorative images in the advertising posters of the time is classified as *art nouveau*. The movement began in France, and the names most closely associated with its development are the Frenchmen Jules Chéret (**Figure 2-1**) and Henri de Toulouse-Lautrec (**Figure 2-2**) and the Czech Alphonse Mucha (Figure 9-19).

Toulouse-Lautrec was primarily a painter and printmaker who produced only about 32 posters as well as music and book jacket designs. Mucha designed furniture, carpets, jewelry, and posters for the famous actress Sarah Bernhardt. Jules Chéret is now called the father of the modern poster. He produced over a thousand posters, some of them close to seven feet

⬤ **2-1** *Jules Chéret.* Pastilles Poncelet. *1895. Color lithograph, 213.8 × 149.16" (54 × 36.8 cm). Milwaukee Art Museum Collection, gift of Mr. and Mrs. Richard E. Vogt.*

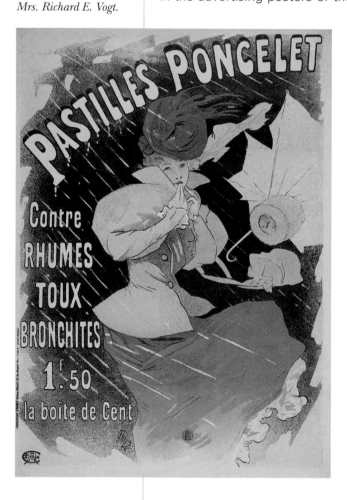

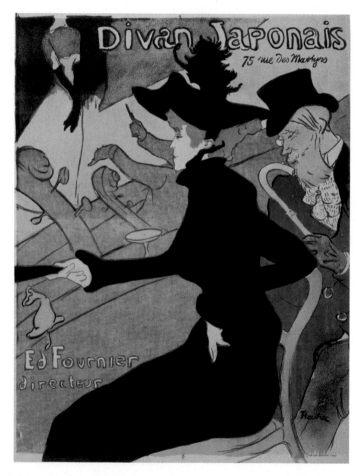

⬤ **2-2** *Henri de Toulouse-Lautrec.* Divan Japonais (Japanese Settee). *1893. Lithograph, printed in color, composition: 315.8 × 237.8" (80.3 × 60.7 cm). The Museum of Modern Art, New York. Abby Aldrich Rockefeller Fund.*

Photograph © 2001 The Museum of Modern Art, New York/Art Resource, NY.

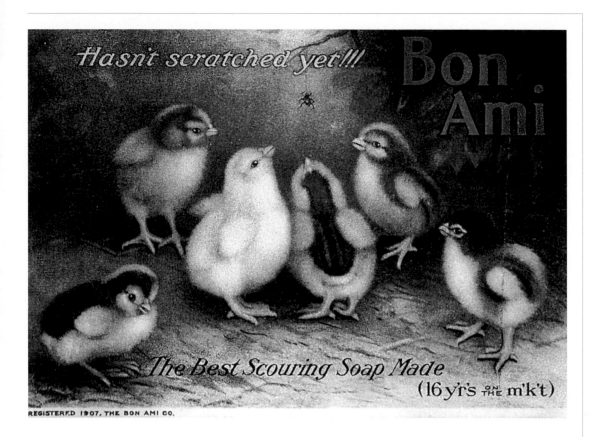

tall. This size was achieved by joining sections mounted on walls. Posters brought art out of the galleries and into the streets and homes of the working class. Art nouveau became an international style that spanned the period from 1890 to 1910. Its organic, decorative quality stressed the invention of original forms that were often inspired by nature. These forms and shapes were applied not only to graphic design but also to product design and crafts. Its influence has lasted much longer than the official dates for the period.

All of the functional arts grew during this time. In the United States, Louis Tiffany created stained glass windows, lamps, and glassware. The illustrations in **Figures 2-3** and **2-4** show early advertising design in the United States flourishing in the form of trade cards. Scottish archi-

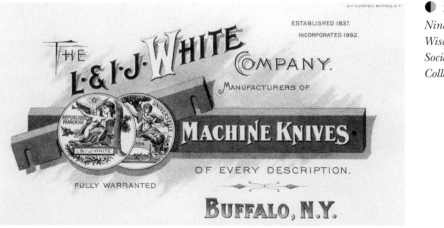

tect, designer, and watercolorist Charles Rennie Mackintosh, his wife, Margaret Macdonald, and her sister Frances Macdonald developed furniture and cutlery designs as well as interior and graphic design that celebrated the organic forms of nature (**Figure 2-5**).

An English artist whose work is an important example of art nouveau style is Aubrey Beardsley. A curving, sensual line and a compelling tension between the figure and background (**Figure 2-6**) characterize his illustrations for Oscar Wilde's *Salome* and other books. A prolific artist with an enduring reputation, Beardsley died at age 26.

Among the many North American art nouveau artists is Maxfield Parrish, an illustrator for *Harper's* and *Life* magazines as well as many other clients (**Figure 2-7**). Parrish worked as an illustrator for the first three decades of the 20th century, creating book, magazine, and advertising illustrations inspired by art nouveau. The legacy of art nouveau is not only its stylistic surface treatments (**Figure 2-8**) but also its concern with the interrelationship of materials, processes, and philosophy.

Not all reactions to the Industrial Revolution embraced progress. William Morris founded the Kelmscott Press in 1890 against what he regarded as the mass-produced, inferior, inhuman product of the machine. Styles of past eras were being copied in art schools and factories with an emphasis on quantity over quality. He and the writer-philosopher John Ruskin wished to renew an appreciation for handcrafted,

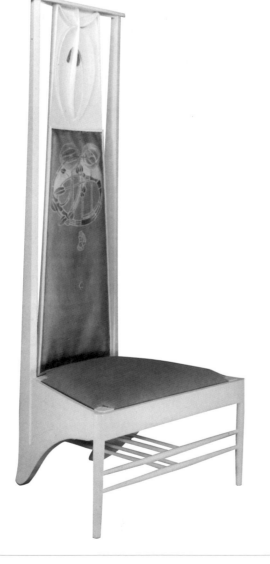

● **2-5** *C. R. Mackintosh.* *Chair designed for the Rose Boudoir, Scottish Section, International Exhibition of Modern Decorative Art, Turin, 1902. The Hunterian Museum and Art Gallery, University of Glasgow.*

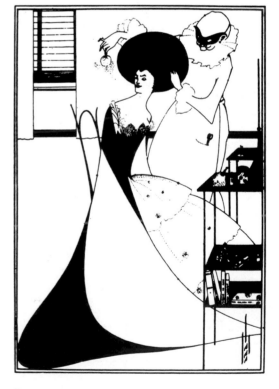

● **2-6** *Aubrey Beardsley.* *Pen-and-ink drawing for an illustration in* Salome. *1894. 813.16 × 65.16" (22 × 17 cm). The British Museum.*

unique, labor-intensive products. Morris worked in many different media, including fabric, rugs, wallpaper, furniture, and typography. Thanks to Morris, the common person's home and furnishings became worthy of an artist's design. His highly stylized hand-printed books and hand-woven tapestries are wonderful examples of English art nouveau. Morris was a key figure in the English arts and crafts movement. This movement originated in England around the middle of the 19th century and its influence spread to continental Europe and the United States. It rejected the heavy ornamentation of the Victorian style in favor of good craftsmanship and clean design. An intensely romantic idealist, Morris was deeply concerned with the ethics of art. He equated bad design with a faulty ethical system. He is credited, along with the Bauhaus, with bringing about a renewal of

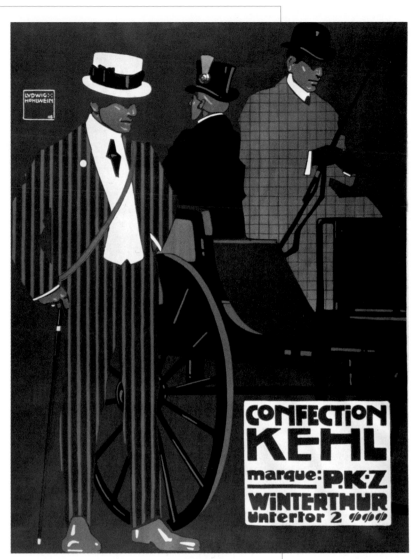

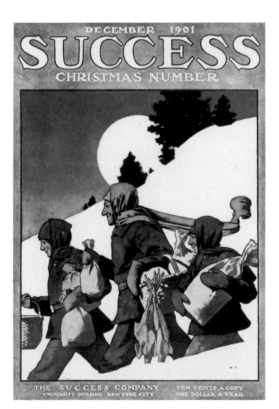

● *2-7 Maxfield Parrish. Cover illustration for* Success *magazine. December 1901. Rare Book and Manuscript Library, Columbia University.*

the standards of craftsmanship (**Figure 2-9**). His work was an inspiration to European modernists who, in turn, greatly influenced American art of the 20th century.

THE TURN OF THE CENTURY

The turn of the 20th century brought fundamental changes in our understanding of the world. In 1905 Albert Einstein made public his theory of relativity and altered our ideas of space and time. They became interrelated variables instead of isolated absolutes. After Sigmund Freud published *The Interpretation of Dreams* in 1909, dreams were no longer considered simply

● *2-8 Ludwig Holwein. Confection Kehl, Marque: PKZ, Winterthur Untertor 2. 1908. Lithograph, printed in color, 481.2 × 361.8" (123.2 × 91.7 cm). The Museum of Modern Art, New York. Gift of Peter Muller-Munk.*

Photograph © 2001 The Museum of Modern Art, New York/Art Resource, NY.

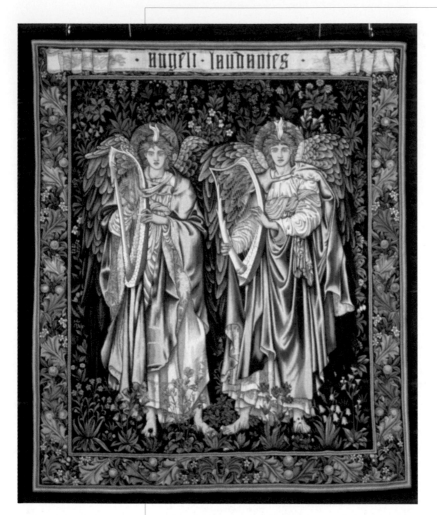

lifestyles, beliefs, and perceptions. This communications explosion continues to be one of the most important influences on society today. As designers we play an important part in its development. Art and design reflect society *and* help shape it.

In 1907 Pablo Picasso completed his painting *Les Demoiselles d'Avignon* (**Figure 2-10**). Pointing the way to cubism, it emphasized the flat surface of the canvas and resembled the symbolic, patterned figures of African art. The relationship between the figures and the picture plane itself was ambiguous. As cubism developed, shapes became increasingly abstracted, showing objects from multiple points of view, with transparent overlapping. Such shapes denied an absolute, inviolate place in space for any single object. In these respects, cubism influenced the subsequent development of 20th-century design. Nature was no longer the only form of reality to depict. The human mind itself played a part in structuring reality, and subjectivity ruled over absolutes. The cubist practice of integrating letterforms into paintings influenced the typography of subsequent art and design movements.

In Germany, Friedrich Nietzsche and the nihilist rebellion contributed to the expressionist movement, which appeared around 1905. The nihilists championed the independence of the individual, questioning the validity of all forms of preconceived ideas and social norms. The expressionist movement aspired to show subjective emotions and responses rather than objective reality. The idea that art is primarily self-expression led to a dramatic non-naturalistic art, typified by Oskar Kokoschka and Ernst Kirchner (**Figure 2-11**).

In Paris in 1905 the first exhibition of a group of artists who would be called "les fauves" ("the wild beasts") was held. Led by Henri Matisse and similar in look to expressionism, with its open disregard of the forms of nature, fauvism favored wildly expressive, subjective, and non-local colors. Fauvism ended around 1908, while

fantastic, clearly divided from reality. Sexuality also was no longer safely reserved for the bedroom but appeared in various symbols in everyday life. The accepted boundaries of reality began to shift. See the accompanying Web site for links that explore these ideas.

The philosophy of existentialism further undermined faith in absolutes by suggesting that there is no single correct answer or moral action. Instead we are individually responsible for shaping meaning. This philosophy argues that humans define themselves by the choices and actions they freely and consciously make. Subjectivity rules over absolutes.

Meanwhile, travel and the growth of a communications network made it possible for us to hear of cultures with different expressionism ended around 1920. Neo-expressionism, influenced by the expressionists and the fauves, shows up today in contemporary illustration. The concept of local color versus arbitrary color continues to contribute to contemporary art and design.

In 1890 the German psychologist Christian von Ehrenfels published an essay called "On Gestalt Qualities." In it he proposed that the *Gestalt* (total entity) is larger than the sum of its parts. Ehrenfels suggested that the parts interact to form a new whole. Our perception of an object is influenced by the arrangement of objects around it. This work pointed the way to another new idea. Reality could be seen as dependent on context rather than as absolute. This is an important part of our contemporary understanding of design and visual perception.

In 1910 at the Frankfurt Institute of Psychology, Max Wertheimer, an admirer of Ehrenfels, began research on apparent movement, which is the basis for the motion picture. He asked why we perceive some images as belonging together and others as not. He arrived at the Gestalt principle of unit forming, which describes how we organize and interpret patterns from our environment. Simply put, things that are similar will be perceptually grouped together. (For a more detailed description of unit-forming factors, see Chapter 5.) Wolfgang Köhler and Kurt Koffka carried on Wertheimer's investigations, and later Rudolf Arnheim applied these principles to art and visual perception throughout much of the 20th century. See the accompanying Web site for links to investigate these ideas.

Germany also gave birth to Peter Behrens, a pictorial and graphic artist who moved into architecture. He was an artist of the Deutsche Werkbund, founded in 1907. Inspired by William Morris and the English arts and crafts movement, the Werkbund artists believed in examining the moral questions inherent in art and

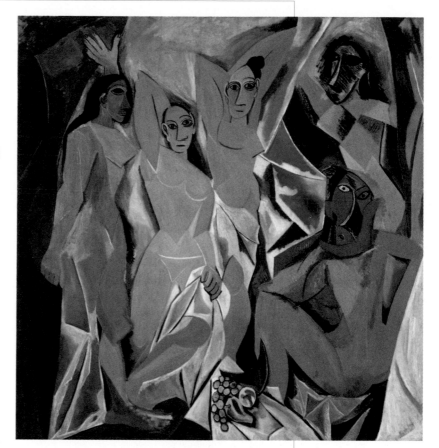

● **2-10** *Pablo Picasso.* Les Demoiselles d'Avignon. *Paris. June–July 1907. Oil on canvas. 8′ × 7′8″ (243.9 × 233.7 cm). The Museum of Modern Art, New York. Acquired through the Lillie P. Bliss Bequest.* Photograph © 2001 The Museum of Modern Art, New York/Art Resource, NY.

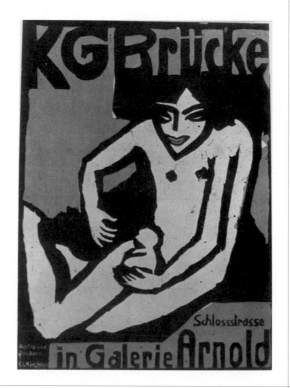

◑ **2-11** *Ernst Kirchner. Cover for catalog of K. G. Brücke exhibition. 1905–1907. 32.7 × 31.9″ (83 × 81 cm). Collection Kaiser Wilhelm Museum.*

25

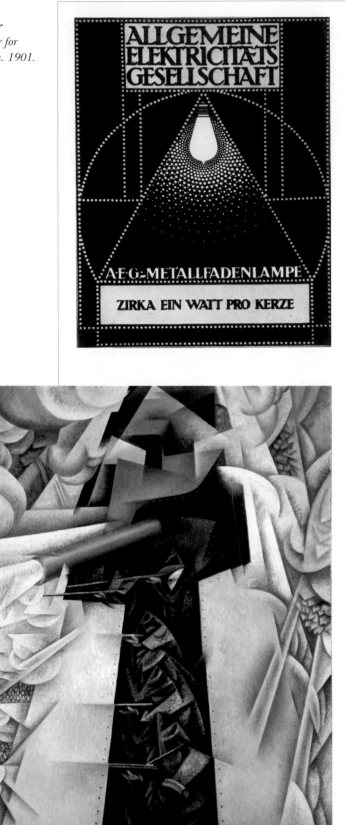

2-12 *Peter Behrens. Poster for AEG lightbulbs. 1901.*

in preventing commercial and industrial abuse. Behrens received the first corporate identity job in the history of design. AEG, a large German corporation, asked him to design everything from its architecture to its advertising and products (**Figure 2-12**). Behrens taught Walter Gropius, who would later become famous as a leader of the Bauhaus, which we will discuss soon.

MODERNISM

The development of the European modernist era spanned roughly 1908 to 1933, from the early days of cubism until Hitler's rise. Modernism encompassed fine art, graphic design, and architecture through various movements, including cubism, futurism, Plakatstil, suprematism, Dada, de Stijl, the Bauhaus, and constructivism. Many artists and designers fit into multiple categories.

The years before World War I brought new movements that continued to expand our notion of reality. *Futurism* showed time itself on canvas by capturing motion through multiple images. The movement was established around 1909 by the Italian poet Emilio Marinetti and developed by artists such as Giacomo Balla, Gino Severini, and artist-designer E. McKnight Kauffer, who spent much of his career as an illustrator. The futurist artists were so named for their optimistic belief that the machines of the Industrial Age would lead to a better future. Ironically and sadly, many artists of the movement were killed in World War I (**Figure 2-13**). Futurism's influence, however, continued. Motion pictures were popular by 1910. They widened our visual reality, creating images that moved

2-13 *Gino Severini.* Armored Train in Action. (Train blindé en action). *1915. Oil on canvas. 455.8 × 347.8″ (115.8 × 88.5 cm). The Museum of Modern Art, New York. Gift of Richard S. Zeisler.* Photograph © 2001 The Museum of Modern Art, New York/Art Resource, NY.

through time, as the futurists hoped their paintings would do.

Plakatstil, a flat-color pictorial design style that maintained a balance between 2-D design structure and imagery, emerged in Germany early in the 20th century. Lucian Bernhard created a compelling series of advertising posters using imagery made from flat colors with an emphasis on shape, combined with the product name (**Figure 2-14**).

Around this same time, another movement surfaced that would strongly influence graphic design. *Dada* was founded in 1916 by a group of poets, chief of whom was the Romanian-born Tristan Tzara. Its name, like the movement itself, had no meaning, according to the Dadaists. The following poem is by Tzara:

> Colonial syllogism
> No one can escape from destiny
> No one can escape from DADA
> Only DADA can enable you to escape
>   from destiny.
> You owe me: 943.50 francs.
> No more drunkards!
> No more aeroplanes!
> No more vigor!
> No more urinary passages!
> No more enigmas!

The Dadaists were extremely important in 20th-century art and philosophy because they questioned meaning itself with an assault on all accepted values and conventional behavior. Marcel Duchamp exhibited such things as bicycle wheels, urinals, and bottle racks, challenging the criteria by which we define something as art. He stated, "I was interested in ideas—not merely in visual products. I wanted to put painting again at the service of the mind." The Dada poet Guillaume Apollinaire created a series of "Calligrammes" around 1918 that seemed to break every known rule of typography. One of the many Dada publications, *Der Dada,* introduced photomontage. It was characterized by an intentional disorder. Letters of all types and sizes, various languages, and dictionary illustrations mingled (**Figures 2-15** and

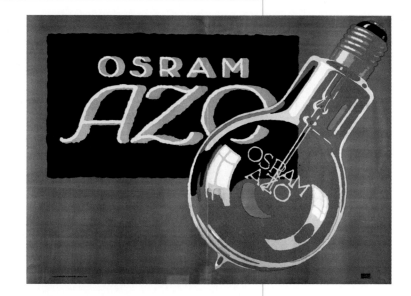

2-16). Figurative photographic images were treated with the same freedom from conventions. With "rayographs" or photograms and techniques such as solarization, Man Ray made an important contribution to graphic design in the form of photomontage.

Hannah Höch and John Heartfield (Figure 5-4) were also important photomontage artists, creating rich, unexpected visual effects. Both Höch and Heartfield made anti-Hitler images that spoke without words about political realities. Kurt Schwitters, another Dada artist, combined

⬤ **2-14** *Lucian Bernhard (Emil Kahn).* Osram AZO. *c. 1910. Lithograph, printed in color, 175.8 × 373.8" (44.7 × 95.9 cm). The Museum of Modern Art, New York. Purchase Fund.*

Photograph © 2001 The Museum of Modern Art, New York/Art Resource, NY.

⬤ **2-15, 2-16** Der Dada *covers. 1920. Collection, The Art Institute of Chicago. Mary Reynolds Collection.*

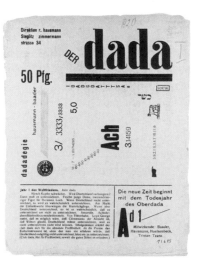

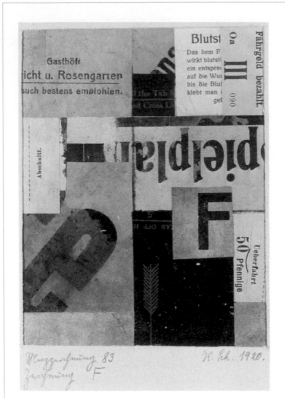

cubism with Dada for a series of collages that remain a rich visual resource for artists today (**Figure 2-17**).

ABSTRACT MOVEMENTS

The first totally abstract poster is attributed to Henry van de Velde in 1897 (**Figure 2-18**). A Belgian art nouveau artist, he moved to Germany in 1906 to teach and became interested in architecture and a more structural approach to art. An architect, designer, educator, and painter, his ideas contributed to the later development of the Bauhaus movement. Van de Velde's work is regarded as a precursor to 20th-century abstract painting. His only poster was for Tropon, a concentrated food product. In his writing he called for a new art that would integrate the best of the decorative and the applied arts of the past.

The first abstract painting is attributed to Wassily Kandinsky. He and others were working in an abstract fashion by 1911

(**Figure 2-19**). Such paintings, in Kandinsky's words, issued from "inner necessity." For Kandinsky a painting was above all "spiritual," an attempt to render insights and awareness transcending obviously descriptive realism. Author of *On the Spiritual in Art,* he joined the Weimar Bauhaus around 1920.

In 1913 the Russian Kazimir Malevich began painting abstract geometric compositions.

Malevich formulated a theoretical basis for his paintings, which he called *suprematism.* He viewed them as the last chapter in easel painting that would point to a universal system of art headed by architecture. This architectonic approach led the way to constructivism, a movement that saw painting as a structurally driven construction, like architecture.

Constructivism began as a Soviet youth movement. The Russian Revolution of 1917

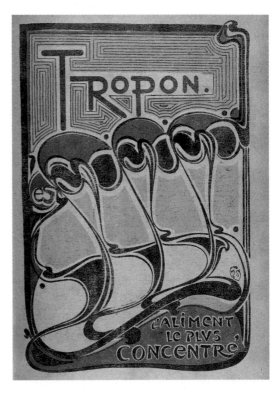

● **2-18** *Henry van de Velde.* Tropon. *1897. Poster, 133.4 × 105.8" (35 × 27 cm).*
Bridgeman Art Library.

Graphic Design Basics

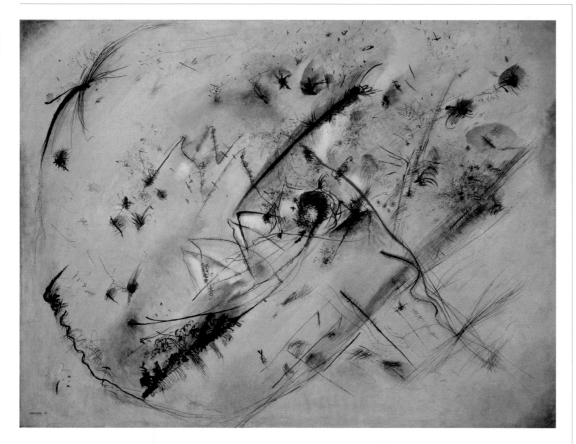

involved many Russian artists, who combined political propaganda and commercial advertising in support of the new state enterprises and revolutionary change. Civic-minded artists designed posters and packaging intended to attract buyers to state products. Advertising became a means for artists, poets, and others to advance the goals of Soviet society. Kasimir Malevich, Aleksandr Rodchenko, and others were abstract painters whose goal to directly reach viewers' consciousness adapted readily to advertising propaganda for the good of Soviet society. The state enterprises flourished with the support of painters turned graphic designers (**Figure 2-20**). Rodchenko worked in a variety of media, including filmmaking and set and costume design for film and theater. He designed posters for several films by using photo collage.

El Lissitzky was a Russian constructivist and designer who devoted a great deal of effort to propaganda work. He also

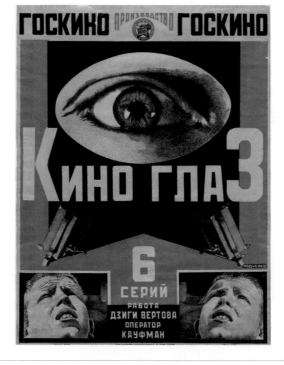

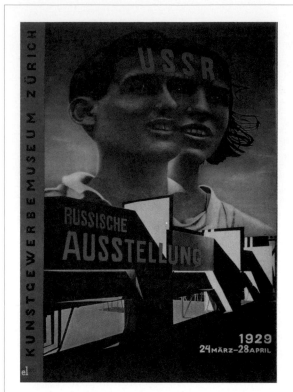

developed the rules of typography and design that laid the groundwork for the development of grid systems. Designing a book of Vladimir Mayakovski's poetry, he wrote, "My pages relate to poetry in a way similar to a piano accompanying a violin. As thought and sound form a united imagination for the poet, namely poetry, so I have wanted to create a unity equivalent to poetry and typographical elements" (**Figure 2-21**). Lissitzky experimented with the photogram and foresaw the importance photography would come to have in graphic design. This innovative thinking and design work spread its vision to other countries. In Germany, Lissitzky and the Bauhaus influenced advertising and packaging design. The contemporary designer Paula Scher uses the strong constructivist approach of Lissitzky's layouts to create a modern design that deliberately mirrors this movement (**Figure 2-22**).

Closely related to constructivism, *de Stijl* developed in Holland, where artists

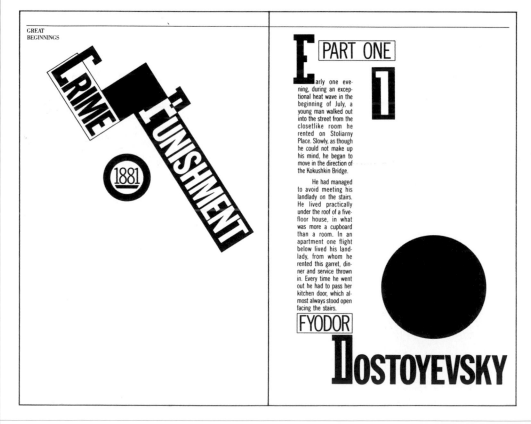

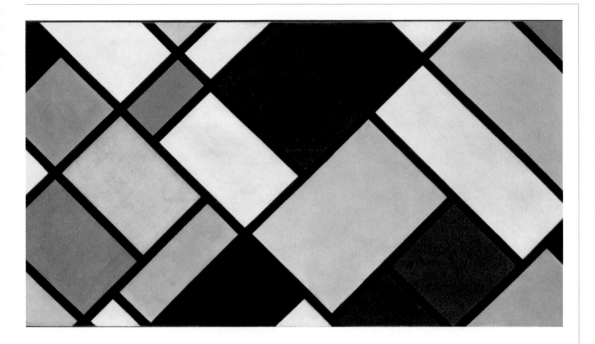

● **2-23** *Theo van Doesburg.* Kontra-Komposition mit Dissonanzen XVI. *1925. Oil on canvas, 391.2 × 71" (100 × 180 cm). Haags Gemeentemuseum, Den Haag-Bridgeman Art Library.*

Copyright 1997 Artists Rights Society (ARS), New York/Beeldrecht, Amsterdam.

fled to avoid direct involvement in World War I (**Figure 2-23**). It flourished during the 1920s in Europe and strongly influenced the later Bauhaus work. De Stijl was anti-emotion and based on a utopian concept of style. At first glance, it may look similar to the Bauhaus movement described later, but de Stijl was more concerned with formal aesthetic problems than with function. The most widely known painters of the period are Piet Mondrian and Theo van Doesburg. Their style is the epitome of de Stijl, with straight black lines set at right angles to one another and a careful asymmetrical balancing of primary colors. **Figure 2-24** shows an armchair by Gerrit Rietveld, a leader of the movement. His design is reduced to its basic components of line, planes, and color. These de Stijl artists strongly influenced graphic design.

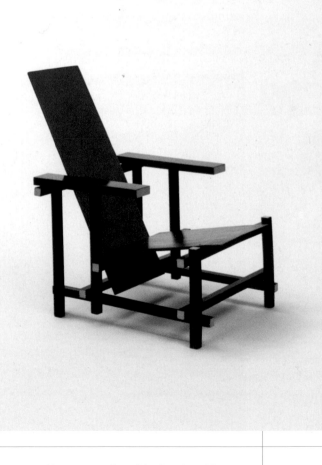

● **2-24** *Gerrit Rietveld,* Red and Blue Chair. *c.1918. Wood, painted, height, 341.8"; width, 26"; depth, 261.2" (86.5 × 66 × 83.8 cm); seat height: 13" (33 cm). The Museum of Modern Art, New York, Gift of Philip Johnson.*

Photograph © 2001 The Museum of Modern Art, New York/Art Resource, NY, copyright 2005 Artists Rights Society (ARS), NY.

The School of Applied Arts and Crafts, founded by Henry van de Velde in 1906, closed at the outbreak of World War I and reopened as the *Bauhaus* at Weimar, Germany, in 1919. Walter Gropius, who worked with Peter Behrens at the Deutsche Werkbund, became the Bauhaus director. In 1922 the constructivist El Lissitzky met with Theo van Doesburg and László Moholy-Nagy in a congress of constructivists and Dadaists in Germany. Their exchange of ideas formed a core for the Bauhaus after 1923. This German design school shaped 20th-century graphic design, product design, furniture, and architecture.

Expressionism, Dada, constructivism, and de Stijl influenced the Bauhaus in its early years. By the late 1920s, the Bauhaus was emphasizing functional graphic design. The Bauhaus trained artists in all areas. It attempted to bridge the gap between pure and applied art, to place equal importance on all areas of arts and crafts. It stressed clean, functional forms. Its weavers, metalsmiths, and carpenters did not attempt to produce works of art, but rather, good and useful designs in which form was tied to function. The industrial designer was born from this movement. Bauhaus publications featured asymmetry, a rectangular grid structure, and sans-serif type.

The contributions by artists of the Bauhaus have been vastly important and continue to exert a strong influence in contemporary design. See the accompanying Web site for links to investigate. Here are a few Bauhaus artists who were influential in the development of graphic design. Josef Albers is known for his research into color and structural relationships (**Figure 2-25**). His wife, Anni Albers, was a gifted fiber artist (**Figure 2-26**). László Moholy-Nagy developed photography as illustration. He saw the camera as a design tool that could be integrated with typography to create a new and better communication.

Herbert Bayer created several typeface designs, including Universal (**Figure 2-27**). In keeping with the Bauhaus philosophy, he believed in removing personal values from the printed page, leaving it purely logical and functional in design (**Figure 2-28**). Bayer typically avoided using capital

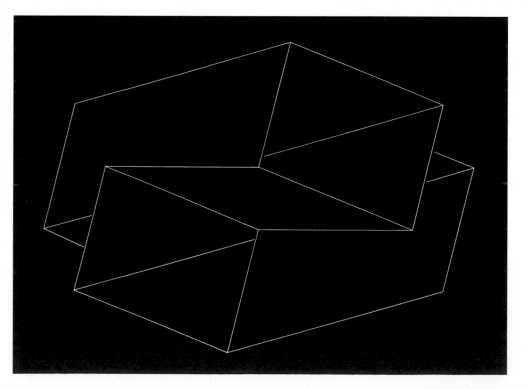

● **2-25** *Josef Albers.* Structural Constellation NN-1. *1962. Machine-engraved vinylite, 20 × 261.2" (50.8 × 67.3 cm).*

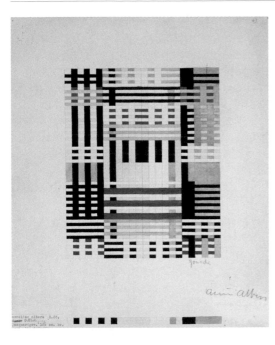

abcdefghi
jklmnopqr
s tuvwxyz
a   dd

◐ **2-26** *Anni Albers. Design for wall hanging. 1926. Gouache and pencil on paper, $14 \times 11^1/_2"$ (35.5 × 29.2 cm). The Museum of Modern Art, New York. Gift of the designer.*

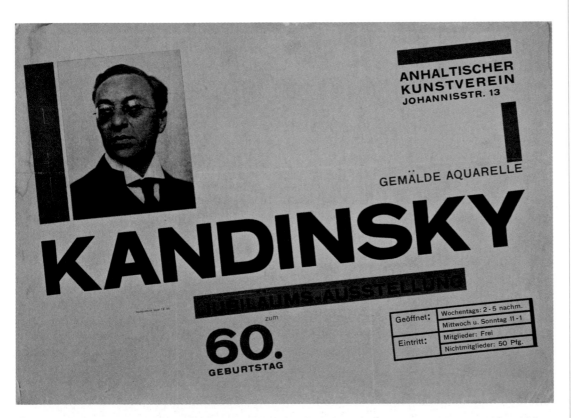

● **2-28** *Herbert Bayer.* Kandinsky zum 60. Geburtstag. *1926. Offset lithograph, printed in color. $19 \times 25"$ (48.2 × 63.5 cm). The Museum of Modern Art, New York. Gift of Mr. and Mrs. Alfred H. Barr, Jr.*

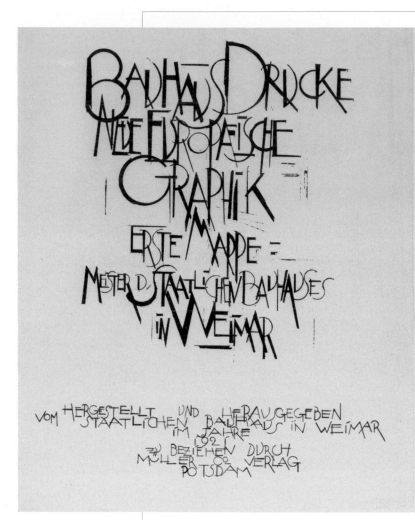

metrical layout. An underlying horizontal and vertical structure unified the page.

The Swiss also continued to develop the ideas of the Bauhaus in typography and layout design from the 1950s onward. Work from this period came to be known as *Swiss Design* or the *International Typographic Style*. Major practitioners included Josef Müller-Brockmann, Emil Ruder, and Armin Hofmann. Their emphasis on visual unity and formal grid elements contributed greatly toward shaping the design field. Personal expression was rejected in favor of order and clarity. The predominant graphic design style in the world by the 1970s, it featured a strong reliance on typographic elements, usually sans serif typefaces in a flush left and ragged right format.

FIGURATIVE MOVEMENTS

Art deco appeared as a definite style in Paris around 1925. It was especially influenced by art nouveau and also by African sculpture and cubism. Although it developed at the same time as the Bauhaus, art deco emphasized the figurative image with decorative appeal. It was applied to architecture, clothing, graphic design, advertising, packaging, crafts, and furniture. Artists associated with this movement included the Russian Erté and Georges Lepape (**Figure 2-30**), who contributed to *Vogue* magazine. Perhaps the best-known and most respected art deco artist, who continues to have a strong influence today, is A. M. Cassandre. His posters and advertisements show the influence of cubism, but the forms retain a recognizable physical identity balanced with an intricate Gestalt unity (**Figure 2-31**). It is a very recognizable style. For a time, art deco was out of favor in the eyes of architects and designers because it did not follow the Bauhaus tenets of functional, non-ornamental design.

Surrealism also surfaced in the 1920s. Now the style is often incorporated into the eclectic mix of contemporary design.

letters in printed material and used extreme contrast of weight and size to establish a visual hierarchy. A looser design by Lyonel Feininger forms the title page for a portfolio featuring the work of many famous Bauhaus artists (**Figure 2-29**).

After the Nazis forced the closing of the Bauhaus in 1933, many of its artists immigrated to the United States. There they greatly influenced American architecture and graphic design.

New typography is a term that came to identify new, Bauhaus-inspired approaches to graphic design. Its chief German proponent, Jan Tschichold, created typography that emphasized clarity. White space was used to create visual intervals in an asym-

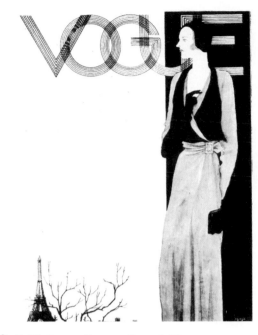

Owing a philosophical debt to Dada for its questioning attitude, it was joined by several Dada artists. This literary and artistic movement was based upon revealing the unconscious mind in dream images, the irrational, and the fantastic by juxtaposing incongruous subject matter. The writer André Breton was influential in starting this movement, which then found visual expression. The surrealists drew inspiration from Freud's *Interpretation of Dreams.* Like the author James Joyce, who used stream-of-consciousness techniques rather than rational, linear development of characters, surrealists sought to reveal the subconscious.

Surrealism has exerted a strong influence on illustration. René Magritte is much imi-

tated today, and in fact he created quite a lot of advertising illustration (**Figure 2-32**). Other surrealists, like Max Ernst and Man Ray, show the influence of Dada in their unorthodox and compelling arrangement of elements. Surrealism's search for unconscious motivation and innovative combinations continues to interest today's designer/advertiser. In the 1930s many surrealist artists were putting found objects in strange combinations that evoked poetic and unconscious associations. **Figure 2-33** is an advertising photo created by a team of women designer-photographers in 1931 that shows

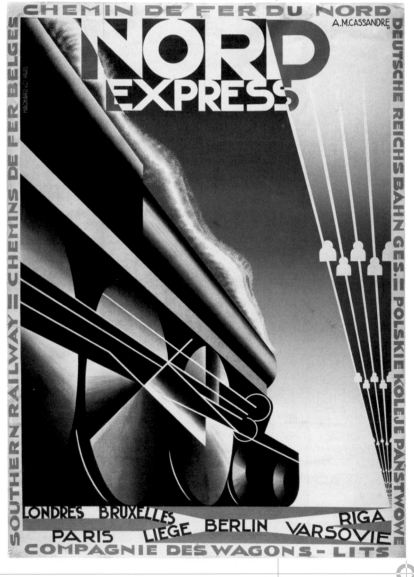

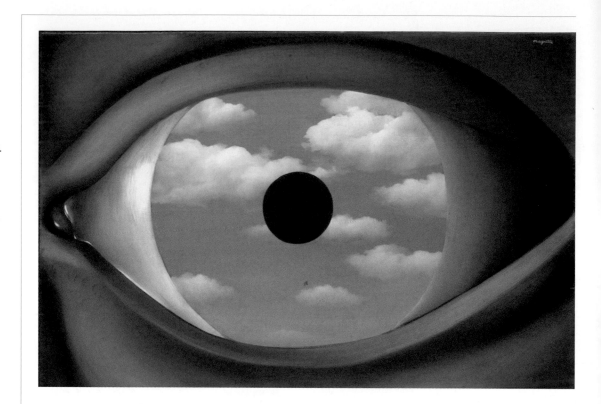

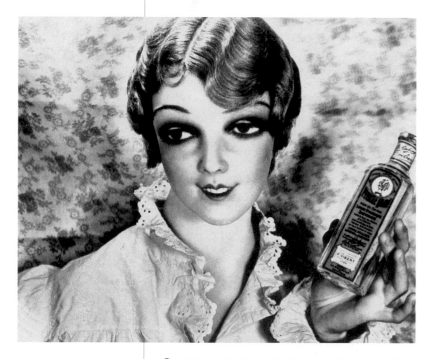

● **2-33** *Studio Ringl & Pit (Grete Stern and Ellen Rosenberg Auerbach).* Pétrole Hahn. *1931. Gelatin silver print. 93.8 × 111.8" (23.8 × 28.3 cm).*

the interest of the time in surrealism. Upon close examination, we realize that what appears to be an attractive woman is actually a mannequin, although her hand is real. This forces the potential buyer to look again, a major aim of an advertisement.

AMERICAN DESIGN

European Modernism (whose movements we've just read about) greatly influenced design in the United States. Modernists believed that each new generation must build on past styles in new ways or break with the past in order to make the next major historical contribution. Modernism is associated with innovation and progress. Its demise is often dated to 1970, although some argue that it continues as a strong influence today, concurrent with postmodernism, especially in the design field. László Moholy-Nagy came to Chicago in 1937 to direct the New Bauhaus. It closed after one year, and Moholy-Nagy operated his own Institute of Design from 1938 to 1946. This school offered the first complete modern design curriculum in America. The Illinois Institute of Technology is a descendant of the New Bauhaus. Many samples of modernist American graphics are shown throughout this text.

Lester Beall, an American-born Chicago artist, embraced modern design and European influences from cubism, constructivism, and Dada. Working in New York in the1940s, he combined drawing, symbols, photography, and mixed typefaces into a coherent, eclectic design. Many young American designers of the time drew inspiration from European modern art and design, including Paul Rand. Rand realized that his role as a designer involved reinventing the problem presented by the client (**Figures 2-34,** 3-18, 10-4, 10-7a, 10-8, and 10-10). He focused on restating the problem, and he drew inspiration from painters such as Klee and Miró. His books on design

and his life's work are extremely important contributions to the field.

Through the 1930s and early 1940s, Cipe Pineles learned editorial art direction from one of the masters of the era, Dr. M. F. Agha, at Condé Nast publications. She became (at *Glamour* magazine) the first autonomous woman art director of a mass-market American publication. She was the first art director to hire fine artists to illustrate mass-market publications. After achieving national prominence as art director for *Glamour,* British *Vogue,* and *Seventeen,* Pineles became the first female member of the New York Art Directors Club. She was one of the few women designers to gain recognition during this period. Until her death in 1991, Cipe Pineles's career spanned almost 60 years. Designers from this period synthesized the influences of European avant-garde and design movements to create new designs for magazines, posters, advertisements, and corporate communications. **Figure 2-35** shows Cipe Pineles at work.

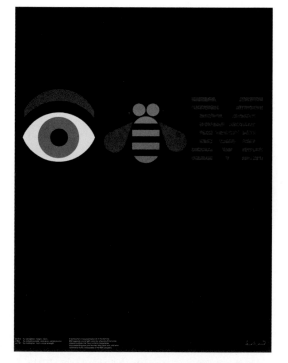

2-34 *Paul Rand.* IBM. *1982. Offset lithograph, printed in color, 36 × 24" (91.4 × 61 cm). The Museum of Modern Art, New York. Gift of the designer.*

The Museum of Modern Art, New York. Gift of the designer. Digital Image © The Museum of Modern Art, New York. Licensed by SCALA/Art Resource, NY.

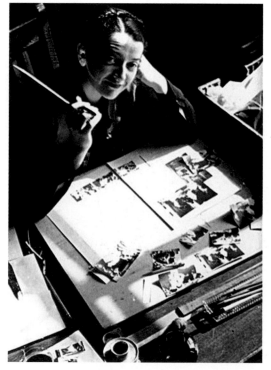

2-35 *Cipe Pineles at Condé Nast, late 1930s or early 1940s.* Copyright AIGA.

By the 1950s, marketing research was an important influence on business decisions.

Advertising designers dealt with the proliferation of national television and radio networks, the emergence of large chain stores, and the importance of public perception and corporate identity. The International Design Conference in Aspen was founded in 1951 to assess and discuss the role of design in the commercial environment. This conference continues to meet in Aspen every summer.

The 1950s saw the emergence of design curricula in universities and art schools and the articulation of an important concept. Leo Lionni—then art director for *Fortune* magazine, as well as an author, an illustrator, and a fine artist—stated that "Whatever [the designer's] activities, they involve, to some, and various, extent, the shaping, interpretation and transmission of values." This issue of values and the role of design in society is an important current topic. See the accompanying Web site for more information related to individuals in this section.

Push Pin Studios was founded in 1955 in opposition to the spirit of Swiss Design. The founders included Seymour Chwast, Reynold Ruffins, Ed Sorel, and Milton Glaser. Glaser stated that "We frequently find corruption more interesting than purity" (see Figures 4-7 and 4-9). This studio revived art nouveau, art deco, and narrative illustration, turning to visual history for inspiration. This attitude, with its historical references, heralded postmodernism. The studio's founders continue to contribute to the shape and direction of design in the 21st century.

During the mid-20th century the media theorist Marshall McLuhan noted the influence of television on communication and wrote about the potential for a global village united by a shared vision. McLuhan saw print media as an isolationist influence, giving rise to categorization, linear sequencing, and dogmatism. Television, according to McLuhan, has the potential to reunite society into a new global village. It certainly exerts a major influence on advertising and communication and, thus, on society. McLuhan's writings remain thought-provoking today as media continue to evolve and influence our societal structures.

Magazine design was a creative area in the 1960s. In 1964 Ruth Ansel and Bea Feitler took charge of *Harper's Bazaar* as co–art directors. Drawing inspiration from pop art and underground images, *Harper's Bazaar* represented the glamour and glitter of the 1960s.

Herb Lubalin, a major figure in the field, was art director for the countercultural magazines *Avant Garde* and *Eros* (**Figures 2-36,** 5-13, 5-17, and 5-29). Alternative publications with political and cultural commentary flourished during the 1960s.

Postmodernism

In the 1970s the term *postmodernism* was first applied to architecture, and a questioning of rational Swiss Design led to New Wave, or postmodern, graphic design. This period has questioned the modernist concept of constant innovation and progress. Contradictory and coexistent trends from a variety of historical periods provide rich concepts for study. April Greiman's work is an example of New Wave design, mixing formal experiments with popular imagery (**Figure 2-37**). The remainder of the 20th century saw history as a shopping mall of styles. Art deco and art nouveau were among the styles that were revived and revised, as decorative and figurative work regained respect.

◗ **2-36** *Herb Lubalin. Logo for* Eros *magazine. A magazine with a graphically beautiful approach to love and sex; only four issues were published.*

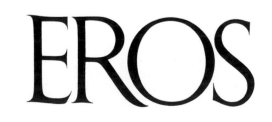

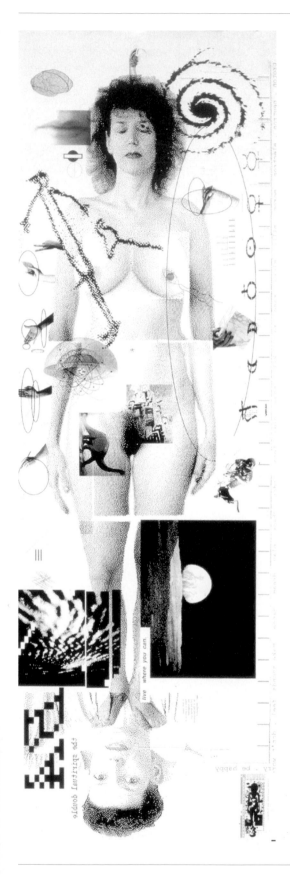

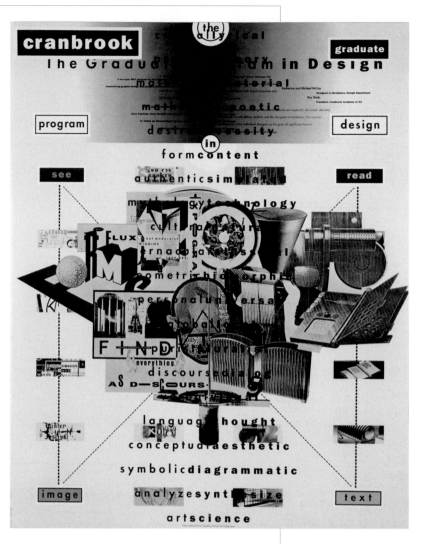

Women had an important impact on design during this time and afterward. Designer and educator Katherine McCoy joined in questioning the modernist ideal of a permanent, universally valid aesthetic. She encouraged the production of visually rich and complex designs, believing that there is more to design than the clear, impartial transmission of information. McCoy believes designers interpret and communicate cultural values through the forms they create. See **Figure 2-38**.

● **2-37** *April Greiman. Art director–designer.* Design Quarterly #133. Does It Make Sense? *Publication insert, Walker Art Center, 1986. MIT Press Publisher.*
Courtesy of the artist.

◗ **2-38** *Katherine McCoy. Cranbrook recruiting poster. 1989. Images of student projects are layered with typography and a diagram related to design theory.*
Courtesy, Katherine McCoy.

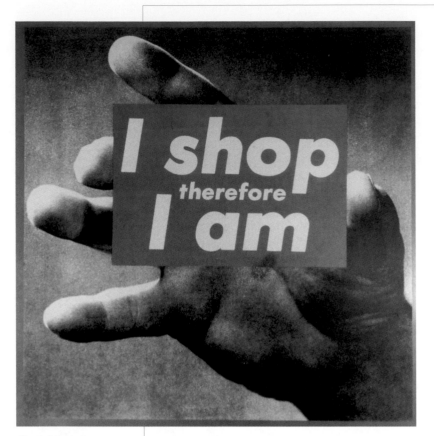

program that brings together artists, designers, computer scientists, sociologists, and others to study communication in the electronic age. Electronic media have been used to explore and invent eclectic, personal art and design work.

During the 1980s the question of style over substance became an important issue. Theorists such as Stuart Ewen questioned the role and impact of advertising design on society. Fine artist Barbara Kruger worked for a time as a layout artist and used those skills to develop an "advertising campaign" that is anti-advertising. Her mock ads and billboards used typographical devices and images to expose the persuasion-consumption cycle of commercial advertising (**Figure 2-39**). **Figure 2-40**

Technology has become an increasingly important issue during the postmodern period. Murial Cooper and others at the Massachusetts Institute of Technology (MIT) developed the Visible Language Workshop—a multidisciplinary, multimedia

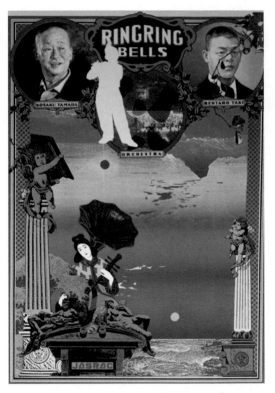

Digital Focus

The computer made possible the visual and conceptual layering that is the hallmark of postmodernism in graphic design. By the late 1980s, as you can see in Figure 2-38 by Katherine McCoy, type could be overlapped to create a rich visual texture and be intertwined with the photographic image. It is much easier to accomplish such an effect totally on the computer today. By the last decade of the 20th century, postmodern typography could be used to explore multiple meanings rather than strictly to clarify a fixed message. The Internet is a very postmodern medium, with its interactive, non-linear flow. The impact of ever-developing computer technology influences our style and our content. Ideas change technology, and technology influences ideas.

is a good example of the visual complexity of Japanese postmodernism. This design combines visual motifs from a variety of cultures and periods, including Édouard Manet's painting *The Fifer* and Michelangelo's Medici tombs.

A concern for the intellectual and historical foundations of design led to the publication, in 1983, of Philip Meggs's *History of Graphic Design*. This is a comprehensive and thoughtful text that provides a foundation for many contemporary design history classes.

NEW TECHNOLOGIES

New technologies always influence the course of graphic design. We can trace our history and development from medieval manuscripts to Gutenberg's printing press to hot type to cold type to computer-generated type and image. Later chapters discuss this development in greater detail. In the opening years of the 21st century, the use of electronic technology in the United States and internationally has revolutionized design. Style and content are affected by the technology used in their creation. This chapter's brief history of design has shown the relationship between design and technology, citing the invention of the printing press and of stone lithography as examples of earlier technologies that affected design and societal patterns of communication. The mid-20th century's emphasis on clarity and structural integrity has been replaced by an interest in rich textural layers of information, as graphics are now generated with software programs that encourage stylistic complexity.

The Development of Computer Graphics

Computer graphics, the use of computers to draw images, dates back to 1953, when a simple visual display of a bouncing ball was used to calculate and show military targets. Funding for the development of computers and computer graphics in the United States originally came from the Defense Department. In 1962 at MIT Ivan Sutherland created the first interactive computer graphics display. A light pen touched to the video screen could draw a line stretched from the previous point. Although its early development was tied to defense and aerospace, computer graphics now has a wide variety of applications, from engineering, medicine, and geology to graphic design, animation, the film industry, and the Internet. **Figure 2-41** shows an excellent Internet site hosted by the National Design Museum, presenting topics on design. Refer to this book's accompanying

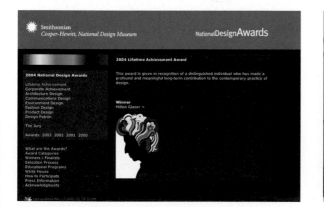 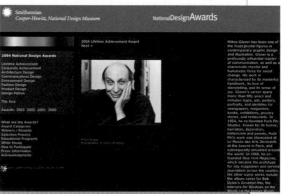

● **2-41** *Jessica Helfand and William Drenttel. Cooper-Hewitt, National Design Museum Web-site pages.*
Courtesy of Cooper-Hewitt, National Design Museum.

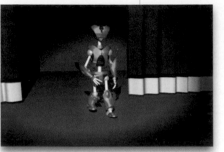 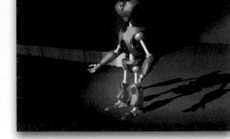

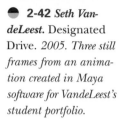
2-42 Seth VandeLeest. Designated Drive. *2005. Three still frames from an animation created in Maya software for VandeLeest's student portfolio.*

Web site to visit this location. **Figure 2-42** shows stills using a 3-D animation program, created by Seth VandeLeest for his student portfolio. Computer graphics today has many different stylistic approaches and methods of delivery.

Interactivity

Text, photography, animation, illustration, sound, and video can now be combined and linked by using a variety of desktop programs. **Figure 2-43** shows two stills from a multimedia installation that artist-educator Coleen Deck created in Adobe After Effects. Unlike books, film, or video that present linear information, the new electronic media are truly interactive and present nonlinear, animated browsing opportunities.

The Internet offers not only interactivity but also freedom from the physical constraints of traditional media. CD-ROM storage and DVDs offer interactivity, but only the Internet travels through time and space

with no physical barrier. This medium promises to transform the nature of communication as well as physical and political boundaries.

THE FUTURE

During the 20th century we have progressed along a visual escalation from photography to film to video to computers to the Internet. Computer graphics has come a long way since the original moving-ball display in the 1950s. The digital desktop has come a long way since the Macintosh was introduced in the mid-1980s. The Internet has become a vehicle for marketing products and disseminating information of all kinds. Web-site production is a growing market for graphic designers, and the complexity of these sites is increasing rapidly. Our ability to communicate with interactive visuals and to create desktop video and 3-D animation is also developing a new market for graphic designers.

2-43 Coleen Deck, artist and educator, created Search Twice *in 2001. This diptych installation uses Adobe After Effects to integrate image and motion.*
Courtesy of the artist.

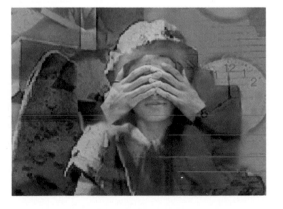 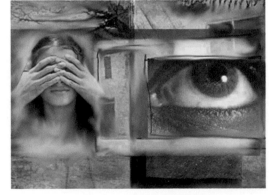

Virtual reality is another developing technology. It extends the senses, allowing a person to move through and interact with a computer-simulated environment by wearing special glasses and clothing or other sensors. These monitor physical movements and gestures in the alternate, virtual world. Psychologist R. L. Gregory stated in his book *Eye and Brain,* "The seeing of objects involves many sources of information beyond those meeting the eye when we look at an object. It involves knowledge of objects from previous experience and not only sight but touch, taste, smell, hearing, and perhaps also temperature or pain." What might the impact of virtual reality be on design and communication?

As we continue into the 21st century, it is interesting to remember the important developments at the turn of the last century. The future will be exciting and challenging for designers intent on maintaining an emphasis on issues of values and content while learning and using a proliferation of new media.

PROJECT

In consultation with your instructor, research a contemporary designer mentioned in this chapter or elsewhere in the text. Prepare a paper and classroom presentation based on your research. Describe the designer's work, philosophy, and background. Shoot slides of the work, or gather and present visual materials on computer. Bring library books to pass around. Schedule this presentation to the class sometime during this term. Check the links for each chapter that are on the accompanying Web site.

Goals and Objectives

By researching this topic, you will learn about the subject and gain appreciation for the artist or period you choose. You will also gain skills in research.

The goal is to enrich the knowledge of everyone in the class with each presentation.

Critique

Did you support your talk with images?

Did you cover the artist's biography as well as discuss his or her style?

Did you explain why you are drawn to this artist or period?

Ask for comments and questions from the audience. The more discussion you get, the better your presentation is likely to be.

TERMINOLOGY

CHAPTER 3

See glossary
for
definitions.

Gestalt	Shape	Type Size
Visual Perception	Volume	X-height
Semiotics	Realism	Ascender
Icon	Abstraction	Descender
Symbol	Nonobjective	Typeface
Index	Counter	Font
Figure/Ground	Serif	Baseline
Stable	Sans Serif	Stress
Reversible		
Ambiguous		

Perception

3

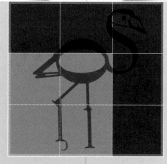

KEY POINTS A successful visual whole, or *Gestalt,* is achieved by the careful combination of parts. A graphic designer works with shapes in both word and image. This chapter stresses parts and shapes in typography, since most beginning designers understand the design structure of images better than that of type. Figure/ground in type and image is also discussed, because it is a vital part of seeing and working with shape. If we are aware of how the eye and brain organize marks on a surface to give them meaning, we will be much more successful in creating designs that do what we intend.

SEEING AND BELIEVING

Graphic designers do more than decorate a surface. They work with the fundamental principles of *visual perception.* When we look at a printed page, whether it is covered with type, illustrations, or a photograph, there is more than meets the eye. The brain is sifting and cataloging the images. We carry a load of experiences, innate responses, and physiological considerations that interact with those images. Designs that effectively use that process have the creative strength of sight itself on their side.

As soon as the first mark is made on a blank sheet of paper, it is interpreted by the eye. We cannot see only a flat mark on a flat piece of paper. Our past experience, our expectations, and the structure of the brain itself filter the information. The visual illusions created through this process are a real part of perception. Realism in art and design is not an absolute but a convention that our culture and personal background create from visual data.

Search for Simplicity

Gestalt psychologists have investigated the way humans process information from a two-dimensional surface. There is an interplay of tensions between shapes on a flat surface because the appearance of any one element or shape depends on its surroundings. Shapes are interpreted by an active eye that seeks the simplest satisfactory explanation for what it sees. Any mark drawn on paper stimulates an active, interpretive response from eye and brain. We finish uncompleted shapes, group similar shapes, and see foreground and background on a flat surface. The experiments of Gestalt psychologists led them to describe a basic law of visual perception: Any stimulus pattern tends to be seen as a structure as simple as conditions permit. This law is similar to the principle of parsimony known to scientists, which states that when several hypotheses fit the facts, the simplest one should be accepted.

In science, elegance and success result from explaining a phenomenon with the minimum number of steps. A similar elegance can be achieved on the printed page. A great deal may be happening on a page although few marks exist. In fact, adding more marks without understanding their effect can often make less happen. That is poor design.

In this and following chapters, we discuss the manner in which Gestalt psychologists believe our brain interprets and groups the images on a flat surface. Gestalt theory is generally recognized as a useful tool for designing visual images so they will be comprehended as we want. No single theory, however, explains all there is to visual perception. Much has yet to be discovered.

Interpretations

The lines in **Figure 3-1** demonstrate our busy interaction with simple marks drawn on a page. The resulting interpretations are influenced by the culture in which we live. We accept the black mark in *a* as nearer than the white field it occupies, although they both exist on the same physical plane on the surface of the page. Adding a second mark of a larger size (*b*) requires another interpretation involving depth. The larger mark seems closer in space than the smaller one. A line placed vertically that divides the space (*c*) will not disturb the two-dimensional quality. Use an angled line (*d*), and a sense of space begins to develop. Add another angled line (*e*), and suddenly the eye may see the perspective of a road or railroad tracks running at an angle into the distance. The addition of changes in size and value enrich our possible interpretations.

Visual perception, and thus communication, is always colored by interpretation. Context, personal experience, and culturally inculcated systems of signs and symbols play a strong role in perception. Later chapters discuss this phenomenon from varying perspectives. *Semiotics* is the study of influences on our perception. It goes beyond linguistics to incorporate the visual language of sign and symbol (**Figure 3-2**). The field of semiotics often breaks down visuals into the categories of icon, symbol, and index. An *icon* looks like the thing it represents. A road sign with an image of a

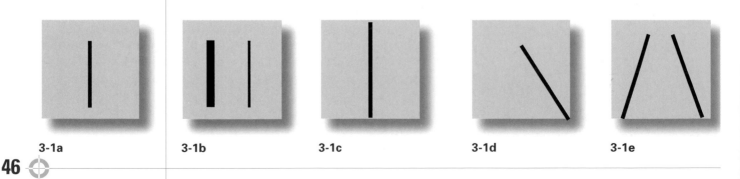

3-1a   3-1b   3-1c   3-1d   3-1e

Graphic Design Basics

deer is an icon. A road sign with a circle and slash, meaning "forbidden," is an example of a *symbol,* which has a culturally accepted meaning. Words are also considered symbols of the thing they reference. An *index* is a visual we have learned to associate with a particular meaning. For example, a thermometer is an index of temperature. A footprint can indicate a deer. The study of semiotics crosses between the field of linguistics and the field of visual language. Apply the concepts of icon, symbol, and index to your thumbnail designs to enrich the range and depth of your solutions.

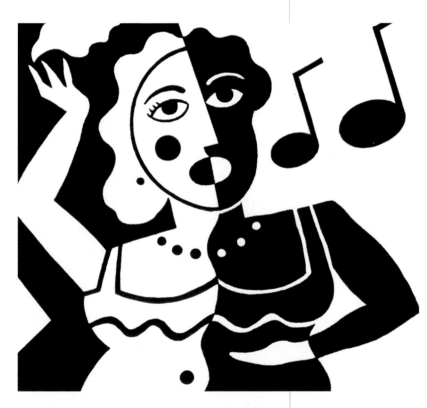

◖ **3-2** *How many different ways can you express the idea of "bird"? This is a good mental exercise to stretch your conceptual muscles.*

FIGURE/GROUND

If we are aware of how the eye and brain organize marks on a flat surface to give them meaning, we will be much more successful in creating designs that do what we intend. The most fundamental organizational principle of sight for an artist working on a flat, two-dimensional surface is *figure/ ground.* It is sometimes called positive/ negative space. An ability to see and structure both figure and ground is crucial to the designer. Whenever we look at a mark on a page, we see it as an object distinct from its background. This distinction is the fundamental first step in perception. A thing (figure) is only visible to the extent that it is seen as separate from its background (ground). This theory applies to every area of perception. A tree, for example, can only be seen in relation to the space around it, the "not-treeness." We can look at the shapes and lines of a photograph and recognize a picture because of figure/ground grouping. **Figure 3-3** shows a contemporary illustration with a dynamic figure/ ground relationship that encourages varied readings. Is the white figure in profile, or do the white and black combine into a single figure? This design is both very abstract and very figurative. The repeated oval shapes in mouth and notes make a symbolic visual tie between mouth and music.

● **3-3** *David McLimans. Freelance illustrator, Madison, WI. An intricate play of figure/ground and repetition of shape makes up this beautifully designed illustration.*
Courtesy of the artist.

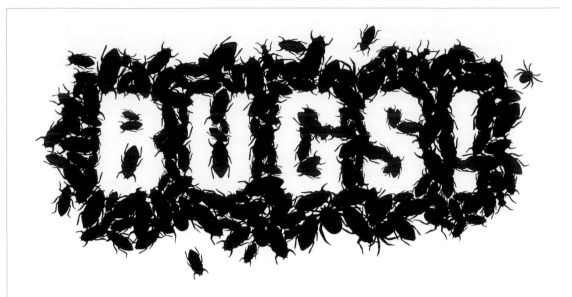

Figure 3-4 makes playful and effective use of reversible figure/ground grouping. We are able to recognize and read the words because we organize the letters into a white figure lying against a black ground. We can change our focus from the insects to the white space and back again. At its best, design becomes inseparable from communication. Form becomes content.

Categories

Every figure seems to lie at some location in front of the ground. Designing well depends on handling both areas. Many beginning artists concentrate only on the mark they make and are not aware of the white space surrounding it. Remember, this space, or ground, is as integral a part of the page as the figure placed on it. The three main categories in figure/ground shaping are *stable, reversible,* and *ambiguous.*

Stable Figure/Ground

Each two-dimensional mark or shape is perceived in an unchanging, stable relationship of object against background. Toulouse-Lautrec (see Figure 2-2) played deliberately with the tension of a stable figure/ground relationship on the verge of breaking down, as did the illustrator Aubrey Beardsley (see Figure 2-6). The poster by Emile

Preetorius also has a great deal of compelling figure/ground tension (**Figure 3-5**).

Reversible Figure/Ground

Figure and ground can be focused on equally. What was initially ground becomes figure (see Figure 3-4). Because we cannot simultaneously perceive both images as figure, we keep switching between them. Many logo designs use some degree of reversible figure/ground (Chapter 5). **Figure 3-6** is a personal logo created by a young designer for his student portfolio that makes good use of figure/ground relationships. As this student did, consider building your portfolio by donating your design skills to a local not-for-profit organization.

Ambiguous Figure/Ground

In some puzzle pictures, one figure may turn out to be made up of another figure, or of several different figures (**Figure 3-7**). The student designs in Figure 3-24 are good examples of a whole figure that is made up of many individual, repeated shapes. In Figure 4-26, the animals created by combining alphabet letters also form an ambiguous figure/ground. The Gestalt notion that the whole is more than the mere sum of its parts is clearly illustrated by these examples.

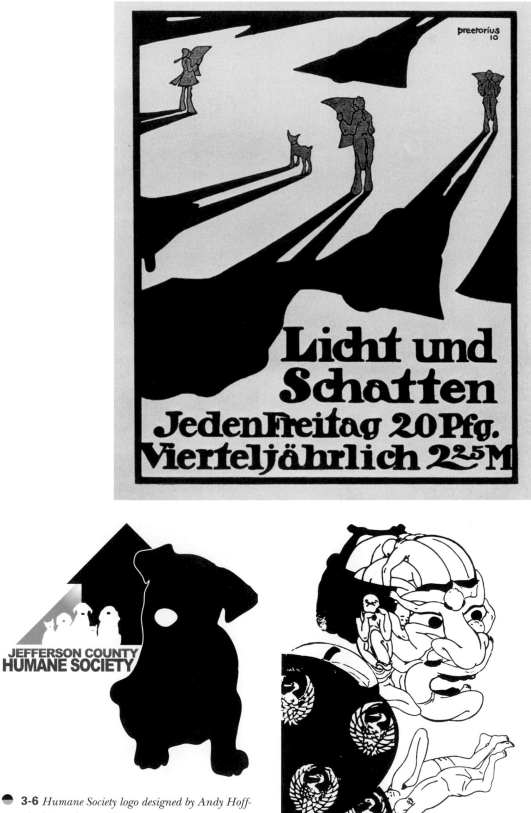

● **3-5** *Emile Preetorius.* Licht und Schatten *(Light and Shadow).* 1910. Lithograph, printed in color, 11³/₄ × 8³/₄" (29.8 × 22.2 cm). The Museum of Modern Art, New York. Gift of The Lauder Foundation, Leonard and Evelyn Lauder Fund.

Photograph © 1998 The Museum of Modern Art, New York/Art Resource, NY.

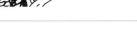

● **3-6** *Humane Society logo designed by Andy Hoffman for his student portfolio.*

● **3-7** *Japanese symbolic picture. Nineteenth century. An example of ambiguous figure/ground.*

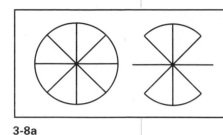

3-8a

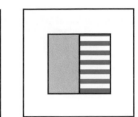

3-8b

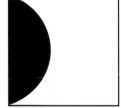

3-9a

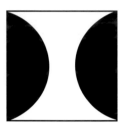

3-9b

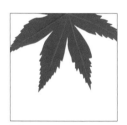

3-9c

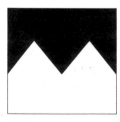

3-9d

Conditions

Once mastered, figure/ground grouping is an invaluable tool. It is complex and deserves study. Here are some conditions under which one area appears as figure and another as ground. Use these principles when completing the first exercise at the end of this chapter.

■ The enclosed or surrounded area tends to be seen as figure; the surrounding, unbounded area as ground (**Figure 3-8a**).

■ Visual texture makes for figure perception. The eye will be drawn to a textured area before it is drawn to a nontextured area (**Figure 3-8b**).

■ Convex shapes are more easily seen as figure than concave (**Figure 3-9a**).

■ Simplicity (especially symmetry) predisposes an area to be seen as figure (**Figure 3-9b**).

■ Familiarity causes a shape to pull out from its surroundings. As we focus on it, it becomes figure while the surroundings become ground (**Figure 3-9c**).

■ The lower half of a horizontally divided area reads as the solid figure to which gravity anchors us (**Figure 3-9d**).

■ There is a tendency for black to be viewed as the predominant figure more readily than white. Rotating Figure 3-9d will help demonstrate this effect.

Letterforms

How does this figure/ground phenomenon affect letterforms, the basic ingredient of

the printed page? Stop now and do Exercise 1. As you do the exercise, you will realize that figure/ground affects letterforms the same as any mark on the page. Using type effectively depends on seeing both the black shapes of the letters and the white shapes between, within, and around them. You must pay close attention to the shape of the ground areas, called counters (**Figure 3-10**). This has direct application in logo and layout design (Chapters 5 and 7).

Because we tend to read for verbal information and not for visual information, we are rarely aware of the appearance of type itself. We read it but do not "see" it, unless we are dealing with designers who deliberately treat typography as a design element to be manipulated.

For the first several chapters, we will be concerned with type as a pure design element while you learn to "see" it. Only display, or headline-size, letterforms are used. Look closely at the letter *a*'s shown in Figure 3-20 and study all the parts of their structure, paying close attention to the different counter shapes. Renaissance artist Albrecht Dürer constructed his own typestyle. His structural diagrams demonstrate the careful shaping and measurements necessary when hand-constructing letterforms (**Figure 3-11**). Computer software has simplified the creation of new typestyles, but a discerning eye is still the most important ingredient.

and
a l o

● **3-10** *The shape of letterform counters can be seen easily when figure/ground is reversed.*

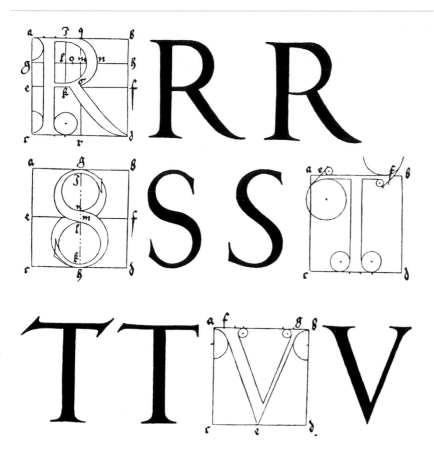

● **3-11** *Albrecht Dürer. From* On the Just Shaping of Letters. *1525.*

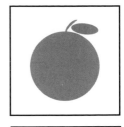

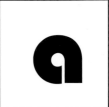

● **3-12** *Look for similarity of shape in type and image.*

SHAPE

Design is the arrangement of shapes. They underlie every drawing, painting, and graphic design. It is easy to become enamored with the subject matter of a design and forget about basic shapes. A designer must develop the ability to see and think in terms of shapes even though those shapes look like dots or apples or oranges or letterforms (**Figure 3-12**). Shape occurs in both figure and ground, in both type and image.

Shape versus Volume

A *shape* is an area created by an enclosing boundary that defines the outer edges. The boundary can be a line, a color, or a value change. Shape describes a two-dimensional artwork; *volume* describes a three-dimensional work, such as a ceramic pot, a sculpture, or a piece of furniture. A rectangle and a circle are 2-D shapes, whereas a box and a sphere are 3-D volumes (**Figure 3-13**). Just as a 2-D surface

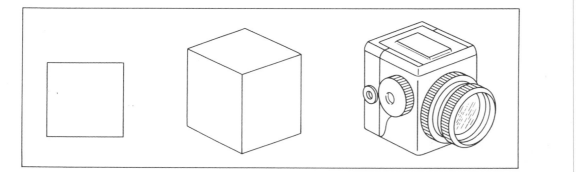

● **3-13** *This rectangle can be made to resemble a camera, but it is still made up of only two-dimensional shapes.*

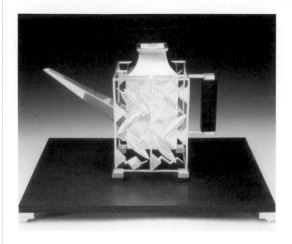

can give the illusion of volume, a 3-D sculpture can use 2-D shape to enrich its surface design. **Figure 3-14** shows a richly textured theme of rectangles in the surface treatment and basic structure of a contemporary teapot design.

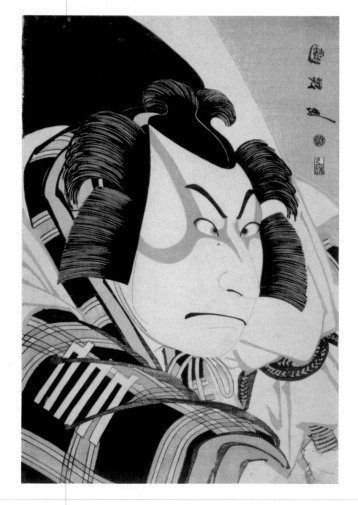

Grouping Shapes

Every visual experience is seen in the context of space and time. Every shape is affected by surrounding shapes. The normal sense of sight grasps shape immediately by identifying an overall pattern. Research has demonstrated that grouping letters into words makes it possible to recall the letters more accurately than when they are presented alone. If it is possible to group marks into a recognizable or repeating shape, the eye will do so, because it is the simplest way to perceive and remember the marks. The letters in *word* are easier to remember than *o, d, w, r.*

Shape versus Subject

For the graphic designer, the shape of a circle may represent the letter *O,* a diagram of a courtyard, a drawing of a wheel, or a photograph of a musical instrument. These objects are not linked by subject matter to any common theme. They are linked by shape. Through basic shape you can bring unity to a group of seemingly disparate objects. The designer works with so many disparate objects that to be blind to their shapes would result in utter chaos on the page. Repeating similar shapes in different objects is an excellent way to bring visual unity to a design.

The Form of Shapes

An artist may choose to represent an object or a person *realistically,* by an image similar to an unaltered photograph. Actually, reality is a little more difficult to define than that. Philosophers have been working on it for centuries. We know that visual reality is a combination of shapes and the viewer's interaction with them. In later chapters we'll discuss other factors that contribute to our 2-D perception.

An artist/designer may also represent an object in a purposeful distortion or stylization that can emphasize an emotional quality, as in **Figure 3-15**—a beautiful example

Raster and Vector

There are two kinds of image files in computer graphics: vector graphics and raster graphics. Vector graphics are like a cross-stitch embroidery pattern in which the yarn stays as separate interwoven strands. Raster graphics, on the other hand, are like a woven fabric in which the color pattern is dyed into the cloth. The vector "strands" can be separated and moved independently, but raster "fabric" cannot.

Vector graphics involve creating shapes that are clean edged and defined as geometric objects. Each vector object, whether a shape or a drawn line, can be easily selected and edited, repositioned, and transformed. Vector graphics are resolution-independent, which means that they retain crisp edges when enlarged. This is a powerful concept. However large or small you transform a vector file, it remains perfectly sharp. Typography, logo design, and some forms of illustration are created in vector programs such as Illustrator and Freehand, and in page layout programs such as InDesign and Quark. Raster programs such as Photoshop and Painter are excellent for image manipulation and can best be used for typography that will not need to be resized.

of shape finding from 18th-century Japan. An illustration that emphasizes shapes like this looks as if it were created in a contemporary vector graphics computer program. The history of art and design offers many such inspirations for computer solutions.

Abstraction is another approach to illustration and design. It implies a simplification of existing shapes. Details are ignored, but the subject is often still recognizable. Often the pure design shapes of the subject are emphasized, as in **Figure 3-16**—a Japanese portrait created in the late 20th century that uses squares.

Purely *nonobjective* shapes are abstractions that have no recognizable realistic shapes. The constructivists worked with nonobjective shapes to give structure and character to their designs. Nonobjective shapes are the basis of the invisible, underlying structure of layout design.

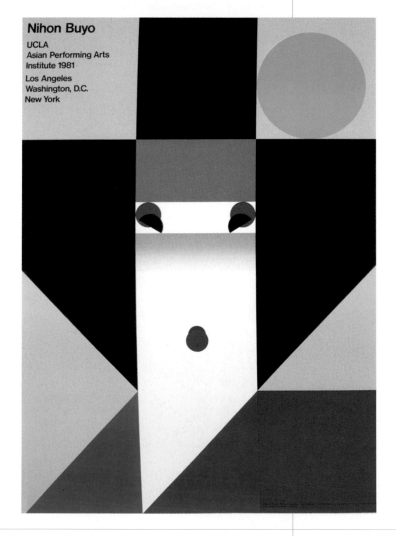

◗ **3-16** *Ikko Tanaka.* Nihon Buyo. *1981. Offset lithograph. $40^1/_2 \times 28^3/_4"$ (102.2 × 73 cm). The Museum of Modern Art, New York. Gift of the College of Fine Arts, UCLA.*

Photograph © 2001 The Museum of Modern Art, New York/Art Resource, NY.

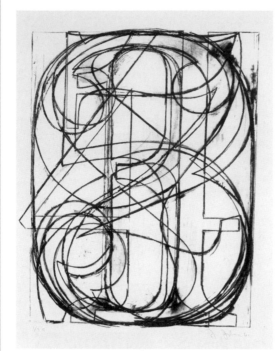
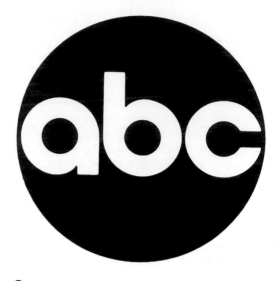

● **3-18** *Paul Rand. Trademark, the American Broadcasting Corporation, 1962.*
Courtesy of Mrs. Marion Rand.

Letterform Shapes

The ability to see shapes is especially important with letterforms. True, they are symbols of something, but first and foremost they are pure shape, a fundamental design element. Successful layout and logo design depend on creating unity through the play of similarity and variety of letterform shapes.

The distinction is often made between geometric shapes and curvilinear, organic shapes. The painter Jasper Johns utilizes a free, expressive, curvilinear, organic line when dealing with letterforms. Our eyes alternate between numerals as we recognize the multiple overlap in **Figure 3-17**. **Figure 3-18** shows the logo for ABC designed by Paul Rand, who skillfully repeated basic geometric shapes.

Typestyles often have different expressive qualities depending on their shapes. Those with hard, straight edges and angular corners have a colder, more reserved feeling than typestyles with graceful curves, which have a relaxed, sensual feeling. To become sensitive to the shapes in a letterform, look carefully at its anatomy (**Figure 3-19**). Then learn the differences between typestyles. Chapter 6 discusses their history and classification. Right now, however, concentrate on making comparisons between a few classic typestyles (**Figure 3-20**).

Terminology

The following list of terms and definitions will help you know what to look for when comparing shapes in letterforms.

COUNTER Counters are the white shapes inside a letter. Duplicating a letterform accurately calls for close attention to both the white and the black shapes (the ground

● **3-19** *Parts of a letterform.*

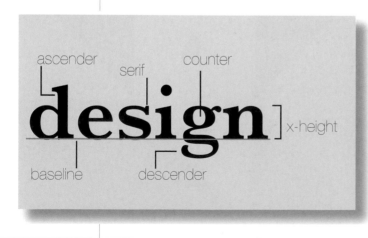

abcdefghijklmn

abcdefghijklmnop

abcdefghijklmnopq

abcdefghijklmnop

abcdeefghijkl

and the figure). When drawing a letterform or designing with one, think of yourself as drawing the white shapes.

SERIF A serif is a stroke that projects off the main stroke of a letter at the bottom or the top. Letters without serifs are called *sans serif.*

TYPE SIZE *Type size* is measured by points. For example, 72-point type is 1 inch high, as measured from the top of the ascender to the bottom of the descender. See **Figure 3-21a.**

X-HEIGHT This is the height of the body of a lowercase letter such as *x* or *a.* It does not include ascender or descender. The x-

height will vary in typefaces even though the point size is identical. This variation makes different typestyles of the same point size appear larger or smaller. Type size is measured from the top of the ascender to the bottom of the descender. Thus 10-point Garamond has a small x-height and long ascenders and descenders;

Type *Type*

3-21a *Ascenders and descenders determine type size. These are both 72 pt.*

55

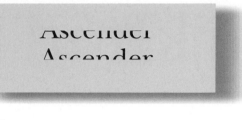

abcde
fgkl*hij*
mnopq
stuvw
xyz

● **3-21b** *The Univers typestyle has a consistent x-height in all its family of font variations.*

● **3-21c** *Ascenders and descenders increase legibility. The ascenders play an especially important part in identifying letterforms.*

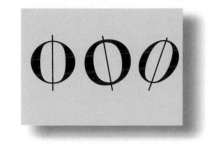

● **3-22** *Stress varies greatly between typestyles.*

10-point Univers has a larger x-height and smaller ascenders and descenders.

The Swiss designer Adrian Frutiger developed Univers in 1954. It was the first typestyle available in many fonts with a consistent x-height throughout (**Figure 3-21b**).

ASCENDER An *ascender* is the part of a lowercase letter that rises above the body of the letter. The letter *a* has no ascender, but the letter *b* does. See **Figure 3-21c**.

DESCENDER A *descender* is the part of a lowercase letter that falls below the body of the letter. The letters *a, b, c, d,* and *e* have no descenders, but the letter *g* does.

TYPEFACE A *typeface* is a style of lettering. Most typefaces vary a great deal, as you can see when you develop an eye for the differences. Each family of typefaces may contain variations such as italic and bold in addition to regular, or roman.

FONT A *font* is a specific size and variation on a typeface. (Bold Baskerville is a

different font from italic Baskerville, for example.)

BASELINE The line that typography sits on is called a *baseline*.

STRESS *Stress* is the distribution of weight through the thinnest part of a letterform. It can be seen easily by drawing a line through the thinnest part of an *o* and observing the slant of the line (**Figure 3-22**).

Using this terminology, look at three typestyles and ask yourself the following questions:

How much variation is there between thick and thin strokes?
Which style has a short x-height?
Which style has a tall x-height?
Which has the longest ascenders and descenders?
What are the differences in the serifs?
Which type has the most vertical stress?
What are the similarities among letters that belong to one style?

EXERCISES

1. a. Place the letter *h* inside a rectangular format. Use a Helvetica typestyle (see **Figure 3-23**). Place the letter and its values so the *H* (upper- or lowercase) becomes ground instead of figure. Familiarity makes this exercise difficult.

b. Group several copies of an arrow to form an interesting symmetrical pattern.

Emphasize the creation of shapes in figure and in ground (**Figure 3-24a, b**).

c. Choose one of the typestyles shown in this chapter. Repeat a letterform in a symmetrical pattern, as shown in **Figure 3-25**. What do you see as figure? Why? Can you change the figure into ground?

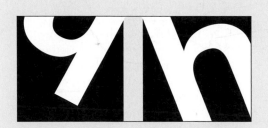

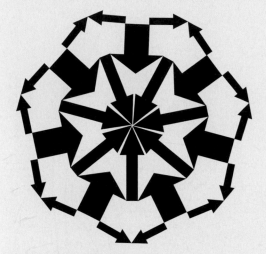

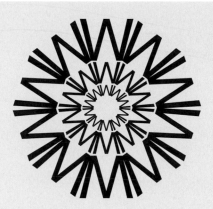

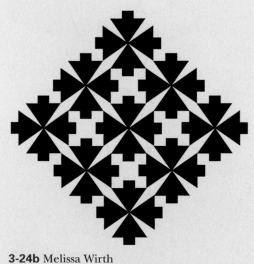

● **3-23** *Reverse, crop, and place the letter* H *to make it read as background.*

3-24a Eric Wuebben

3-24b Melissa Wirth

● **3-24** *Student solutions to Exercise 1b.*

● **3-25** *Lindsay Riesop's symmetrical letterform design.*

2. The letter *a* has been shown to you in five different typefaces (Figure 3-20). To help you recognize the shapes of different typestyles and learn to handle your tools, trace each of these letters and transfer them to drawing paper or illustration board. Reproduce them in ink or pencil so they are "letter perfect." Hand skills continue to be valuable to the graphic designer in the planning, conceptual, and sketching stages. When you have finished and your work has been critiqued, you will be ready to proceed with the following project. You may choose to work with pencil and ink throughout this next assignment or to finish executing your design sketches on the computer in a vector graphics program.

PROJECT

Figure/Ground and Letterforms

Applying figure/ground to letterform shapes is the best way to really see typography. Choose two letterforms from the typestyles shown in this chapter. If they are your initials, you might choose to use your design for a business card and letterhead later. Create a design that uses one letter as the figure and another as the ground. This relationship can be stable, reversible, or ambiguous as long as it remains possible to read both letterforms. Remember the importance of thumbnails, exploring a minimum of 15 possibilities.

Fit your design within an 8 × 10" (20 × 25 cm) format. Keep your letters "true to form" and "letter perfect." Use solid black or white shapes without outlining, cross-hatching, or screening. You can (1) extend the edge of a shape, (2) overlap a form, or (3) hide an edge by placing a black letter against a black background or white against white. Do not, however, distort the letters'

basic shapes. Bring out the beauty, variety, and personality of those shapes. **Figures 3-26a, b, c** are student designs based on this project. **Figure 3-26d** shows a page of thumbnails based on this assignment. Once this problem is solved successfully, do your own experiments with figure/ground and letterforms. Feel free to experiment with color and a variety of typestyles.

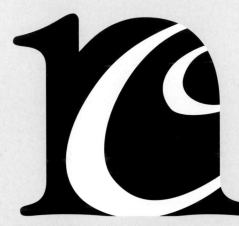

3-26a Christy Niewolny

3-26 *Student solutions to the Figure/Ground and Letterforms project.*

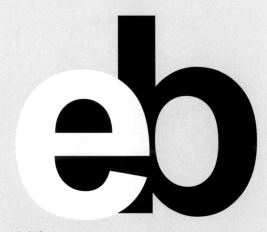

3-26b Erin Bartelson

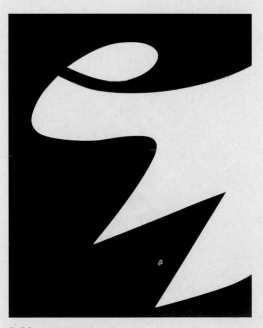

3-26c Eric Wuebben

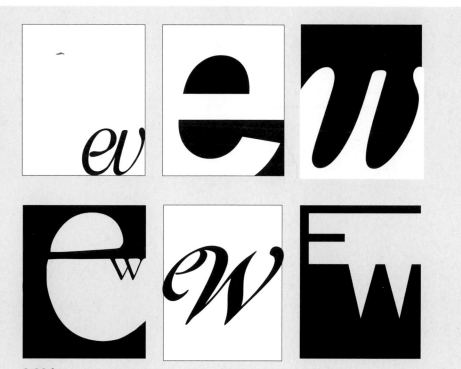

3-26d Eric Wuebben's thumbnail explorations.

Goals and Objectives

Learn to see the shapes in typography as well as image and begin to recognize fonts.

Use thumbnails to explore and evaluate alternative solutions.

Experiment with creating figure/ground relationships.

Learn to manipulate tools and software.

Critique

Begin by looking at the results of the exercises. What forms of figure/ground do you see? Which are the most successful and interesting examples of reversible and of ambiguous figure/ground? Identify the typestyle used in your two favorites. How does the anatomy of this typestyle contribute to the look of the final piece? Where do you see repetition of shape? Which is the best example of Gestalt, where the whole is more than the sum of the parts? Spend some time looking, learn-ing, and talking about these exercises, with everyone participating. You won't agree about everything. That can make for a good discussion. The instructor will make comments, identifying which designs he or she thinks are most successful and explain-ing why.

When finished with the final project you are ready for the second critique. Pre-sent your solution to the class, along with your thumbnails. Tell which typestyle you've chosen and why. Explain why you chose this design from your thumbnails. Discuss your use of symmetry or asymme-try and repetition of shape. What is the figure/ground relationship in your design? How do you think the design might be improved? Ask the class for com-ments on how to improve it. Hopefully, the instructor will let you make changes based on the class critique. That way, criti-cal comments can be used constructively. Again, ask the instructor to make some final comments about what works and why.

TERMINOLOGY

CHAPTER 4

See glossary
for
definitions.

Intellectual Unity	Symmetry	Visual Weight
Visual Unity	Asymmetry	Visual Direction
Kinesthetic Projection	Radial Symmetry	Visual Texture

Toward a Dynamic Balance

4

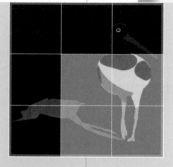

KEY POINTS The elements on a page are a combination of type and image, of photography and illustration. Understanding how to make these diverse elements work together calls for a knowledge of the visual language of balance. This chapter examines how type and image are placed in a composition intentionally to direct the eye and achieve visual unity. The final assignments are type based, to emphasize that placement and command of the visual language of typography is crucial in page layout.

VISUAL AND INTELLECTUAL UNITY

Two kinds of unified communication occur in graphic design. *Intellectual unity* is idea generated and word dominated. The mind, not the eye, makes the grouping. *Visual unity,* in contrast, is created by placement of design elements perceptible to the eye.

The poster in **Figure 4-1** by the famous early-20th-century designer A. M. Cassandre is unified both intellectually and visually. It is a poster for an optician, so it is intellectually unified by the slogan, the emphasis on the eyeglasses, and the bright, clear area of vision through which the eyes peer at us. It is visually unified through a complex series of events as the small type frames the subject's eyes and leads our eyes down and into the *O* of *Leroy.* The size of this small type echoes the size of the serifs on the larger name. The verticality of the typography in *Leroy* is echoed by the bright rectangle surrounding the face.

Imagine that a designer and a writer are hanging a gallery show of a photojournalist's work. The designer is hanging photographs together that have similar value and shapes. The writer is following behind, rehanging the photos together according to subject matter: a picture of a burning building next to one of firefighters. One is *thinking* of subject matter

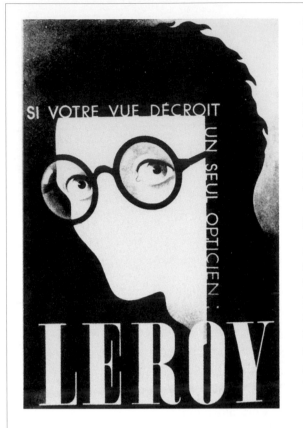

(intellectual unity); the other is *looking* at design (visual unity).

As a design student, you are learning to see the visual unity in a composition and to create with an eye for it. Few people have this skill. Study the <u>form</u> of your design. Once you have mastered the visual "language," you will be able to use it to strengthen both visual and intellectual communication. Both are important and should work together.

Design as Abstraction

Abstract art drew attention to pure visual design. It was "about" color, value, shape, texture, and direction, although often incorporating recognizable imagery. In a purely nonobjective painting by Piet Mondrian (**Figure 4-2**), we are intrigued by the breakup of space and the distribution of value and color. There is no "picture" to distract us from the visual information. The de Stijl

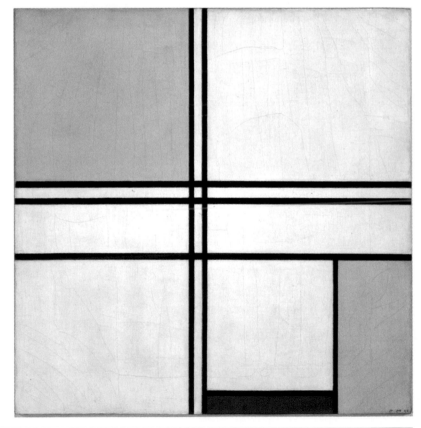

movement had a tremendous influence on graphic design as layout artists began arranging their shapes and blocks of type into asymmetrically balanced compositions.

A good graphic artist must be a good abstract artist, using both pictorial and non-objective elements. **Figure 4-3** shows an International Typographic Style layout by Swiss designer J. Müller-Brockmann that demonstrates a strong eye for pure design shapes reminiscent of Mondrian's surface divisions and strong horizontal/vertical orientation. **Figure 4-4** by contemporary Louisville designer Julius Friedman shows a de Stijl influence on letterhead design.

Graphic design is essentially an abstract art that combines a greatly varied array of elements into a formal 2-D structure. A work should be balanced and visually compelling in its own right as well as supportive of an idea. *Design is a visual language.* The 20th-century movements in art and

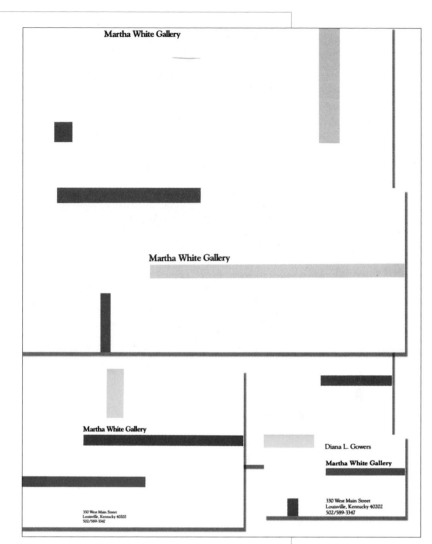

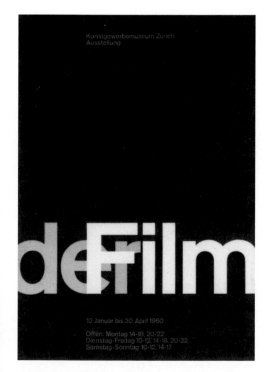

● *4-4 Julius Friedman. Art director, designer. Images design firm. Louisville, KY.* Courtesy of the artist.

design contributed greatly to our current understanding of that language. The fields of Gestalt psychology and semiotics have also helped us understand how meaning is formed.

Working Together

In a design firm, the visual design of a project is given full consideration. In an ad agency, however, copywriters often dominate. Many other places that employ designers also have word people in key positions. These people tend to be sensitive primarily to words and ideas (intellectual unity). They are not trained in visual communication. For this angle they will rely on you. Together you can ensure, as the Bauhaus would say, that the _form_ of a design matches its _function_.

Constructivist El Lissitzky said, "The words on the printed page are meant to be looked at, not listened to." How do we _look_ at designs, and how do we _create_ visually unified ones? The answer has a great deal to do with balance.

VISUAL DYNAMICS

A ladder leaning precariously against a wall will make us tense with a sense of impending collapse. A diver poised at the top of the high dive fills us with suspense. We are not passive viewers. We project our experience into all that we see, including the printed page. How do we project our physical experience into that flat, rectangular surface? _Kinesthetic projection_ (sensory experience stimulated by bodily movements and tensions) is operating, whether we deal with pictures of people or the abstract shapes of type design. **Figure 4-5** by Don Egensteiner demonstrates the attraction of gravity on type. Our culture reads a page from top to bottom, a movement that matches our experience with gravity. It is harder for us to read a design of words or images that asks the eye to go from bottom to top.

4-5 _Don Egensteiner. (Young & Rubicam, Inc.) Ad in_ Fortune _magazine. 1960._
Courtesy of the artist.

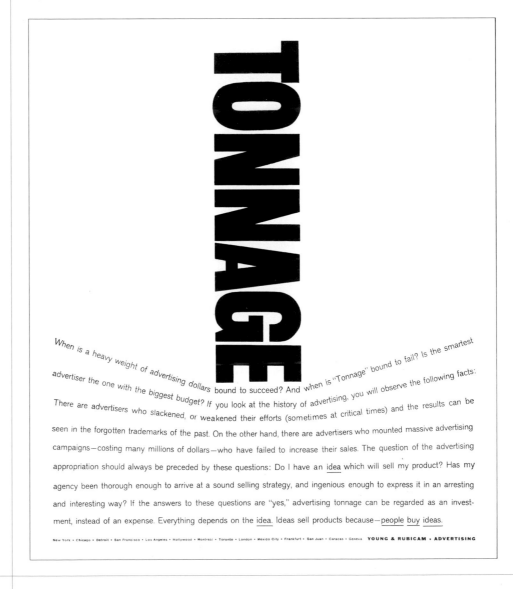

When is a heavy weight of advertising dollars bound to succeed? And when is "Tonnage" bound to fail? Is the smartest advertiser the one with the biggest budget? If you look at the history of advertising, you will observe the following facts: There are advertisers who slackened, or weakened their efforts (sometimes at critical times) and the results can be seen in the forgotten trademarks of the past. On the other hand, there are advertisers who mounted massive advertising campaigns—costing many millions of dollars—who have failed to increase their sales. The question of the advertising appropriation should always be preceded by these questions: Do I have an idea which will sell my product? Has my agency been thorough enough to arrive at a sound selling strategy, and ingenious enough to express it in an arresting and interesting way? If the answers to these questions are "yes," advertising tonnage can be regarded as an investment, instead of an expense. Everything depends on the idea. Ideas sell products because—people buy ideas.

New York • Chicago • Detroit • San Francisco • Los Angeles • Hollywood • Montreal • Toronto • London • Mexico City • Frankfurt • San Juan • Caracas • Geneva   **YOUNG & RUBICAM • ADVERTISING**

We project emotional as well as physical experience onto the page. An illustration of a man stabbed causes discomfort due to such projection. Visual form stirs up memories and expectations. That is why visual perception is so dynamic.

Loose strokes that allow the process of construction to show through also arouse this dynamic tension. The visible brush stroke or "mark of the maker" pulls viewers into the process of creation. Many interesting and appealing printed pieces are created by allowing the tension of the creative process to show through, as in this delightful visual pun on the Saint Louis arch (**Figure 4-6**).

As you saw in Chapter 3, any mark made on a sheet of paper upsets the surface and organizes the space around the mark. *This dynamic tension is not contained*

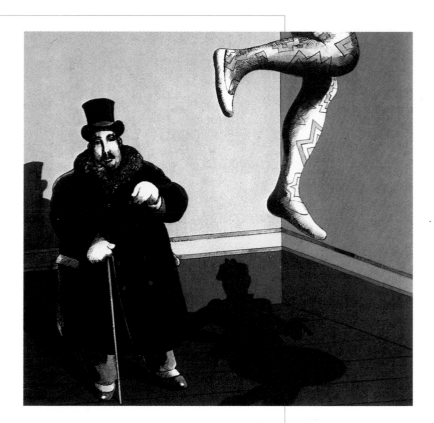

in the paper itself, or in the graphite, ink, or computers we use. It is created by our interaction with the image.

Top to Bottom

We are uncomfortable with shapes clustered at the top of a page, with open space beneath them. We have observed in the world around us that many more things are at rest on the ground than in the sky. If they are not "standing" on anything, we feel suspense as we wait for them to fall. We experience a design as top-heavy much more quickly than as bottom-heavy.

Milton Glaser—a contemporary designer and illustrator, and one of the founders of Push Pin Studios—has been a major force in graphic design for over 45 years (see Chapter 2 and links on the accompanying Web site). He deliberately plays with this top-to-bottom tension in his double portrait of dancer Nijinsky (**Figure 4-7**). All that anchors the dancing, gravity-defying feet is the line of the baseboard under the left foot and the vertical line at the corner.

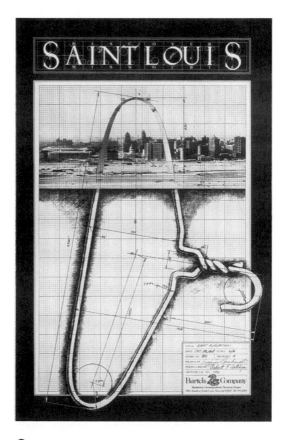

● **4-6** *Self-Promotional Ad. Bartels and Company, St. Louis, MO.*
Courtesy of the studio.

● **4-7** *Milton Glaser.* Portrait of Nijinsky & Diaghilev *designed and illustrated for* Audience *magazine.*
Courtesy of the artist.

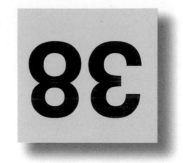

Type designers have long believed in the importance of putting extra weight at the bottom of a letterform to make it look firm and stable. The *8* and *3* in **Figure 4-8** look top-heavy when viewed upside down. Book designers customarily leave more space at the bottom than at the top of a page. They understand that a sense of balance cannot be achieved by placing identical margins at the top and bottom of a composition. This is the same principle used when matting artwork. The bottom measurement is slightly greater than the top, allowing for an optical center that is slightly different from the mathematical center.

Vertical and Horizontal

We find horizontal and vertical lines stable, probably because they remind us of our vertical bodies on the horizontal earth. Milton Glaser again deliberately violates this sense of stability in **Figure 4-9.** As he comments, "The diagonal of this figure gives the illustration its surreal perversity."

We find diagonal lines dynamic because they seem in a state of flux, poised for movement toward the more stable horizontal or vertical. The de Stijl artist Theo van Doesburg (Figure 2-23) deviated from Mondrian's horizontal and vertical compositions, stating that the modern human spirit felt a need to express a sharp contrast to the right angles found in architecture and landscape. An oblique angle is one of the quickest, most effective means of showing tension.

This tension can be created by placing a single shape at an oblique angle or by placing the entire composition at an angle. Part of the delight in Figure 4-9 is the unusual and unanticipated angled figure. This kind of design solution can surprise and interest the viewer.

Left to Right

In Western cultures, we read from the left side of the page to the right, and this experience may influence the way we look for balance between the sides of a design. The left side is the more important, as our attention goes there first. Pictorial movement from the left toward the right seems to require less effort than movement in the opposite direction. An animal speeding from right to left, for example, seems to be overcoming more resistance than one shown moving from left to right. You can explore this left-to-right balance by holding your designs up to a mirror. They may now appear unbalanced.

Overall

Every two-dimensional shape, line, figure/ground relationship, value, and color possesses visual dynamics. We have seen the dynamic value of a kinesthetic reaction, or empathy with the image. There is more to the dynamic of perception, however. We have all seen images of a supposedly moving figure that appears in awkward, static immobility. The objects of dancer or automobile can lead us to expect movement, but only skillful control of visual language can evoke it. Successful communication requires balance, the directing and conducting of visual tensions.

BALANCE

Every healthy person has a sense of balance. It allows us to remain upright and walk, run, or ride a bicycle. Our eyes are pleased with a balanced composition, just as we are pleased with our ability to ride a bicycle and not wobble. **Figure 4-10** creates a focus on the bicycle product, as the large

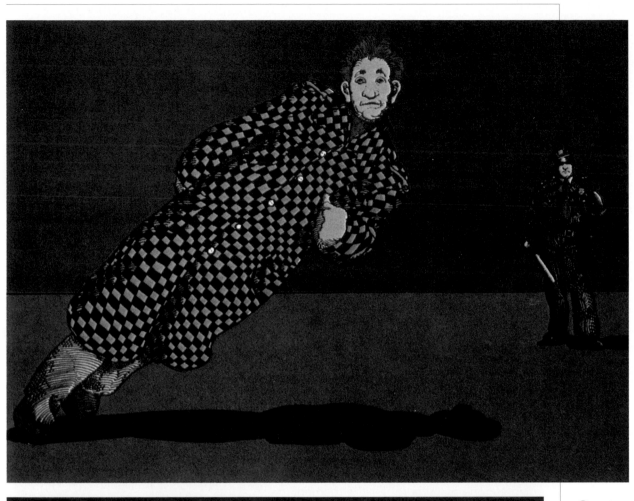

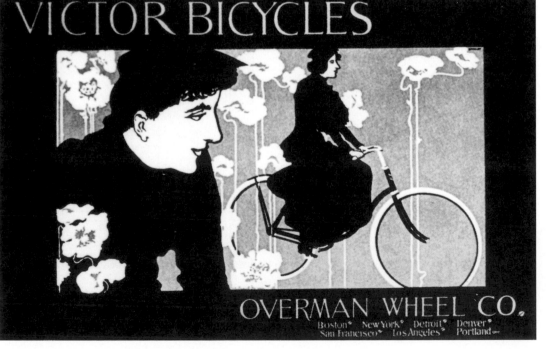

figure on the left directs our gaze at the riding woman. The interwoven dark values help unite the composition, and the placement of the typography again draws our gaze across the bicycle. All of this is a visual balancing act. Lack of balance in a design will irritate viewers and impair the communication. In isomorphic terms, we identify our physical structure with the physical layout/structure of the page and can feel in danger of "falling off the bicycle." How do we create a unified, "ridable," and well-balanced design?

When the dynamic tension between elements is balanced, we are most likely to communicate our intended message. Otherwise, the eye is confused. It shifts from element to element, wanting to move things so they sit right on the page, as we want to straighten a picture hanging crooked on a wall. The viewer so bothered will pay less attention to the quality or content of the picture.

Balance is achieved by two forces of equal strength that pull in opposite directions, or by multiple forces pulling in different directions whose strengths offset one another. Think of visual balance as a multiple rope pull where, for the moment, all teams are exerting the same strength on the rope. It is not a state of rest, but a state of equal tension (**Figure 4-11**).

If artists always employed the simplest and quietest form of balance, their art would seem dull. Too much predictability and unity disturbs us just as too much chaos does. We are animals of change and tension. We strive for growth and life. A simple decrease in visual tension result-

ing in a quiet balance will not satisfy us for long. An interplay between tension-heightening and tension-reducing visual devices seems to satisfy us and match our kinesthetic and emotional experience. *We yearn for diversity as well as unity.*

Symmetry

The two basic types of balance are *symmetry* and *asymmetry*. In symmetrical balance identical shapes are repeated from left to right in mirrored positions on either side of a central vertical axis. **Figure 4-12** is a symmetrical stained-glass window design by architect Frank Lloyd Wright. **Figure 4-13** is a symmetrical logo design. Some symmetrical designs also repeat from top to bottom, often in a *radial* pattern (in which the elements radiate from a central point). Symmetrical balance dominated Western painting and architecture until the Renais-

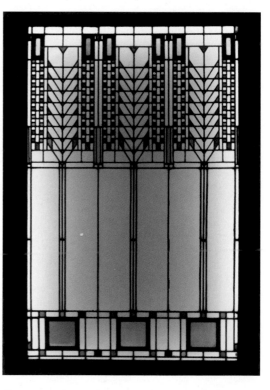

● **4-12** *Tree of Life Window, 1904, by Frank Lloyd Wright.*

Photo © Legion of Honor, Fine Arts Museums of San Francisco. Copyright 2005 Artists Rights Society (ARS), NY.

◗ **4-11** *Elements in symmetrical and asymmetrical balance.*

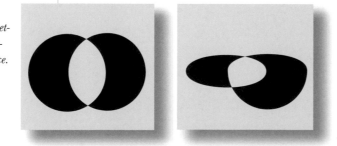

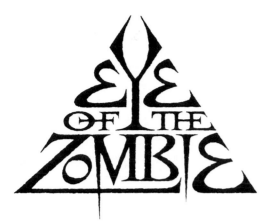

4-13 *Margo Chase. Logo design for John Fogerty's* Eye of the Zombie *album cover.*
Courtesy of the artist.

sance. It dominated graphic design throughout the first centuries of the printing trade, when type was carefully set in centered, formally ordered pages. The traditional book form is a classic example of symmetry (**Figure 4-14a**). **Figure 4-14b** shows a Web page that uses a symmetrical design based on the overall repetition of shape.

Symmetrical design, with its quiet sense of order, is useful whenever stability and a sense of tradition are important. It uses

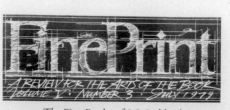

The Five Books of J.G. Lubbock

BY COLIN FRANKLIN

Mr. J.G. Lubbock, book artist, printmaker and author, lives in an obscure corner of Suffolk well protected by a confusing maze of lanes; thus there need be no fear of mass intrusion if I suggest that to know his books one should visit him. Since 1966 his surprising productions have grown among us, bearing his varied and splendid prints and his own struggling cosmic prose printed with the Cambridge taste of Will and Sebastian Carter of The Rampant Lions Press, and nobody has known quite what to make of it all. "Prints are okay," people say, "so long as you don't have to read the books." The sea comes into his writing, and he lives near an estuary. Thinking of another member of his family, Basil Lubbock, whose book *The Last of the Windjammers* I desired as a boy, I had imagined a blustery bearded sailor, talented as seamen often are with their hobbies but greatly out of depth in prose. Mostly it was rather high-flying stuff, like this from his first book:

> The process of production of the work of art is of more interest than the results even to the spectator, because the work must always, by virtue of the artist's imperfection as a transmitter, be inferior to the transcendent reality aimed by him.

He seemed to range rather casually over the universe, taking in science or the sea as a cat needs to pause at the garage. Was it all rather peculiar and pretentious?

It was not. Mr. Lubbock looks a little like portraits of James Joyce, and keeps the Cambridge diffidence of his youth. Few men preserve themselves without worldly corruption through a full span of professional life and return to complete their proper artistic purpose, but he appears to be achieving just that. "Art in books" had appealed to him since undergraduate years at Trinity, where varied Books of Hours and the Trinity College Apocalypse had

provided an enduring wish. As an engraver and living at the edge of London, there had simply been no time for all that; the vanity and indulgence of art waited, and at his retirement burst with energy upon a sudden summer.

He works in mixed method — etching, aquatint, engraving — but always with color and using one plate only. In his studio by the sloping field he was coloring a large chrome-surfaced plate which went through the etching press as he heaved spokes of the old wheel like a sailor at his helm. And out came one of the astonishing religious landscapes, everything looking easy apart from the effort. Hand-coloring of sky and forest background occupied less than two minutes. Later, the laying of a resin-dust ground for aquatint looked simple, the brushing of acid-resist anyone's job. But the vision and energy of these prints. . . . (See illustrations, page 89.)

It has all happened fast for J.G. Lubbock, at an unusual phase of life. Raymond Lister in his book on *British Romantic Art* wrote that "the fuller development and complete synthesis of the aesthetic possibilities of form in Nature have, even now, only just begun to be realized, in the work of artists like Graham Sutherland, Paul Nash, and Ivon Hitchens; but most of all in such works as some little known, but extremely beautiful engravings by J.G. Lubbock, and Morris Cox." The link with Morris Cox and the Gogmagog Press, with comparable and complex examples of color printing, is apt, of course, and I find it entirely sympathetic, though deep differences suggest themselves if one thinks of the two together. Morris Cox has spent his life as an artist, humbly and with a single mind; Lubbock's religion art has survived a conventional career in one of the professions, showing its strength in release. The Gogmagog Press of Morris Cox makes everything, prints, binds, adapts to a table-press and by laborious improvisation produces "form in Nature," as Mr. Lister phrases it.

4-14a *Scott Walker and Tim Girvin. Page design for* Fine Print. *1979.*

4-14b *This web page makes use of an overall symmetrical balance based on repeated shapes. Each of these active shapes leads the visitor to award-winning designs archived on this AIGA (American Institute for Graphic Arts) site.*

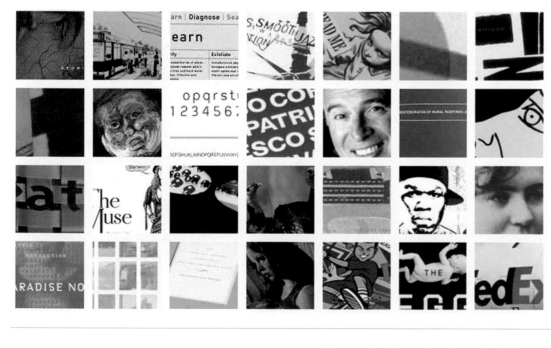

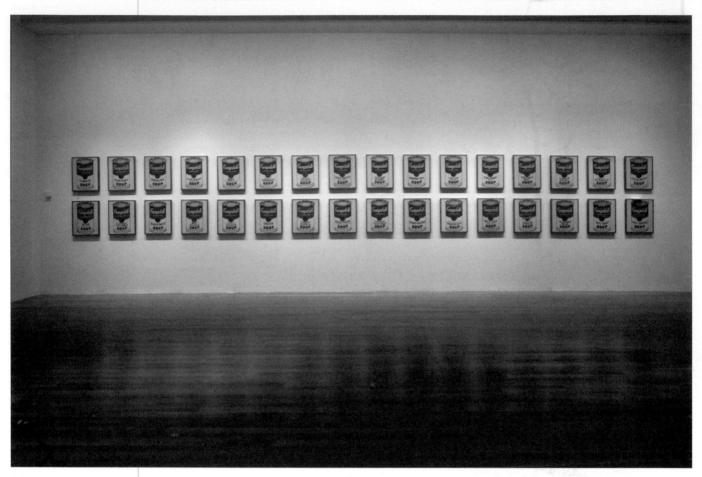

(a)

● **4-15a, b** *Andy Warhol.* Campbell's Soup Cans. *1962. Synthetic polymer paint on canvas, thirty-two works, each 20 × 16" (50.8 × 40.6 cm). The Museum of Modern Art, New York. Purchase and partial gift of Irving Blum.*

Photograph © 2001 The Museum of Modern Art, New York/Art Resource, NY, copyright 2005 Artists Rights Society (ARS), NY.

contrasts of value, texture, and shape to relieve boredom and introduce variety. **Figure 4-15,** by pop artist Andy Warhol, deliberately introduces boredom through repetition of shape and placement. In the process, Warhol examines the nature of, and blurs the boundaries between, fine art and applied design.

There are various ways to achieve symmetry. The most common has a similarity of form on either side of a central dividing line. Symmetrical balance can happen even when images are not precisely identical on either side of this axis. Some differences may occur in shape, color, or value. The important consideration is whether the overall balance of shape, value, and color remains primarily symmetrical. That symmetry may be vertical, horizontal, radial, or overall.

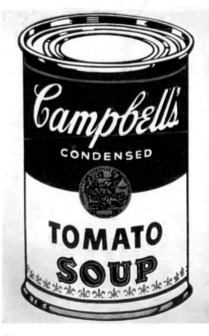

(b)

Graphic Design Basics

Asymmetry

Asymmetrical design evokes a greater sense of movement and change, of possible instability and relative weights. It is like taking your bicycle through an obstacle course. It is a contemporary balance that reflects the changing times. Symmetrical design has a logical certainty that is lacking in asymmetrical design. In symmetrical design, a 2" (5 cm) square in the upper left dictates another such square in the upper right. In asymmetrical design, that square could be balanced by a vast number of shapes, values, colors, or textures. The effects can be difficult, challenging, and visually exciting.

Asymmetrical designs are balanced through contrast to achieve equal visual weight among elements. To be effective, contrast must be definitive. Shapes that are almost but not definitely different are irritating to the eye. **Figure 4-16** is an asymmetrical design that uses several forms of contrast in both figures and letterforms to achieve a balanced, intriguing design.

Balance through Contrast

Symmetry achieves balance through likeness; asymmetry achieves balance through contrast. The easiest way to achieve visual unity would be to make one shape into an overall symmetrical pattern on the page. A

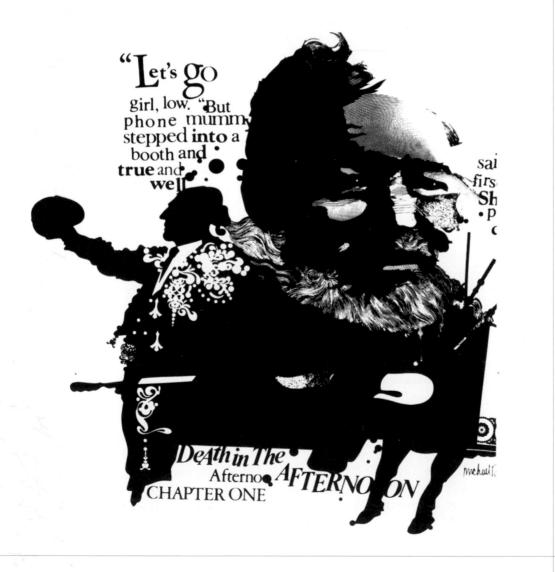

4-16 *Michael David Brown.* Death in the Afternoon *from* Creativity Illustrated. *1983. An example of asymmetrical balance.*

full book page with nothing on it but a solid block of type is visually unified, no matter what the words say. It is also visually dull. In the case of novels, this visual dullness is deliberate. The reader is directed to the content of the words without distraction. In most publications and advertising design, however, this unity must be tempered with contrast if it is to attract and hold the viewer. The designer is usually working with many different elements. Most successful designs rely on a carefully juggled balance of similarities and contrasts.

There are two considerations in setting up balance through contrast: weight and direction. *Visual weight* is the strength or dominance of the visual object. *Visual direction* is the way the eye is drawn between elements over the flat surface. Balance is determined by the natural weight of an element and by the directional forces in the composition. Weight and direction are influenced by several forces that are listed below.

LOCATION The center of a composition will support more weight than the edges. Although a shape is most stable when in the center, it is also visually "light." Small shapes at the edges of a composition can balance large ones in the middle (**Figure 4-17a**).

SPATIAL DEPTH Vistas that lead the eye into the page have great visual strength. We project ourselves into the spatial illusion, so it seems to have greater presence of size (**Figure 4-17b**).

SIZE Visual weight also depends on size (**Figure 4-17c**)—the larger the heavier. Size is the most basic and often used form of contrast in graphic design. The contrast between large and small should be sharp and definite without overpowering the smaller elements so they cannot contribute their share. Most successful designs benefit greatly from size contrast in type or in image. In layout design, the contrast is often between large and small photographs and between headline and text type, as in this 1931 poster design by Max Bill (**Figure 4-18**).

An interesting sort of size contrast is contrast in expected size. The expectedly large element is played small and vice versa, resulting in a visual double take, as in this 1935 poster depicting skiing and ski goggles (**Figure 4-19**).

TEXTURE A small, highly textured area will contrast with and balance a larger area of simple texture (**Figure 4-20a**). This rule refers to *visual texture,* not tactile texture. Contrast of texture is especially useful with text type (type smaller than 14 points, used to set the body of copy).

ISOLATION A shape that appears isolated from its surroundings will draw attention to itself more quickly, and have greater

4-17a *Balance through placement.*

4-17b *Balance through the illusion of spatial depth.*

4-17c *Balance through size contrast.*

| negerkunst |
| prähistorische
felsbilder südafrikas |
| kunstgewerbemuseum   zürich |
| ausstellung 2.—30. august 1931 |
| geöffnet   10—12 14—18 uhr |
| sonntag   —17 uhr |
| montag   geschlossen |
| eintritt —.50 |
| nachmittag und sonntag frei |

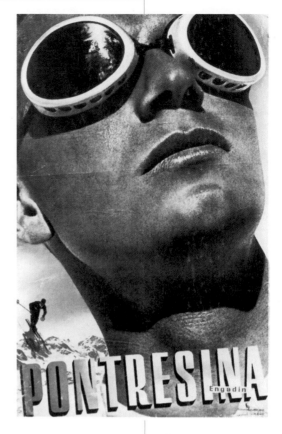

4-18 *Max Bill.* Negerkunst, Prähistorische Felsbilder Südafrikas *(Negro Art, Prehistoric Rock Paintings of South Africa). 1931. Linoleum cut and letterpress, printed in color, 49⁷/₈ × 34³/₄" (126.6 × 88.2 cm). The Museum of Modern Art, New York. Gift of the designer.*

Photograph © The Museum of Modern Art, New York/Art Resource, NY, copyright 2005 Artists Rights Society (ARS), NY.

4-19 *Herbert Matter.* Pontresina Engadin. *1935. Gravure printed in color, 41 × 25¹/₈" (104.1 × 63.8 cm). The Museum of Modern Art, New York. Gift of the designer.*

Photograph © 1998 The Museum of Modern Art, New York/Art Resource, NY.

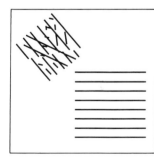

4-20a

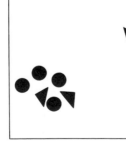

4-20b

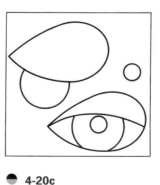

4-20c

4-20d

visual weight, than one surrounded by other shapes (**Figure 4-20b**).

SUBJECT MATTER The natural interest of subject matter will draw the viewer's eye and increase visual weight. It can also create directional movement as we move our eyes between lovers or follow the eye direction of a figure. Our eyes are drawn to the realistic representation of something that interests us (**Figure 4-20c**). The design in **Figure 4-21** is by Herb Lubalin, an important American designer from the last half of the 20th century. The subject is playfully suggested with placement.

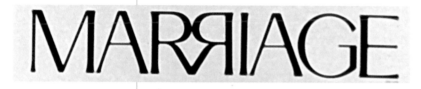

VALUE Areas of high contrast have strong visual weight. A small area of deep black will contrast with and balance a larger area of gray when both are placed against a white background (**Figure 4-20d**). The creation of light and dark areas in a drawing, a painting, a photograph, or an illustration produces a dramatic play of values that delights the eye. Alexey Brodovitch designed these pages for a visual arts magazine in the 1950s (**Figure 4-22**). The high contrast of texture and size, and the cropping of images, create an extremely well-balanced and very dynamic layout.

Typography also uses value contrast. The contrast of a black, heavy type against a light one helps relieve boredom and makes the page more readable. Contrasts between headings and body text and the white areas of paper can create three distinct weights: the black bar of the heading is played against the gray, textured rectangle of the body text, both of which contrast with the white areas of the background page. Designers will sometimes alternate boldface and regular-weight type for a visual pattern.

SHAPE The shape of objects generates a directional pull along the main structural lines. Complicated contours also have a greater visual weight than simple ones. Therefore a small complex shape will contrast with and balance a larger simple shape (**Figure 4-23a**). One block of type might be set in a long, thin ragged rectangle while another is set in a large, square block form. Contrast in shape also works with single letterforms. You might play the round openness of an *O* against the pointed complexities of a *W*, or the shape of an uppercase *A* against a lowercase *c* (**Figure 4-23b**).

STRUCTURE In type design, *structure* refers to the contrasting characteristics of type families. It is a kind of contrast of shape. Compare the *G* in Baskerville with the *G* in Helvetica (Figure 4-23c). They are the same basic shape, but their differences are important in typography. Their structures—thick/thin, serif/sans serif—are different. The logo design in **Figure 4-24** plays with both contrast and similarity, as well as delivering a clever visual pun equating the *V* with facial structure.

COLOR The brighter and more intense the color, the heavier it will be visually. A large gray-blue shape will be balanced by a small bright red shape. A small bright intense

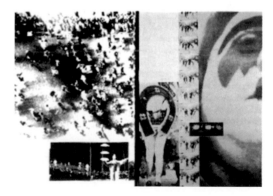

● **4-22** *Alexey Brodovitch. Pages from* Portfolio, *1951.*
Photo courtesy of the UW-Whitewater slide library.

● **4-21** *Herb Lubalin. 1965.*
Photo © The Herb Lubalin Study Center of Design and Typography, The Cooper Union School of Art, NY.

Graphic Design Basics

4-23a

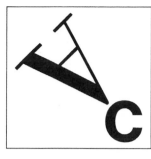

4-23b

GG

4-23c

green will contrast with and balance a large toned-down, low-intensity green. In graphic design, each additional color costs money, so it must be used wisely. A second color can be used to enliven a magazine from cover to cover or only on those pages that are cut from the same printed signature. Remember, in one-color design, that color need not be black. It can be a rich gray, a deep green, or any color you can envision working with your combination of type and image.

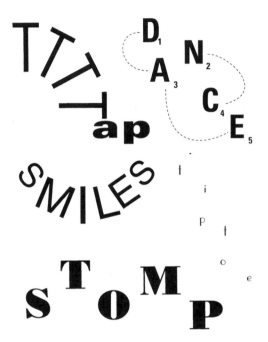

4-25 *Becky Kliese. Word illustration, "Movement," created in response to project 1.*

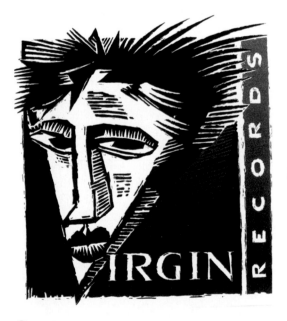

4-24 *Margo Chase. Margo Chase Design, Los Angeles. Logo design for Virgin Records.*
Courtesy of the artist.

Digital Focus

Vector programs like Illustrator and Freehand allow you to type in a letterform and transform it by typestyle and placement, as well as by using the commands for rotate, reflect, scale, and shear. These functions were used in **Figure 4-25. Figure 4-26** is more involved. The cut-and-paste function is used to make a collage of type parts. In some cases, the pen tool is used to add and subtract vector points, and the scissors tool is used to eliminate points. Converting type to outline is a good way to gain control of vector points, but the type tools will no longer work on the letterforms.

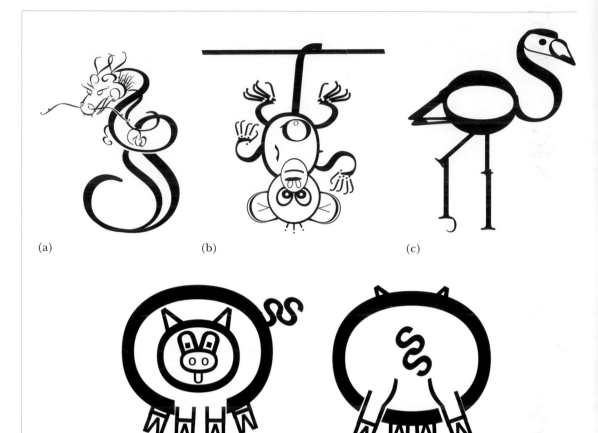

(a) (b) (c)

(d)

EXERCISES

1. Do some thumbnail sketches to experiment with statements a–d. For these sketches, start with letterforms to become better acquainted with them before you try images. The principles of balance function the same, whether applied to type or image. It is easier to understand the fundamentals of an abstract visual language if you begin with simple shapes and letterforms and progress to pictorial designs. What design dynamics are influencing each of these situations?

a. A shape placed in a corner is protected by two sides of a rectangle. Place the same shape farther out into the space around it, and it seems more vulnerable.

b. Two shapes placed side by side will look less lonely than one.

c. Two shapes (an *e* and an *a* work well) placed back to back will appear uncommunicative, unfriendly.

d. A point placed against a soft curve will cause a sensation of discomfort. (An *A* and an *e* work well.)

2. Using traditional collage and/or computer software such as Freehand or Illustrator, select letterforms or simple shapes to demonstrate the following principles. It can be fun to use a font like Webdings for clip art shapes.

a. A single shape can balance several shapes.

b. A large shape can be balanced by a group of smaller shapes.

c. Shapes can be balanced by negative space.

d. A dark shape can be balanced by a larger, lighter shape.

e. A large flat shape can be balanced by a smaller textured shape.

3. Prepare a classroom presentation based on a written critique of a poster, an advertisement, or an illustration. Describe how the design achieves or fails to achieve visual and intellectual unity.

PROJECT 1: WORD ILLUSTRATION

This project asks you to concentrate on placement, contrast, and kinesthetic projection to create a balanced and interesting design. Figure 4-25 shows student designs based on this project.

Choose a word to illustrate. Practice on those listed below. Then find your own word from class discussion or your own research. A dictionary can be useful. Do a minimum of 15 thumbnails. Base these thumbnails and your project on existing typestyles. Search for an appropriate one. Do not use pictures or distort your letterforms into pictures to tell your story. Let the letterforms communicate their message *visually* through size, color, value, shape, structure, texture, placement, and kinesthetic projection. Tell visually what the word says intellectually. Be able to describe the tensions and balancing forces.

Execute your design so it fits within an 11 × 14" (28 × 36 cm) format. Use black and one shade of gray if it will strengthen your design. If you use a computer-generated solution, stay within the same design limitations of size and color. Do not allow the seductive nature of the software to lure you into distorting the basic shape of the letterform. Enjoy it for its clarity and beauty of design. Retain its integrity.

Practice Words

Rain	Allover
Elephant	Black and Blue
Reflection	Wrong Font
Divide	Alone
Dance	Repeat
Invisible	Swiss Cheese

PROJECT 2: ELEPFONTS

Create an animal out of typographic forms. Choose a typestyle and stay with its family of fonts, resizing and rotating as desired. Choose the typography carefully, looking for both shapes and the feeling the typestyle communicates. Feel free to reverse values, overlap, and cut and paste to create your animal, but again, avoid stretching and distorting the proportions of the type. Place your animal somewhere within the rectangle of an $8^1/_2 \times 11"$ (21.5 × 28 cm) page, in either a vertical or a horizontal format. Be sensitive to the edges of the overall composition and the open spaces. **Figure 4-26** shows several playful and creative student solutions.

Goals and Objectives

Practice creating a visually balanced design.

Explore the personalities of varying typestyles.

Increase your control of media, tools, and software, as well as your respect for precision.

Critique
Project 1.

Which solution seems most successful? Make your choice and talk to the class about the characteristics of the typestyle and how it contributes to the solution. What is happening with symmetrical and asymmetrical balance? How does kinesthesia contribute to this design?

Project 2.

How do the parts contribute to the whole? Identify the letterforms in your favorite design. Ask the class and the instructor how your design could be improved. Make changes for the final portfolio piece.

TERMINOLOGY

CHAPTER 5

See glossary
for
definitions.

Gestalt	Figure/Ground	Icon
Similarity	Trademark	Index
Proximity	Symbol	Logo
Continuation	Pictogram	Combination
Closure	Semiotics	Mark

Good Gestalt

5

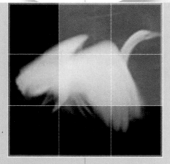

KEY POINTS This chapter introduces the fundamental concepts of visual gestalt that underlie all design structure. Gestalt theory is explained and examined by showing its practical application to symbol and logo design. The function of symbol and logo design in the graphic design field is discussed in terms of the relationship between form and content. All gestalt principles introduced here can be applied in future chapter assignments in layout, illustration, Web design, and more.

THE WHOLE AND THE PARTS

The Gestalt school of psychology, which began in Germany around 1912, investigated how we see and organize visual information into a meaningful whole. The conviction developed that the whole is more than the sum of its parts. This whole cannot be perceived by a simple addition of isolated parts. Each part is influenced by those around it.

WHOLE

As you read the word above, you perceive the whole word, not the individual letterforms that make it up. You can still examine each letter individually, but however you add it up, the *word* is more than the sum of those separate letterforms (**Figure 5-1**).

When you sew a shirt, you begin with pieces of fabric cut into parts. When the parts have been assembled, a new thing has been created. The collar, the facing, and the sleeve still exist, but they have a new "whole" identity called a shirt.

Giuseppe Arcimboldo, a painter from the 16th century, demonstrated the principle clearly in the portrait in **Figure 5-2.** A close examination reveals the separate parts that

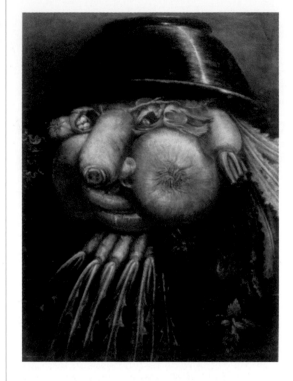

⬤ **5-1** *The whole is more than the sum of the separate letterforms in this diagram, where individual letters in a word are rearranged.*

⬤ **5-2** *Giuseppe Arcimboldo. Sixteenth-century painting in which the separate parts combine to form a new whole.*

GESTALT PRINCIPLES

A designer works not simply with lines on paper, but with perceptual structure. Learn these gestalt perceptual principles and you can take advantage of the way object, eye, and graphic creation interweave. A beautiful example can be found in the editorial illustration by John Heartfield (**Figure 5-4**). This image makes a powerful comment through its use of similarity. The figure on the top is a medieval depiction of a man being "broken on the wheel." In this form of torture, the victim would be tied to a wagon wheel and struck with a blunt weapon to break the bones. The figure on the bottom is a photo collage by Heartfield that shows a man symbolically caught and tortured in the swastika symbol for Hitler's regime. The similar shape and placement make the artist's point that "As in the Middle Ages . . . so in the Third Reich."

Similarity

When we see things that are similar, we naturally group them. Grouping by similarity occurs when we see similar shape, size, color, spatial location (proximity), angle, or value. All things are similar in some respects and different in others. In a group of similar shapes and angles, we will notice a dissimilar shape or angle. In **Figure 5-5** the gray square draws attention because it is different from the squares surrounding it. The

make up this head. A similar example is the contemporary alphabet made up of objects in **Figure 5-3.**

The early Gestalt psychologists and many other researchers into visual perception have discovered that the eye seeks a unified whole, or *gestalt*. Knowing how the eye seeks a gestalt can help you analyze and create successful designs. By knowing what connections the eye will draw for itself, you eliminate clutter and produce a clearly articulated design.

⬤ **5-3** *Julius Friedman and Walter McCord. Co-designers. Logo for Images design firm in which many different images make up the whole word.*

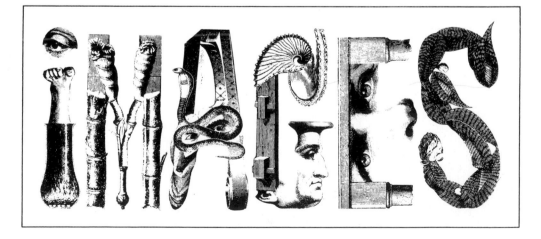

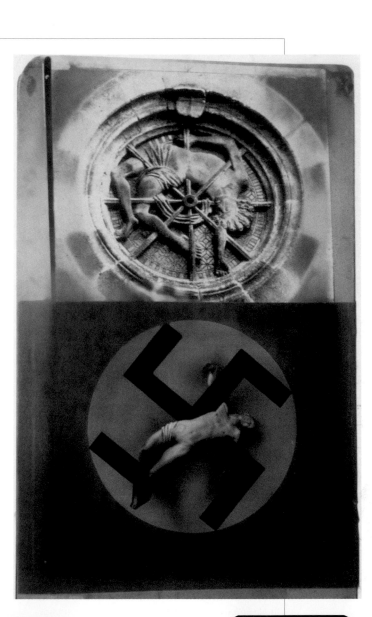

three *i* letters in "similarity" are shown to be similar by treating them in a similar fashion to each other but differently from the other letterforms.

Similarity is necessary before we can compare differences. In the photograph by Gordon Baer (**Figure 5-6**), we are attracted by a similarity of sleeping forms and then begin an internal dialogue about their message. It is useful for the designer to know that the eye will notice and group similarities while separating differences. This is true for subject matter and for nonfigurative design forms. The symbol and logotype created for Alcoa by Saul Bass, a renowned American designer, relies on similarity of shape. Count the triangles in **Figure 5-7**.

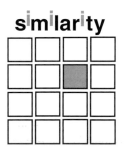

5-5 *The use of similarity also draws attention to differences.*

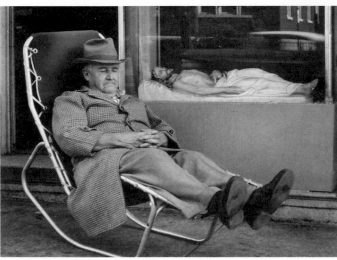

5-6 Gordon Baer. *Freelance photographer, Cincinnati, OH.* Two Old Men. *The photographer's eye noticed that these two men are similar but different.*

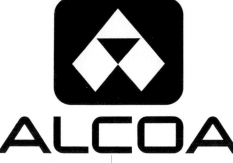

5-7 Saul Bass. *Trademark for Alcoa.*
Courtesy, Aluminum Company of America.

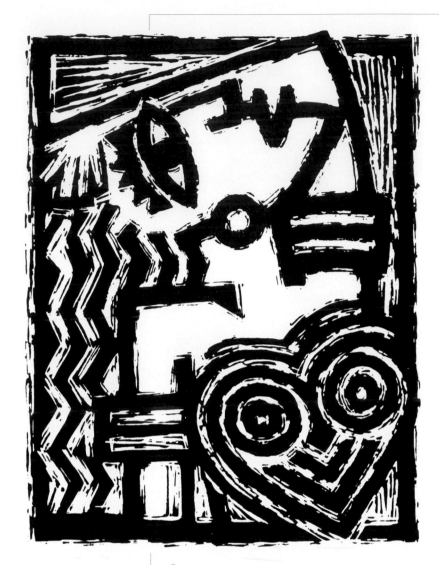

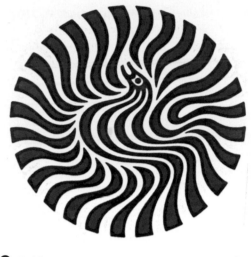

● **5-10** *Stefan Kantscheff,* *Bulgarian designer, created this beautiful example of rhythm and repetition in symbol design.*

The proximity of lines or edges makes it easier for the eye to group them to form a figure. **Figure 5-10** places shapes in close proximity that never touch but form a dynamic whole through proximity and three other gestalt unit-forming principles, listed next.

Continuation

The viewer's eye will follow along a line or curve. *Continuation* occurs when the eye is carried smoothly into a line or curve that links adjoining objects. The diagram in **Figure 5-11** shows how the eye will follow the interruption of the black outline, seeing a continued, implied shape. This principle is used extensively in layout design to unite various elements, often by placing them along invisible grid lines.

Shapes that are not interrupted but form a harmonious relationship with adjoining

● **5-8** *Margo Chase.* Logo for Esprit woman. *A repetitive textural line gives this design its unique visual energy.*

In **Figure 5-8,** contemporary designer Margo Chase uses a similarity of line quality to create a dynamic, unified logo for Esprit.

Proximity

Grouping by similarity in spatial location is called *proximity,* or nearness. The closer two visual elements are, the more likely we will see them as a group. In **Figure 5-9** the four squares on top seem to form a group while the eight squares on the bottom appear to belong to a different group.

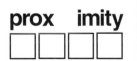

● **5-9** *Proximity grouping is grouping by similarity in spatial location.*

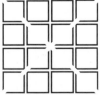

◑ **5-11** *Continuation occurs when the eye is carried smoothly along a suggested line or curve.*

Graphic Design Basics

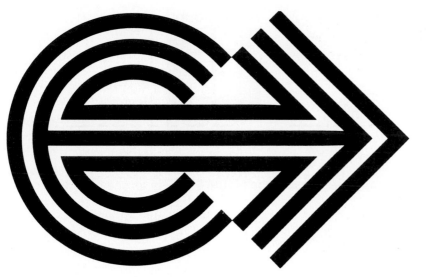

● **5-12** *George Jad-owski*, *designer*, **Danny C. Jones**, *art director. Symbol for the U.S. Energy Extension Service. This symbol illustrates energy with its use of continuation.*

shapes please the eye. The symbol of the U.S. Energy Extension Service (**Figure 5-12**) uses continuation to emphasize the moving, dynamic nature of energy. In this example the ends of the *e* line up with the ends of the arrowhead, forming a continued line that harmoniously unites the shapes. The *Family Circle* logo in **Figure 5-13** creates continuation by lining up the verticals of the two *i* letterforms and also lining up the *l* and *r* forms. The eye draws a line down those vertical shapes that makes a new whole out of two different words.

Closure

Familiar shapes are more readily seen as complete than incomplete. When the eye completes (closes) a line or curve in order to form a familiar shape, *closure* has occurred. **Figure 5-14** shows white circles appearing as the eye and brain close the open areas

into a familiar shape. **Figure 5-15** is a symbol created by the 1 + 1 Design firm. Do you see the white plus sign created by the figure/ground relationship? Part of the closure in this example includes a sudden connection with the name of the firm. This sort of connection is especially useful in trademark design. Closure is sometimes

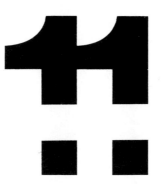

● **5-15** *Pat Hughes* and **Steve Quinn**. *This elegantly constructed symbol for 1 + 1 Design uses a rich combination of similarity, reversible figure/ground, and closure.*

closure

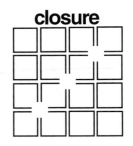

● **5-14** *The eye and brain close the white areas into circles. This demonstrates a highly active partnership between eye and brain and graphic image that is at the heart of visual gestalt.*

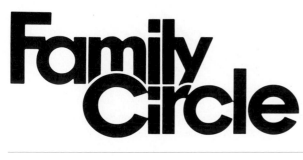

● **5-13** *Herb Lubalin (art director) and* **Alan Peckolick** *(designer). Family Circle. 1967. This magazine logo makes quiet but elegant use of placement and continuation.*

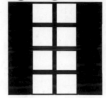

5-16 *Stefan Kantscheff. Symbol for the Staatliches Operettentheater in Sofia, Bulgaria.*

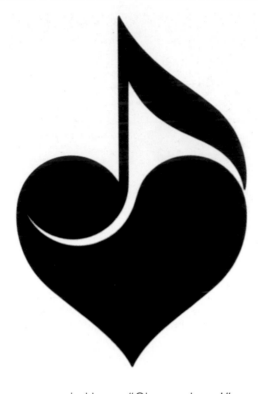

figureground

5-18 *The perception of figure/ground underlies much of symbol and logo construction.*

than one solution to the searching eye, as we discussed in Chapter 3. The diagram in **Figure 5-18** lets us see black bars on a white central background or see white squares on a black ground. Gestalt relationships in graphic design are always intended to help structure an appropriate communication. The most structurally beautiful design is not successful if it fails to present the subject appropriately. **Figure 5-19** presents a fairly abstract symbolic notion of the delivery and exchange of information. It creates a lively figure/ground relationship with the white squares in the background. Similarity in the linear treatment and repeated arrow shapes unite the overall symbol. Finally, the two directional arrows suggest the notion of interactivity.

Sometimes referred to as positive and negative space relationship, the figure/

accompanied by an "Oh, now I see!" reaction. An elegant editorial statement is made in **Figure 5-16** in this opera symbol when we recognize the link between a musical note and a heart.

Figure 5-17 by Herb Lubalin calls for active conceptual participation by the viewer to achieve an intellectual closure with the *O* shape and a womb.

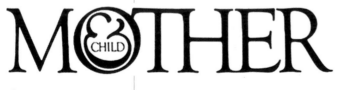

5-17 *Herb Lubalin. 1965. This creation by an important 20th-century designer relies on an anthropomorphic identification with the shape of letterforms to bring closure.*

Figure/Ground

The fundamental law of perception that makes it possible to discern objects is the *figure/ground* relationship. The eye and mind separate an object (figure) from its surroundings (ground). As you read this page, your eyes are separating out words (figure) from ground (paper). Often the relationship between figure and ground is dynamic and ambiguous, offering more

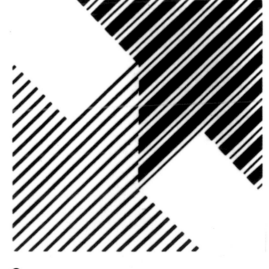

5-19 *A. E. Arntson. 1985. This symbol for Inter-active Financial Learning Systems uses a variety of gestalt principles to illustrate the nature of the company.*

Graphic Design Basics

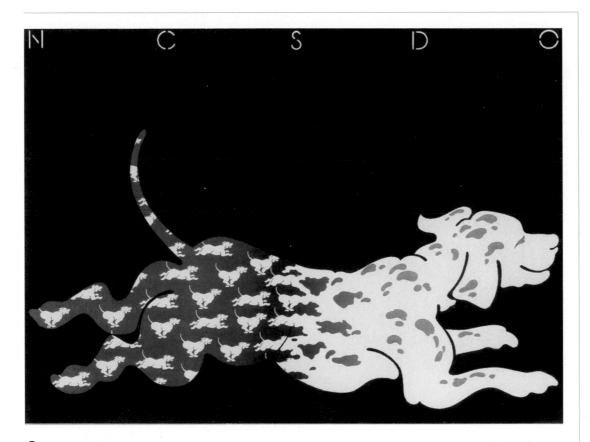

● **5-20** *Whitney Sherman*, *illustrator*; *Martin Bennett* and *Mary Pat Andrea*, *designers. North Charles Street Design Organization. This poster uses the gestalt principle of figure ground to announce an upcoming move to a new location.*

ground principle is crucial to shaping a strong design (see Chapter 4). You must be aware of creating shapes in the "leftover" ground every time you create a figure. **Figure 5-20** uses this principle in an entertaining way, perhaps inspired by the work of the 20th-century printmaker M. C. Escher. The small dogs become spots, emphasizing the notion of forward movement and change. Escher created the wonderful example of a reversible figure/ground relationship shown in **Figure 5-21.** There is no dominant foreground. As soon as our eyes fasten on an image, the surrounding background lays claim to our attention, reversing the figure. **Figure 5-22** is a contemporary illustration that uses an ambiguous figure/ground relationship as an inherent part of its rich structure. One figure is made up of several different pictures.

TRADEMARKS

The interplay of gestalt principles occurs in all areas of design but is clearest in the creation of logo and symbol trademarks. Here form and function are closely related. We have examined the gestalt formal structure of trademarks. Next we consider the function of these marks. The final project in this chapter will ask you to relate these two considerations.

Functions

Symbols and trademarks have served many functions in history. The early Christians relied on the symbol of the fish to identify themselves to one another secretly. In the Dark Ages, family trademarks were used. No nobleman in the same region could

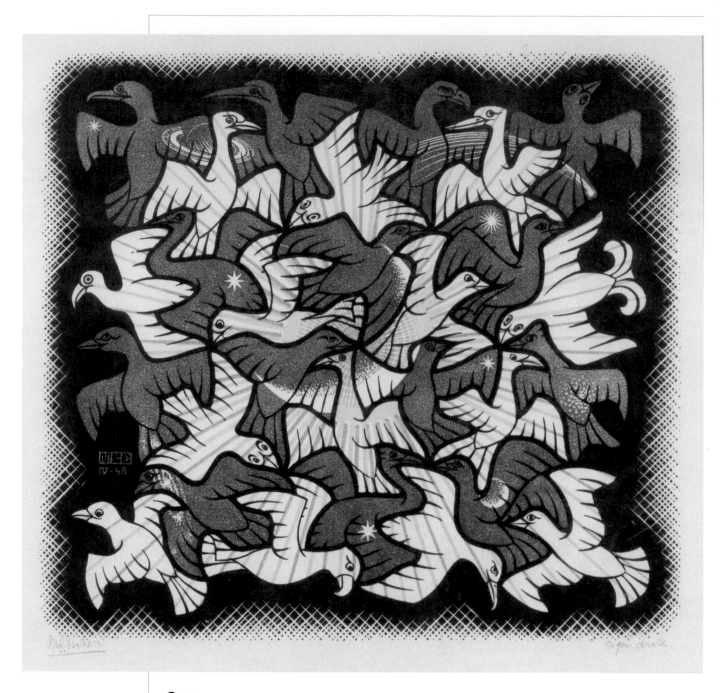

● **5-21** *M. C. Escher.* Sun and Moon. *1948 woodcut. 25.1 × 27cm.*
Art Resource, NY.

wear the same coat of arms. **Figure 5-23** shows a typical coat of arms. These "arms" came to mark the owner's possessions. Peasants used simpler "housemarks," which were especially useful because few people could read. Also, each medieval craftsman inscribed a personal mark on his or her products and hung out a sign showing his calling. During the Renaissance, the three golden balls of the Medici family symbolized money lending. The Medici mark can still be seen today, pirated by modern pawnbrokers. More recently, in the western United States each cattle rancher has

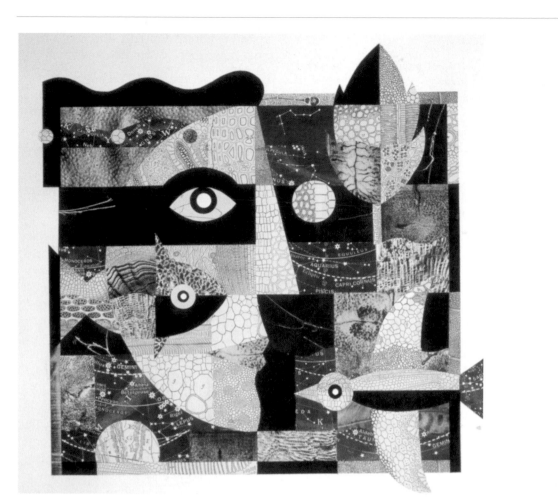

5-22 *David McLimans.*
Illustration courtesy of the artist.

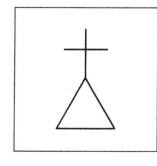

5-23 *A medieval coat of arms is an early example of a trademark.*

used a brand or mark to identify the ranch that owns individual cattle (**Figure 5-24**).

Today trademarks are widely used by corporations. A *trademark* is any unique name or symbol used to identify a product and to distinguish it from others. These unique marks can be registered and protected by law. Their primary use is to increase brand recognition and advertise products and services. The use of trademarks, or logos, flourishes as individuals identify themselves on letterheads, résumés, and home pages. Consumers come to rely on the quality associated with a trademark (think of Coca-Cola) and are willing to try new products identified with that recognized trademark.

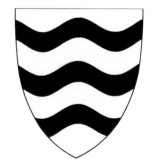

5-24 *Cattle brands are also examples of trademarks.*

Making "Marks"

Unlike other forms of advertising, the modern trademark is often a long-term design. It may appear on letterhead, company trucks, packaging, employee uniforms, newsletters, and so on. Designers can spend months developing and testing one trademark. Only a strong design with a simple, unified gestalt will stand the test of repeated exposure.

Keep several points in mind when developing a mark:

1. You are not just "making your mark on the world"; you are making a mark to symbolize your client and your client's product. It must reflect the nature and quality of that product to an audience. Research the company, product, and audience. As designer Paul Rand said, "A trademark is created by a designer, but *made* by a corporation. A trademark is a picture, an image . . . of a corporation."

2. The mark is often reproduced in many different sizes, from the company vehicle to a business card. Your design must remain legible and strong in all circumstances.

3. Because this mark may be reproduced in newspaper advertising or with severely limited in-house duplicating facilities, it must reproduce well in one color.

4. Many trademarks are seen in adverse viewing conditions, such as short exposure, poor lighting, competitive surroundings, and lack of viewer interest. Under such conditions, simplicity is a virtue. A simple, interesting shape with a good gestalt is easier to remember than a more complex design.

Some designers refer to all trademarks as logos, whereas others have a complex system of subtle categories. The two most common categories of trademarks, however, are symbol and logo.

Symbols

Webster's Eleventh New Collegiate Dictionary says a *symbol* is "something that stands for or suggests something else by reason of relationship, association, convention, or accidental resemblance; *especially:* a visible sign of something invisible. . . . An arbitrary or conventional sign used in writing or printing relating to a particular field to represent operations, quantities, elements, relations, or qualities." Historically important symbols include national flags, the cross, and the swastika (**Figure 5-25**).

● **5-25** *The flag, cross, and swastika are examples of historically important visual symbols.*

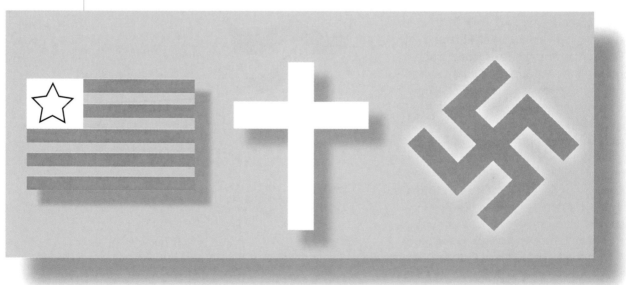

The symbol is a type of trademark used to represent a company or product. It can be abstract or representational, but it does not usually include letterforms. It represents invisible qualities of a product, such as reliability, durability, strength, or warmth.

A symbol has several advantages, including:

1. Original construction
2. Simple gestalt, resulting in quick recognition
3. A strong association that "colors" the symbol's interpretation

Figure 5-26, a symbol proposed for the California Conservation Corps by the critically acclaimed designer Michael Vanderbyl, demonstrates all three qualities. It is an original mark, unlike any other, and it makes excellent use of the figure/ground relationship. We cannot see the baby without the presence of the parent. The whole that is formed by these strong, seemingly simple shapes can be quickly recognized. The associations that this symbol stimulates are very positive and nurturing. Form and content reinforce one another in this fine design.

A *pictogram* is a symbol used to cross language barriers for international signage. It is found in bilingual cities, such as Mon-

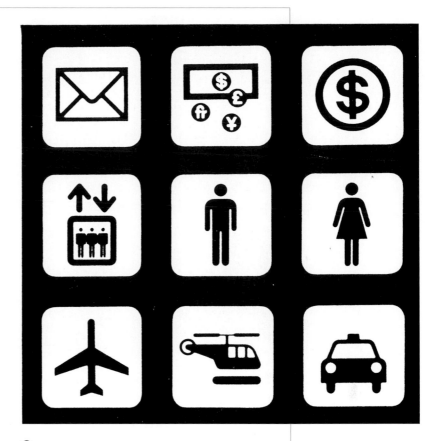

● **5-27** *Roger Cook and Don Shanosky. (Cook and Shanosky Associates). Department of Transportation pictograms prepared by the American Institute of Graphic Arts (AIGA).*

treal, for traffic signs. It is also found in airports and on safety instructions inside airplanes. It is representational rather than abstract, as shown in **Figure 5-27.**

Symbols can also be examined in the light of *semiotics,* which shows how an image takes on a culturally accepted meaning that goes beyond its merely recognizable shape. An *icon* is a sign that bears a direct relationship to the object described. Realistic drawings and photographs are examples. Semiotics goes on to define an *index* as a sign that bears a direct relationship to the object it represents without simply showing that object. For example, the shadow of a building indicates its presence. An index can be a useful way to approach the creation of a mark. Symbol, icon, and index are all considered good approaches

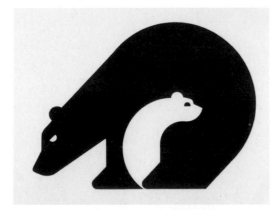

● **5-26** *Michael Vanderbyl. This symbol proposed but not adopted for the California Conservation Corps is an excellent integration of form and content.*
Courtesy of the artist.

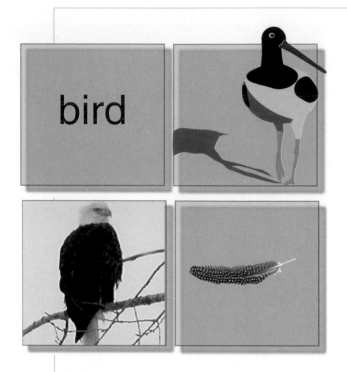

5-28 *The study of semiotics presents an icon, a symbol, and an index as ways of examining an image or idea and developing a trademark.*

in the creation of a trademark symbol. See the diagram in **Figure 5-28.**

Logos

The second category of trademark is called a *logo* or *logotype*. The logo is a unique type or lettering that spells out the name of a company or product. It may be hand lettered, but it is usually constructed out of variations on an existing typeface. Historically, it developed after the symbol, because it requires a literate audience.

When you create a logo, choose type that suits the nature of your client and audience. **Figure 5-29** was created for *Reader's Digest* by one of the most respected and influential logo designers, Herb Lubalin. The clean, bold typestyle makes it easy to see the play on similar shapes that creates the "family connection" hidden in the word. **Figure 5-30** was created for the Ditto Corporation, a duplication products manufacturer. Compare this typestyle with the one before. Although both are sans serif, each is distinctively suited to its use.

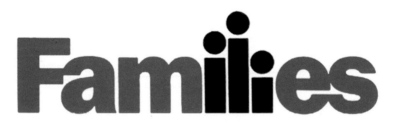

5-29 *Herb Lubalin.* Trademark created for Reader's Digest. *Assigned to Military Family Communication, publisher of* Families *magazine.*

5-30 *Logotype for Ditto Corporation. The Ditto trademark is a federally registered trademark of Starkey Chemical Process Co. of LaGrange, IL.*

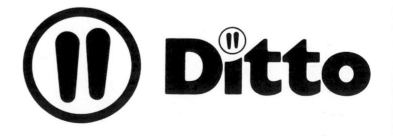

The advantages of a <u>logotype</u> include (1) original construction and (2) easy identification with company or product because the name is included.

A *combination mark* is a symbol and logo used together. These marks can be more difficult to construct with a good gestalt because of their complexity. They are often used, however, because they combine the advantages of symbol and logo.

In all these marks, gestalt principles help create a unified and striking design. With good gestalt, form and function interweave in a powerful whole.

Digital Focus

The majority of logo designs are created using vector graphics. Since vectors can be enlarged or reduced with no loss of detail or resolution, they are the logical choice for logos that will appear on trucks, Web graphics, letterhead, and other applications. Raster graphics can form the underlying basis for scanned imagery that is imported into a vector program and traced over. Examine the accompanying Web site for software solutions to the following exercises and assignments.

EXERCISES

This assignment is best done with graph paper or a vector graphics program with the grid turned on, utilizing guides and rulers (**Figure 5-31**).

1. Select a circle $1/2$" (4 cm) in diameter (or slightly more), and practice overlapping two circles to create new and varied shapes. Then try three circles. Do not use line—only shape and black-and-white values. Reverse one out of another for more interesting effects.

2. Place a circle in various positions within a square. Do not use line. Use black-and-white shapes. Experiment with size and border violations.

3. Set up a series of vertical lines so the white lines gradually diminish while the black lines expand. Start by making a series of vertical lines $1/4$" (5 mm) apart. Each line can then be thickened.

4. Create a break or anomaly in a series of vertical lines.

5. Examine the illustrations in this chapter and identify the unifying gestalt features in each mark.

6. Use one or more of these exercises to develop an appropriate symbol for a company of your choice.

PROJECT

Combination Mark

Design a combination mark for a company mentioned in this chapter. Consider doing Internet research to learn about the character and purpose of this company. You may combine logo and symbol into one image or present them as two images, carefully placed together. Experiment with many options in your thumbnail sketches. Incorporate each of the gestalt principles discussed in this chapter into your thumbnail investigation.

Begin with an existing typestyle and make careful alterations. Spend time looking through type choices. Experiment with fonts, finding which are appropriate for the company you have selected. List the name of the font next to your initial sketch.

After consulting with the instructor, select two thumbnails to create as full-size roughs for final review. Fine-tune and execute the strongest within an 8 × 10" (19 × 25 cm) format. Using only one color, execute it in paint, ink, cut paper, or a vector graphics computer program.

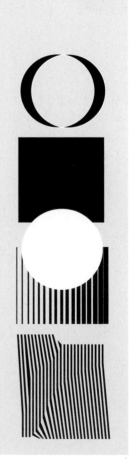

◗ **5-31** *Eric Wuebben. Line variations using an anomaly, or change, in an expected pattern.*

Keep your design visually strong and uncluttered. Be prepared to discuss the gestalt principles involved during the critique. Use at least two of them in your final trademark. Also consider the audience your trademark will be reaching. What will appeal to them? Consider the company. What will be an accurate and positive image? Be prepared to discuss the function of your trademark and why the design suits it. **Figure 5-32** is a combination mark that makes excellent use of an integration of type and image.

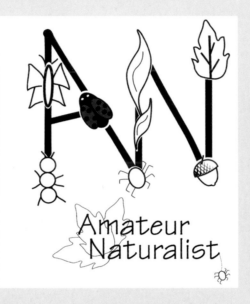

● **5-32** *Valerie Murname created this combination mark for the Amateur Naturalist, a store specializing in products for families interested in studying the outdoors.*

Trademark Design

1. The Museum of Transportation Logo

The Museum of Transportation is a new museum in your state, and it needs a logo. It has a permanent collection that includes all forms of personal and mass transport vehicles in the state from the history of transportation. Consider things as diverse as the first wheel, children's scooters, boats, and Lear jets. Consider the places people go and things people use transportation for. Include the name of

the institution along with an image to create a combination mark. Examine the accompanying Web site to see posters created for this exhibition (**Fig 5-33**).

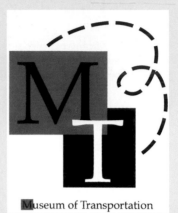

Museum of Transportation

● **5-33** *Logo design by Nicolae Slamar for the Museum of Transportation.*

2. Narnia Zoo

This is a large, well-funded, but new zoo. It hosts everything from aardvarks to insects to zebras and emphasizes preservation of endangered species and habitats. It is planning a special exhibition for which you will create a name and design a poster in a later assignment. Design a symbol or combination mark for this zoo. Consider creating signage for different areas of the zoo. Second, optional assignment: Design a logo, symbol, or combination mark for the special exhibition (see **Figure 5-34**).

Process

Begin this assignment with a series of 10 to 20 thumbnails. You may want to experiment with trademarks for both institutions.

Refine the best into two or three roughs, doing all necessary visual research.

Proceed with the final trademark design after class discussion.

Goals and Objectives

Learn to apply gestalt principles to logo design that reflects the client's needs.

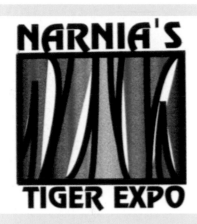

● **5-34** *Russ Jacobs.* *Continuation unites type and image in this combination mark for a special exhibition at the zoo. Notice how the abstract tiger stripes connect the lines of the type on top and bottom.*

Communicate the nature of an institution with a design that appeals to the public.

Apply gestalt principles to develop a trademark that appropriately represents a company or product.

Research for inspirational solutions in periodicals, the library, original photos, or the Internet. Collect or create images for symbol reference.

Critique

How does your design utilize the gestalt principles of similarity, proximity, continuation, closure, and figure/ground?

What is the nature of the institution? How does your design capture the nature of the institution or product? What typeface have you have chosen, and why is it appropriate?

How does your symbol or logo embody the qualities of a successful trademark as discussed in this chapter?

How can your design be improved?

What is the most successful example of each gestalt principle in the various class solutions?

Variations

Ask your instructor to assign existing corporations that need a new trademark design.

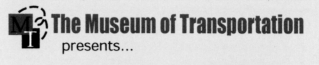

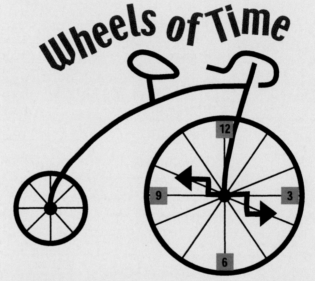

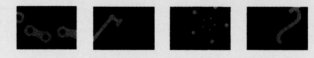

October 31st ~ January 2nd 2002

● **5-35** *Poster design for the Museum of Transportation created for her student portfolio by Nicolae Slamar.*

TERMINOLOGY

CHAPTER 6

Using Text Type

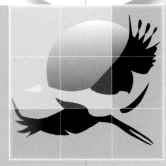

KEY POINTS Innovations in technology have greatly affected the development of our visual record of the spoken language. Historically, the tools used to create letterforms have largely determined the shape of those letterforms. This chapter briefly introduces the historical development of typestyles, explaining the relationship between style and technology. It describes the role of text type in page layout, including size, line length, style, leading, spacing, and format.

THE DEVELOPMENT OF WRITTEN COMMUNICATION

Since a person first made a mark in the sand for another to find, we have been communicating with a visual language. The earliest forms of visual communication were pictorial drawings of everyday objects, such as weapons and animals. As the desire to communicate grew, these pictures were combined to convey thoughts and ideas.

With visual language, it became possible to conquer time. An individual's mark could be seen and understood after the maker had moved on or even died. Civilization developed along with our visual record of the spoken language. So did the importance of the individual.

Alphabets

The earliest known alphabet emerged in Egypt some 4,000 years ago. Its inventors adopted pictorial characters from Egyptian writing to represent sounds in a different language. That language was spoken by a western Asian people then living in Egypt. For the most part, characters in Egyptian writing represented entire words or other meaningful units of language. In contrast, each character in the first alphabet represented a single sound within a word. The development of the alphabet revolutionized communication. To master Egyptian writing required memorizing hundreds of characters; to master the alphabet, one needed to learn fewer than 30.

By 1,000 BC the Phoenicians were using the alphabet. A nation of traders, they needed an efficient, condensed writing system to record business transactions. As time passed, the Phoenician letterforms grew more abstract and linear. The Greeks adopted the alphabet from the Phoenicians a few centuries later. Unlike the Phoenicians, however, the Greeks developed letters to represent vowels as well as consonants. By 700 BC the Greek alphabet had spread to the Italian peninsula, where the Romans eventually learned it, further modifying it to suit the sounds of Latin. Gradually the Roman alphabet evolved into a form almost identical to that used in most western European alphabets today (**Figure 6-1**).

As designers working with the letters of the alphabet, we have thousands of years of history behind us. The shape of letters has been largely determined by the tools used to create them. The Phoenicians, Greeks, and Romans applied ink to reed brushes or pens for writing on papyrus. This method created letters with a pattern of thick and thin strokes and frequently rounded forms. The Greeks and Romans also used a sharp, pointed stylus to write on a wax-coated tablet, resulting in strokes of even thickness. Important inscriptions were carved into stone with a chisel. In early stone inscriptions letters tended to have simpler straighter lines, perhaps because curves were more difficult to carve. Eventually, however, the Roman

alphabet, even as cut into stone, came to have a greater variety of straight and curved forms than its predecessors. Also, this alphabet came to have a finishing line, or serif, at the top and/or foot of vertical elements. A by-product of the way the letters were carved, serifs gave the Roman alphabet an unprecedented sense of overall harmony. But these letterforms were difficult to write and took up a lot of space on increasingly expensive papyrus. So a simpler, more condensed, more easily written script developed. Eventually the classic capital letters came to be used with smaller letters, setting a precedent for our upper and lowercase style. Handwritten papyrus scrolls kept the alphabet alive during the early Middle Ages. These scrolls, produced mostly by Christian monks, were eventually superseded by folded parchment manuscript books.

Our most common typefaces are imitations of early handwriting or modifications of early typefaces modeled after the lettering in manuscript books. From the invention of the first printing press with a system of movable type in the 15th century until the 18th century, type designs were based on handwriting.

INFLUENCE OF TECHNOLOGY Innovation in printing technology during the Industrial Revolution contributed to the development of new typestyles. Advances in mechanical design and cast-iron parts were applied

● **6-1** *The Phoenician, Greek, and Roman alphabets.*

1. Phoenician alphabet

2. Greek alphabet

3. Roman alphabet

Graphic Design Basics

to the printing press in the early 1800s, allowing for a much larger printed sheet. The London Times was the first publisher to replace the hand press with a steam-powered printing press, which could make more than a thousand impressions an hour. Another important innovation of the 1800s was the invention of the Linotype machine in 1886 by Ottmar Mergenthaler. It replaced hand typesetting with a keyboard-operated machine that generated lines of type cast in melted lead. These lines of type were locked into slim wooden cases before printing. The invention of phototypography in the 1960s heralded the Age of Information, as it became increasingly easy and important to disseminate information by word and image. Computers now make it possible to develop variations on existing typestyles quickly. Specialized software makes the creation of new styles simpler and more accessible than ever before, and digital presses continue to speed print production. Whatever technology has been used, in whatever century, the eye and mind of the designer has remained a vital factor.

TYPE CATEGORIES

Like the alphabet, typography has undergone a long development. A brief look at its history will help you assemble and recognize types with similar attributes. History provides a key to proper use.

The type category we refer to as old style, with gently blended serifs leading into thick and thin strokes, was created around 1470 by Nicolas Jenson, a French printer working out of Venice. French typographer Claude Garamond based a typestyle, now known as Garamond, on Jenson's design. This classic remains in use today. Around 1530 Garamond established the first type foundry—a business set up specifically to market "type faces" to printers. The many fonts Garamond cut were extremely precise and legible, setting a standard for typographic beauty that is still recognized today. During the early 1700s William Caslon designed a typeface based on Garamond's classic typestyles that became so widely adopted it became the standard for British newspapers.

A modern revival of 15th-century Italian types occurred in Europe and the United States around 1890. Englishman William Morris produced a type called Golden that recalled the spirit of the 15th century. Golden was based on type designs by Nicolas Jenson in the 1470s. Typefounding of Golden began in 1890, and Morris set up a handpress in a rented cottage, establishing Kelmscott Press. Committed to meticulous hand-printing, handmade paper, and hand-cut woodblocks, the press celebrated the book as an art form. From 1891 until 1898, the Kelmscott Press produced fifty-three different titles and over eighteen thousand volumes. Golden, Troy, and a smaller version of Troy, called Chaucer, were all Morris's typeface creations based on Jenson and Gothic styles (see **Figure 6-2**).

Most roman types today have variations available called italics. Italics are slanted letterforms that relate to the original

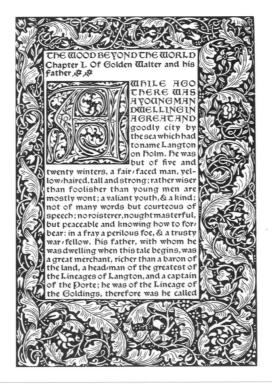

6-2 *William Morris. Page from* The Wood Beyond the World. *1894. 9^1/$_2$ × 6^3/$_4$" (24 × 17 cm). Kelmscott Press.*

typestyle but do not duplicate it. Around the turn of the 16th century, Venetian printer Aldus Manutius (credited with being the first publisher) and his type designer, Francesco Griffo, developed italics as a way of fitting more letters on a line to save space. For about 40 years, italic was simply another style of type, until an italic was consciously developed from an upright roman mold. Today most roman types have matching italics as well as several other variations, such as bold and condensed.

Roman faces with strong contrast between thick and thin strokes and with thin serifs were developed in the 18th century. These faces are generally classified as transitional. Because they were designed specifically for the printing industry, they printed more clearly and precisely than their predecessors. A widespread interest in copperplate engraving at the time encouraged the development of types that incorporated a very fine line.

The typefaces Didot and Bodoni imitated the engraver's tool with precise hairline strokes. The term modern is used to describe these 18th-century typestyles. The Italian type designer and printer Giambatista Bodoni was influenced by Didot and Caslon. His entire Bodoni type family ushered in the Modern era of hairline serifs and strong contrast between thick and thin strokes.

The 19th century saw the development of many new typefaces with a wide variety of looks. Among these faces were sans serifs and the Egyptians. William Morris's revival of the old, classic typefaces occurred during this time.

Since the early 19th century, serif and sans-serif types have alternated in popularity. Great interest surrounded sans serif during much of the 20th century. Bauhaus designers in Germany during the 1920s began designing sans-serif faces such as Futura. In the 1950s Univers and Helvetica became the dominant typefaces used by design professionals. The sans-serif dominance lasted throughout the 1960s and 1970s. Newer versions of Helvetica show more consistency among font variations. Large x-height and beautiful positive and negative shapes accompany a clean precision and understated elegance of line. The horizontals are cut along a common line.

Figure 6-3 is a layout by contemporary designer Paula Scher that uses sans-serif type to evoke an earlier era. Today's designers choose from a rich array of old and new typestyles. In fact, such an extensive array of fonts is available on computer that selecting one can be quite difficult. A basic familiarity with typography will help you develop a discerning eye.

Historic Type Families

OLD STYLE Characteristics of old-style faces (**Figure 6-4**) include thick- and thin-stroke serifs that seem to merge into the main strokes. This feature is called bracketing. Garamond and Caslon are examples. Created in the early 1600s, Garamond was the first typeface designed to appear uniformly printed rather than hand lettered. It remained the principal typeface for over 200 years, with many derivatives.

TRANSITIONAL Transitional, a category of type combining features of both old style and modern, emphasizes thicks and thins and gracefully bracketed serifs (**Figure 6-5**).

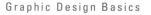
● **6-3** *Paula Scher.*
This layout design for The Magic Mountain *is part of the Great Beginnings series.*
Courtesy of the artist.

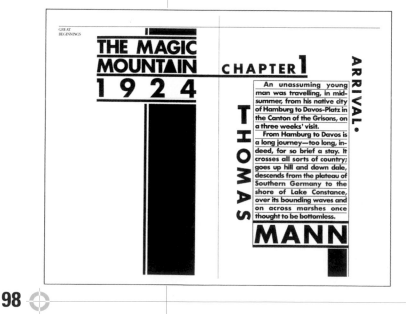

abcdefghijklmn
opqrstuvwxyz
ABCDEFGHIJK
LMNOPQRSTU
VWXYZ$12344
567890 (.,""";:!)?&

6-4 *Garamond Book, a revised old-style typeface.*

abcdefghijklmnop
qrstuvwxyzAB
CDEFGHIJKLM
NOPQRSTUV
WXYZ$1234567
890(.,"""-;:!)?&

6-5 *Baskerville, a transitional typeface.*

It is lighter than old style and has a more precise, controlled character. It is less mechanical and upright than the modern faces.

The transitional Baskerville was designed in the 1750s by John Baskerville, an amateur printer. Baskerville has straighter and more mechanical lines than the old-style typefaces, with flatter serifs that come to a fine tip. Increased contrast between the thick and thin strokes of the letterforms, as well as rounded brackets, give it more delicacy than old-style faces such as Caslon.

John Baskerville made several technical innovations that affected the appearance of his type. He passed printed sheets through heated copper cylinders to smooth out the rough texture of the paper then in use. This smooth surface made it possible to reproduce delicate serifs clearly. **Figure 6-6** shows text-size Garamond and Baskerville fonts in different leading. The three factors—typestyle, point size, and leading—are interrelated.

MODERN The modern styles evolved from transitional types. They show still greater contrast between thicks and thins. Modern typefaces are characterized by hairline-thin serifs that join the body with a stiff unbracketed corner. There is strong vertical stress to the letters.

Bodoni (**Figure 6-7**) fits this category. It was created in the late 1700s by Italian printer Giambattista Bodoni. Bodoni was influenced by the work of Baskerville and François Ambroise Didot, a Frenchman who also gave Europe a fully developed type measurement system.

EGYPTIAN The first slab-serif typestyle was introduced around 1815. The category was dubbed "Egyptian" because Egyptian artifacts and Egyptian travel were in vogue. Napoleon's conquest of Egypt aroused great enthusiasm for that country. During this period, type design became less predictable and more eclectic. Type characteristics were mixed and recombined, producing many variations. The heavy square serifs in this category often match the strokes in

● **6-6** *Point size and leading affect one another.*

Baskerville

Since the first person made a mark in the sand for another to find, we have been communicating with a visual language. The earliest forms of visual communication were pictorial drawings of everyday objects such as weapons and animals. As the desire to communicate grew, these pictures were combined to convey

8/11

Since the first person made a mark in the sand for another to find, we have been communicating with a visual language. The earliest forms of visual communication were pictorial drawings of everyday objects such as weapons and animals. As the desire to communicate

9/10

Since the first person made a mark in the sand for another to find, we have been communicating with a visual language. The earliest forms of visual communication were pictorial drawings of everyday objects such as weapons and animals. As the desire to communicate

9/11

Garamond Book

Since the first person made a mark in the sand for another to find, we have been communicating with a visual language. The earliest forms of visual communication were pictorial drawings of everyday objects such as weapons and animals. As the desire to communicate grew, these pictures were combined to convey

8/11

Since the first person made a mark in the sand for another to find, we have been communicating with a visual language. The earliest forms of visual communication were pictorial drawings of everyday objects such as weapons and animals. As the desire to communicate grew, these

9/10

Since the first person made a mark in the sand for another to find, we have been communicating with a visual language. The earliest forms of visual communication were pictorial drawings of everyday objects such as weapons and animals. As the desire to communicate grew, these

9/11

abcdefghijklmnopq
rstuvwxyzABCDEFG
HIJKLMNOPQRST
UVWXYZ$12345678
90(.,""''''-;:!)?&

6-7 *Bodoni, a modern typeface.*

abcdeefghijkl
mnopqrstuvwx
yzABCDEFGHI
JKLMNOPQRST
UVWXYZ$123
4567890(.,''""-,;!)?&

6-8 *Lubalin Graph, an Egyptian slab-serif typeface.*

thickness. There is less difference between thicks and thins than in the modern and transitional periods. Clarendon and Century are examples of this group.

The popularity of square slab-serif type decreased greatly in the early 20th century but then revived somewhat in its latter decades. Lubalin Graph (**Figure 6-8**), designed in 1974 by Herb Lubalin and drawn by Tony DiSpigna and Joe Sundwall, has the characteristics of Egyptian typestyles.

SANS SERIF William Caslon created the original sans serif in the early 1800s. The 1920s saw the development of sans-serif type families including Gill Sans, created by Eric Gill, as well as Herbert Bayer's Universal. In the 1950s designers of the International Typographic Style examined available typefaces and found them lacking. Weight changes were not subtle enough, and the various weights and widths in a type family often lacked coherency. This disorder was natural, because fonts within a family were often designed by different people. Then a young Swiss type designer named Adrian Frutiger developed a sans-serif face called Univers. He created a completely consistent family of types in all possible weights and widths (Figure 3-21b).

Several classic sans-serif typefaces were designed at the German Bauhaus (see Chapter 2). Influenced by the Bauhaus, the Swiss firm Haas worked with the German Stempel foundry to produce Helvetica (**Figure 6-9**). It is still considered by many designers to be the perfect type—versatile, legible, and elegant.

Figure 6-10 shows a design from 1923 using a grid layout and sans-serif type by

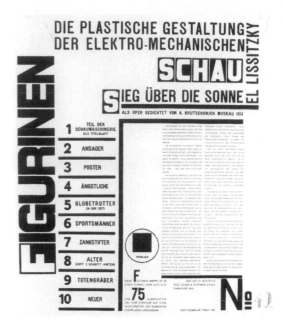

● **6-10** *El Lissitzky. Table of Contents from Plastic Figures of the Electro-Mechanical Show: Victory over the Sun. 1923. Collection, The Art Institute of Chicago. Gift of the Print and Drawing Club. Gaylord Donnelley and Wm. McCallin Mckee Fund, 1966.*

● **6-9** *Helvetica, a sans-serif typeface.*

ABCDEFGHIJKL MNOPQRSTUV WXYZ&abcdefg hijklmnopqrstuvw xyz1234567890 $.,"-:;!?

Graphic Design Basics

El Lissitzky. A leading Russian constructivist, Lissitzky believed in the power of graphic design to influence social order. He helped export constructivist theory and style to the rest of Europe through his printed work and lectures.

MISCELLANEOUS FACES Many fonts do not seem to belong to any category. They are often experimental, ornamental styles of limited application, sometimes created by hand. These eccentric types are rarely suitable for text type, but they do find appropriate usage in display headings, such as the book cover in **Figure 6-11,** where type and image are delicately integrated.

It is possible to use specialized ornate styles in display headlines and not hamper readability too greatly. In large amounts of body copy, however, every subtle variation has a cumulative effect that can seriously hinder readability. A classic all-purpose typestyle will remain legible and unobtrusive as body type. Selecting an appropriate legible and beautiful text type calls for a sensitive, educated eye. **Figure 6-12** shows a few of the all-purpose styles.

TYPE FAMILIES

The five categories of type we have discussed are filled with type families, such as Bodoni and Baskerville. Each family comes in a variety of weights and sizes. A type family is all the variations of a particular typeface. Helvetica, for example, now comes in a series of variations described as light condensed, medium condensed, bold condensed, ultra light, ultra light condensed, ultra light italic, light, medium, regular, medium light, bold, bold italic, and bold extended. **Figure 6-13** displays the Helvetica family.

A specific variation in a specific size is called a font. For example, 18-point Helvetica italic is a font. A great variety of shapes exist in a single font. There are 26 capitals, 26 lowercase letterforms, and assorted numerals and punctuation marks.

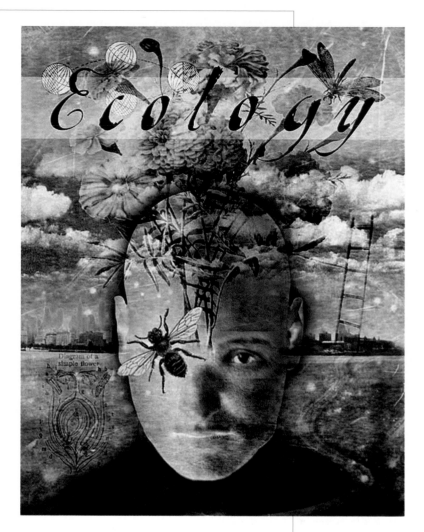

These various shapes can be successfully combined into a unified design because of the similarities in width, brackets, serifs, and x-height. A well-designed type font is an excellent example of the interplay of repetition and variety that makes for good design.

Computerized layout gives the designer the ability to make a wide variety of changes in these carefully designed fonts. Vector programs allow type to be mirrored, scaled with varying horizontal and vertical values, and otherwise manipulated for effect. The pre-computer hot type technology was based on actual physical pieces of metal shaped into letterforms. These could not be stretched or set to overlap unless the

⊕ **103**

6-12 *Some highly legible typestyles for body copy as well as display type.*

American typewriter light	Benguiat medium cond	Beton light	ITC Bookman light italic
ABCDEFGHIJ KLMNOPQR.R STUVWXYZØ abcdeefgh ijkl mnopqrstuv ?! wxyzæœø12 34567890£¢$	ABCDEFGHIJKL" MNOPQRSTUVW XYZÆŒÇØabcd efghijklmnopqrs tuvwxyzæœçø1 234567890ß£$¢ ?!&%§()/«--~~*::	ABCDEFGHIJKL MNOPQRSTUV WXYZabcdefghi jklmnopqrstuvwx yz 1234567890 Æ ŒÇØæœçøß £$ ¢&%?!()«»/*;--~~.	ABCDEFGHIJKLMNO PQRSTUVWXYZAB ABCDEFGHIJK LMNOPQRR STU VVWWWXYZÇTh ÆŒØabcdefghijklm nopqrstuvwxyze-fifiç fihk mno-pqr ˜æœø ß1234567890 1234567 890£$¢&%?!§@#[(5:˜:˜:/)]
American typewriter med	Benguiat medium cond	Beton bold	Bookman
ABCDEFGHIJ! KLMNOPQRŒ STUVWXYZØ ÆÇabcdefghij klmnopqrstu? vwxyzæœçøß 1234567890£ $¢&%§(«»:;-*/)	ABCDEFGHIJKL MNOPQRSTUV*:: WXYZÆŒÇØab cdefghijklmnop» qrstuvwxyz æœ çø1234567890ß £$¢?!&%§()/«--~~.	ABCDEFGHIJK LMNOPQRST() UVWXYZabcd efghijklmnopq, rstuvwxyz1234! 567890ÆŒÇØ? æœçøß£$¢&%.	AˆAˆ ABBCDDEF EˆFGˆHIˆIJKˆKL LˆMMˆNNOPQR, PRSTUˆUVˆVWX ˆWˆXYˆYZÆabcde fghijklmnopqrrˆstu vwxyyˆzæœçl234 567890ÆŒØÇB&! ?ˆ@,$(˜:˜:)
American typewriter bold	Benguiat bold cond	Beton extra bold	Bookman italic
ABCDEFGHI JKLMNOPQ RSTUVWX? YZ!abcdeefg hijklmnopq rstuvwxyz1 234567890ˆ*	**ABCDEFGHIJKL" MNOPQRSTUVW XYZÆŒÇØ abcd efghijklmnopqr stuvwxyzæœçø* 1234567890 ß£$ ¢?!&%§()/«--~~:;**	**ABCDEFGHIJ KLMNOPQR STUVWXYZ? abcdefghijkm lnopqrstuvwx yzæœçø:1234 567890ÆŒØ! £$¢%&ß(ˆ˜:˜÷;)**	*AˆAˆABBCˆGD DˆEˆEFFGGˆHIˆ HJˆJKKˆKLˆLMM ˆMNNˆNOPQR PRˆRRˆSSTTˆU! UVˆVWˆWˆXYZa bcdefghˆhijkkˆlmnŋ opqrrˆStuvwwˆxyˆz 1234567890&ˆGhˆ&,*

6-13 *The Helvetica family.*

Helvetica LIGHT CONDENSED
Helvetica MEDIUM CONDENSED
Helvetica BOLD CONDENSED
Helvetica ULTRA LIGHT
Helvetica ULTRA LIGHT ITALIC
Helvetica LIGHT
Helvetica MEDIUM
Helvetica REGULAR
Helvetica MEDIUM ITALIC
Helvetica BOLD
Helvetica BOLD ITALIC
Helvetica BOLD EXTENDED
HELVETICA OUTLINE

sheet was printed twice and the font recast. Now that nearly everything is possible, an enthusiasm for exploration needs to be tempered by respect for the subtle and complex beauty of a font.

Selection

How do you select which style of type to use? What factors are involved in designing with text type? Selecting the type for a given layout means making decisions in six inter-related areas: type size, line length, type-style, leading, spacing, and format.

Designers sometimes set their own type as they develop a layout design. But whether you set the type yourself or someone else prepares it, the six characteristics mentioned earlier need to be specified. It is important to develop a fine critical eye for type quality, watching for problems such as uneven letterspacing and low resolution.

This is an example of a reversed 9 point serif font. Often such delicate lines will be overwhelmed by a reversal.

6-14

Often the type printed on a desktop laser or inkjet printer is not as sharp as offset, especially if the type is reversed and in a small serif font (**Figure 6-14**).

Size

Text type is any type that is under 14 points in size. A point is a unit of measurement based on the pica. There are 12 points in a pica and approximately 6 picas in an inch, so there are 72 points in an inch. The point system of measurement was introduced in the 18th century, because the small sizes of text type called for a measuring system with extremely fine increments (**Figure 6-15**). Type size is measured in points until it reaches about 2″ (5 cm) high. It is available from 5 points to 72 points on desktop computer menus, or larger sizes can be specified (**Figure 6-16**). When measuring type size by hand, include the ascender and descender in the measurement.

The easiest way to measure type without a computer is by comparing it with a type specimen book and matching the size visually. It can also be measured with a point

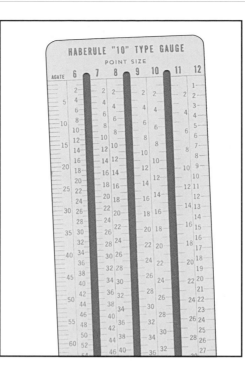

and pica ruler. Remember to measure from top of ascender to bottom of descender.

When choosing a type size, keep the audience in mind. Type smaller than 10 points is often difficult for older people to read.

Type size can be difficult to judge on the computer monitor, because the screen image may not be the same size as your final printed page. Also, the vertical, backlit quality of a monitor is a very different medium from the printed page, and we interact with it differently. Student designers have a tendency to choose sizes that are too large when they first begin designing with type on the computer. It is easier

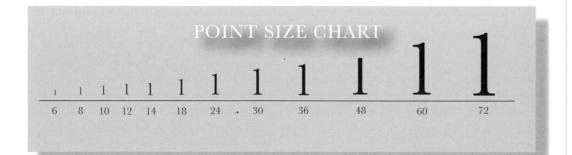

6-16 *Type is measured in points until it reaches about 2″ (5 cm) high.*

to judge the effect of typography accurately in a printed proof than on-screen. However, if the final format will be a Web page, its effectiveness should be judged on the screen rather than in printed form.

Line Length

Line length also is measured by the pica system. It is the length in picas of a line of text type. The dimensions of the page itself, however, are usually expressed in inches (or centimeters). For example, an 8-point type may be set in a 22-pica line length on an $8^1/_2 \times 11$" (22×28 cm) page format. Or it may simply flow to fill a predetermined column layout in your layout program.

The length of a line is closely related to the size of type. A small point size such as 6 point or 8 point on a line 44 picas long is difficult to read. The type seems to jump around along the midsection of the line, and the eye must search for the beginning of each new line. This trouble is worse when there is insufficient space between lines. Usually you want the reader's eyes to move smoothly, never being forced to slow down or lose their place. The standard line length and point size ratio for optimal legibility is a line of 50 to 70 characters long. To remember this ratio, keep in mind that line length should be approximately double the point size. An 8-point type sits well on a 16-pica line. Variations on this theme can be used purposely to slow the reader down.

Style

When you choose text type, legibility is a prime consideration. Although there are many elegant and accessible styles, stay away from styles with an excess of ornamentation.

Next, seek a type appropriate to the audience, the publication, and your own sense of aesthetics. Sans serif has a modern feel and is highly legible in the limited amounts of copy used in most annual reports, newsletters, and so on. The serif types are generally more traditional and classical in feeling. They are easier to read in large amounts. Many of the newer styles strive to combine the virtues of serif and sans-serif type.

Trends arise in type just as in music, clothes, and lifestyles. Notice how they change from year to year. Use the fashionable typestyles only when they seem both appropriate and aesthetically pleasing.

The printing process can help determine typestyle selection. Delicate hairline serifs are not appropriate when a heavy ink coverage is required, because the ink will block up the serifs and result in a blotchy look. Heavily textured paper will also make a delicate serif unadvisable. The texture of the paper will cause the finely inked serifs to break up.

Beginning designers often combine several typestyles in a typographical layout. They choose each for its own beauty and interest but forget the effect of the whole design. Diverse styles usually refuse to combine into an organized whole and have an undisciplined and chaotic look. Many experienced designers prefer to work within one type family, drawing on its bold, italic, and roman faces (see Figure 6-13). They achieve a look of variety without risking going outside one family. This course is certainly the safest for a new designer.

Exciting layouts, however, often do mix distinctively different typefaces. Mixing takes sensitivity to how the styles affect one another and contribute to the whole. A good rule of thumb when mixing type families is to make certain they are very different. The composition will work if there is either deliberate similarity or definite variety. It can confuse and displease the eye if the distinctions are muddy. **Figure 6-17** is a design by well-known and influential designer Paula Scher that combines typestyles, sizes, and format to make a point that is consistent with the content of the book *Metamorphosis* by Franz Kafka. Contemporary designers have many more choices of typefaces and design effects than ever before (**Figure 6-18**).

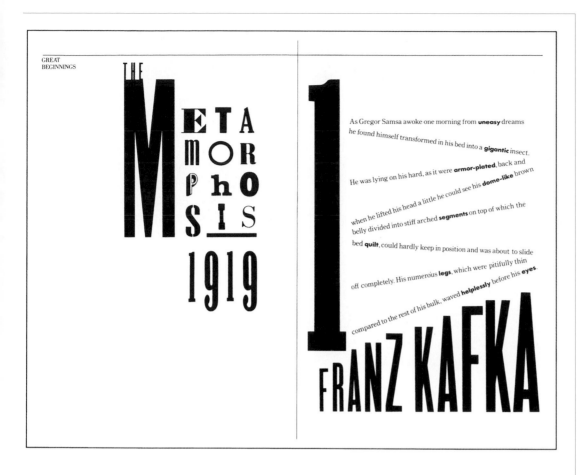

THE METAMORPHOSIS 1919

As Gregor Samsa awoke one morning from **uneasy** dreams he found himself transformed in his bed into a **gigantic** insect.

He was lying on his hard, as it were **armor-plated**, back and when he lifted his head a little he could see his **dome-like** brown belly divided into stiff arched **segments** on top of which the bed **quilt**, could hardly keep in position and was about to slide off completely. His numerous **legs**, which were pitifully thin compared to the rest of his bulk, waved **helplessly** before his **eyes**.

1 FRANZ KAFKA

6-17 *Paula Scher.*
Layout design for The
Metamorphosis *in a*
brochure for the Great
Beginnings series.
Courtesy of the artist.

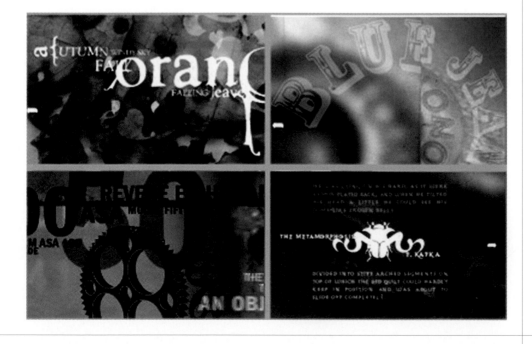

6-18 *Graphic*
designer **Luis Escorial**
created these Web pages
as part of his personal
Web site.

Leading

Leading (pronounced like the metal lead) describes the vertical spacing between lines of type. The historical origin of the term goes back to hot-metal typesetting, when a thin strip of lead was inserted as a spacer between lines of metal type. This type and leading were locked together into a galley, inked, and printed. Leading strongly affects the look and readability of the layout. Type is considered to be set solid when no space is inserted between the descender of the top line and the ascender of the bottom line. A 10-point type set on a 10-point leading is an example of solid leading. Herb Lubalin's design for *Avant Garde* magazine in 1967 uses very tight leading (see Figure 7-9). How much leading you use is important. Several factors affect that decision, including type size, line length, and typestyle.

TYPE SIZE Leading must be proportionate to the size of the type. Although there is no standard, correct leading for a certain type size, we often find 10-point type set on 12-point leading. An extra 2 points of space have been inserted between the lines of type. A larger or smaller type size will require less extra leading. A 14-point type might need only 14- or 15-point leading, for instance. It is rare to find minus leading, or a 10-point type set on 9-point leading. Current typesetting technology makes it possible to set one line of type on top of another and to weave entire paragraphs over each other for visual texture. The important criteria are always Is it appropriate? and Is it good design? Does the form follow and enhance the function?

LINE LENGTH Line length is an important factor in determining leading. The longer the line, the more leading is appropriate. With longer line lengths, the eye has a tendency to wander. If there is insufficient space between lines, you will find yourself reading the line above or beneath and having difficulty finding the beginning of each line.

TYPESTYLE Three aspects of the typestyle also affect leading: x-height, vertical stress, and serif versus sans serif. The x-height, as you know, refers to the size of the body of the letter, without its ascender or descender. The x-height of Helvetica is much greater than the x-height of an older type such as Garamond. Consequently Helvetica probably requires more leading. It does not have lots of extra white space packed around its body, because it has relatively short ascenders and descenders, so the lines of type appear closer together (**Figure 6-19a**).

The vertical stress of a typestyle also affects leading, because the stronger the vertical emphasis, the more the eye is drawn up and down instead of along the line of type. Hence the greater the vertical stress, the more leading is required. A typestyle such as Baskerville has a stronger vertical stress than Garamond and therefore requires more leading.

A serif helps draw the eye along in a horizontal direction, so serif type is generally considered easier to read than sans-serif type. Sans-serif type usually requires more leading than the serif style to keep the eye moving smoothly along.

Spacing

Letterspacing is the amount of space between letters of a word (**Figure 6-19b**). A good figure/ground relationship between letterforms is as important with text type as with display type. If the letters are spaced too far apart, the eye must jump between letters, and reading becomes strained.

Whether designing with text type or display type, keep an eye out for the creation of equal volumes of white space between individual letterforms. Kerning is a term that describes the specific adjustment of space between individual letterforms. IO, for example, will require spacing different from MN (**Figure 6-20**).

The amount of space between words is called word spacing. If it is too great, it is difficult for the eye to move quickly along

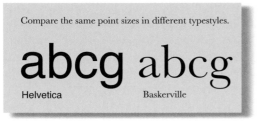

Compare the same point sizes in different typestyles.

abcg abcg

Helvetica   Baskerville

● **6-19a** *Identical point sizes can have very different x-heights.*

the line of type. There is a tendency to pause between individual words. The reader should be unaware of the space between words and aware instead of their content.

Word spacing usually is not a problem with text type, unless the type is being set in a justified format (flush left and flush right edges). To make the lines come out even, the computer will insert extra space between words. If a line is long, with many words, this addition is not noticeable. However, if the line is short, great white holes seem to appear in the copy (**Figure 6-21**). Look at your local newspaper, and squint. Often rivers of white will appear in the columns of text type as a result of poor word spacing.

Format

Format design refers to the arrangement of lines of type on the page (**Figure 6-22**). There are two basic categories: justified and

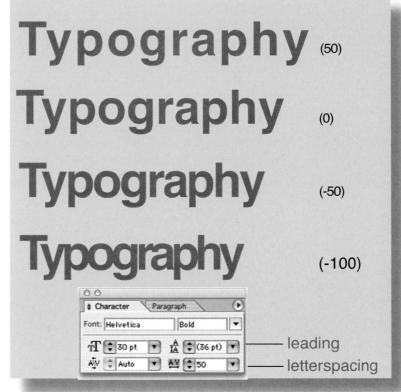

Typography (50)

Typography (0)

Typography (-50)

Typography (-100)

leading

letterspacing

● **6-19b** *Letterspacing can vary from very loose to very tight. It is easily adjusted in many software programs. This is called tracking.*

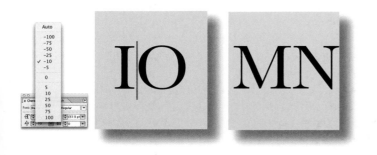

● **6-20** *Spacing between individual letterforms must vary to please the eye. This is called kerning.*

In justified type the lines are all the same length, so that the left and right edges of the column of type are straight. This format is used in newspaper layout and text and trade books. It is useful when speed reading is the primary consideration.

◑ **6-21** *Justifying copy in a short line will cause white holes to appear.*

109

The flush right format is unusal, and somewhat difficult to read. It has a ragged left edge and is used for design effect in special situations.

The flush left format has a straight left edge and a ragged right. This format is commonly used in annual reports, brochures, and identification lines under artwork. One of the benefits of this format, compared with justified copy is that it is possible to avoid hyphenated words.

Centered copy is often found in headlines or invitations, but rarely in standard copy. It is a slow-reading, classical format that encourages the reader to pause after each line.

Asymmetrically
arranged type
can enhance the message
of a poem.
It was used early in the
20th century by the poet
Apollinaire.

unjustified. In justified type, all the lines are the same length, so that the left and right edges of the column of type are straight. This format is commonly used in newspaper layout and in text and trade books. It is appropriate when speed and ease of reading are the primary considerations. Justified copy is considered by many to be slightly easier to read than unjustified copy. The straight, squared-off columns of type give an orderly, classical feeling to the page.

Unjustified copy can be arranged in a variety of ways: flush left, flush right, centered, and asymmetrically. The New Typography proponents of the 1920s believed ragged-right type was more readable than justified type. Unequal line length was also an important part of the International Typographic Style.

FLUSH LEFT The flush-left format calls for a straight left edge and a ragged right edge. Typewritten copy is usually flush left. This format is commonly used in annual reports, brochures, identification lines under photographs, and whenever you want a slightly

less formal look than can be achieved with justified type. One of the benefits of this format is that it is possible to avoid hyphenated words. Page layout software programs usually allow the user to set parameters for hyphenation. A designer can specify how many hyphenated line endings can happen in succession and just how ragged the right or left edge can become.

FLUSH RIGHT The flush right format is unusual and difficult to read. It has a ragged left edge and is used for design effect in special situations. It is difficult for the eye to search out the beginning of each new line without a common starting point.

CENTERED Centered copy is often found in headlines or invitations but rarely in standard copy. It is a slow-reading, classical format that encourages the reader to pause after each line. It is important to make logical breaks at the end of each line. This format has a pronounced irregular shape and packs a lot of space around itself. The white space and irregular outline can draw the eye strongly. Consider the content of your material, how rapidly it should be read, and the overall look of the page before deciding on a centered format.

ASYMMETRICAL Asymmetrically arranged type can put across the point of a poem or an important statement. Asymmetry is also used in display type to achieve better balance among letterforms. Contour type is a form of asymmetry that fits the shape of an illustration, following its contour. Type that is set around the squared edge of a photo is called a runaround. Occasionally type will be set in the shape of a contour itself.

The ancient Egyptians and Greeks originally experimented with this format. It was used early in the 20th century by the poet Apollinaire and more recently by contemporary designers. **Figure 6-23** is an asymmetrical typographic illustration created by a recent design graduate.

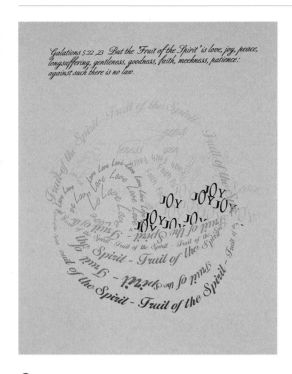

6-23a *An asymmetrical typographic illustration by Donna McWilliams for her student portfolio. Based on Galatians 5:22–23.*

Style and Content

Typography sets a visual tone depending on the variables we have just examined. The style, the leading, and the format all contribute to a nonverbal communication that has a great deal to say. This visual communication, or visual language, affects the image of the client. It is a function of the choices the designer has made—partly as a personal preference, partly in response to the client's needs, and partly in response to contemporary design trends.

Specific typestyles and layout designs are associated with historical periods. Typestyles can evoke the mood of an era just through careful type selection and usage. The 20th century in the United States saw many styles come into vogue and then fade out. Typestyles reflect their era's philosophical and technological status.

Wood display type was widely used in the 1800s. By the latter part of the century, these wooden typestyles became elaborate, beautifully decorative designs. Typestyles and trends continued to change, reflecting the sensibilities and technology of the time. The Broadway typestyle was popular in the 1930s; the sans-serif styles of Helvetica and Univers were widely used in the 1950s and 1960s. Today's styles show an appreciation for classic style as well as an eclectic willingness to experiment with unusual graphic effects, as digital typesetting encourages stylistic innovation.

With the advent of digital typography, special effects with type and layout design have become easier to achieve than ever before. Experimentation is good, especially when tempered by a firm knowledge of traditional typographic design principles. Figure 6-23b shows some examples of digital options for type placement.

6-23b *Type inside a shaped area, type on a path, and vertical-area type are shown here.*

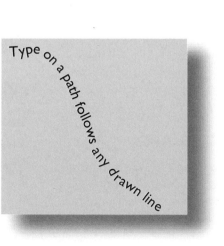

| Type inside a shaped area can fit inside a geometric or an organically shaped form as here. | Type on a path follows any drawn line | Vertical Type | Vertical Type | VERTICAL TYPE | Vertical Type |

Computer programs that work with vector graphic typography can generate a wide variety of typographic effects. Type can be keystroked directly (or placed from word processing programs) into Illustrator, Freehand, InDesign, or Quark with a wide variety of effects to choose from. The same block of type can be placed with a variety of sizes, fonts, spacing, and formats using these programs. With all these choices available, it is more important than ever to develop a good eye for type use. In your program of choice, experiment with type on a path, type inside an area, and varying formats, and become familiar with an array of fonts and spacing options. Keep an eye out for elegance, understatement, clarity, and beauty. But an element of "fun" can be a great addition.

Some Problems

Once the format for the layout is selected and the type is set, some awkward accidents may occur. If you are aware of these potential problems, you can avoid them.

Widows and orphans are romantic names designating short, isolated paragraph-ending lines. A widow appears at the top of a printed column and is most distressing when it appears at the top of a new page. An orphan is a short line that appears at the bottom of a column or page, or a single word or word part that appears on a line by itself at the end of a paragraph.

Hyphenation can also become a problem, especially if the line length is short and the format is justified. Too many hyphenated words will interfere with readability. Hyphens should always fall between syllables, and they should not chop a word into unrecognizable segments.

A DESIGN SUMMARY

Designing well with typography is a delicate thing. It relies on so many interrelated variables that it cannot be reduced to a simple formula. Here, however, are a few general guidelines:

■ When choosing typestyles, remember that it is wise to either mix different fonts or to stay within the same type family. For example, two fairly similar serif fonts will be more difficult to use together than a serif and a sans serif. Staying within a family gives a wide but unified choice.

■ Multiple fonts with strong personalities and highly distinctive styles are difficult to use together because they all call for attention. Thus it becomes difficult to establish a visual hierarchy.

■ The design principles of proximity, similarity grouping, and focal point are all important to consider in layout design. Variations in point size and font style function like a code to guide the reader. The heading and subheading formats in this text, for example, were carefully chosen to visually group information and highlight topics. Each heading should be placed closer to the information it introduces than to the unrelated paragraph above it.

■ Decide what kind of speed you want from your reader. A justified format is the quickest read; ragged right takes a little more intimate involvement on the part of the reader. A centered format is a very slow read, presenting itself line by line rather than as a grouped paragraph. Mixing these formats can give the reader visual clues about the content. The running text in a chapter may be justified, for example, while the photo captions are all ragged right.

■ Every element that goes onto a page is important. Every element contributes to the whole. Take nothing for granted.

EXECUTION

Specifying Copy

If the designer is sending copy to someone else for typesetting, the first step is to specify the copy. When you spec copy, you provide all the information necessary to set the final type for layout: typestyle, point size, leading, format, line length,

Delete ℒ	Close up ⌒
Insert here ∧	Elevate a word ⌐⌐
Move to left ⌐	Move to right ⌐
Lower a letter ⌐⌐	Insert an Em space ▢
Insert 2 Em spaces ▢▢	Broken type, please reset ✕
New paragraph ⁋	No new paragraph *no* ⁋
Open up a space #	Close up a space
Restore to original *stet*	Wrong font *wf*
Transpose ∩	Set in caps and lower case
Set in all caps ☰	Set in small caps
Set in boldface	Set in roman *rom*
Set in italics	Change to lower case *lc*
Insert period ⊙	

sometimes letterspacing, and special instructions.

Making Corrections

Almost always some corrections are needed in typeset copy, due to last-minute revisions or errors caught late. Proofreading is an easier job now, with the spelling check feature available on layout programs. Use it always.

You will need to know proofreader's marks to correct errors from a design point of view, such as damaged copy, poor breaks in words, or incorrect fonts. The standard proofreader's marks are shown in **Figure 6-24.** It is a good idea to use one color for corrections. The color you choose will function as a symbol signaling your corrections.

EXERCISE

Study various magazines, newspapers, and other publications for samples of different formats. Which are successful, and which are flawed? **Figure 6-25** is a lovely sample of a layout that integrates type and image. Choose two of the less effective samples for analysis. Determine their line length, leading, point size, and typestyle. Make recommendations for improvement. Prepare these for a class discussion.

PROJECTS

Typographical Illustration of a Poem

Select a poem or a portion of an interesting and emotive piece of prose (song lyrics are OK) that is no longer than 20 lines. Set it twice, using the typesetting equipment available to you. The first time,

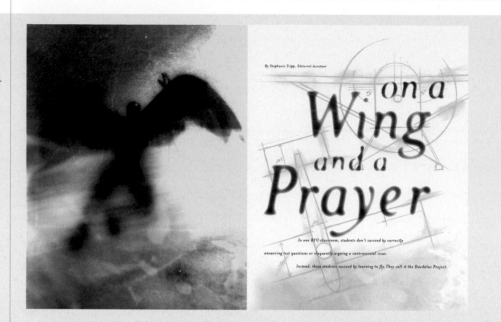

◗ **6-25** *Spread from BYU Magazine. Design studio: BYU Publications & Graphics, Provo, Utah. Art Director: Bruce Patrick. Designer/Illustrator: Emily Johnson. John Rees photographer/ johnrees@qwest.net.* Courtesy of the artist.

follow the standard guidelines for typography to enhance readability, paying close attention to leading, line length, spacing (kerning and tracking), and format. Select one type family, limit the fonts, and restrict the point-size variation.

The second time you set the copy, break as many rules as you wish while creating an effect appropriate to the piece and your feelings about it. Experiment with complexity and diversity. Freehand, Illustrator, Quark, InDesign, or another vector graphics program is suitable for this project. If you are planning for online output, raster graphics programs such as Adobe Photoshop and Corel Painter can provide rich results.

Book Cover Design

Book covers are like small posters. They attract readers with their strong visuals. Create covers for two books that are part of a reissued series by a 20th-century author. The covers for this series should be visually united to indicate that the books are part of a series. Consider similar color, layout, graphic technique, and so on. Be sure the covers are also varied enough to hold interest. Use a primarily typographic treatment, but consider including abstract or nonobjective shapes. Paula Scher's designs for the Great Beginnings series shown in this chapter may provide good inspiration for this project. **Figure 6-26** is a professional cover design that effectively uses type to frame an illustration.

Design the entire cover, including front, spine, back, and flaps. Include appropriate information. Print the finished pieces and fold them around an actual book for final presentation. The research part of this assignment is important. Be familiar with the author's writing so that your design reflects the content and tone of the writing. Spend time at a local bookstore looking at the competition's cover designs. Look at a series, and consider how the cover designs are united. Look for designs that are primarily typographic. The accompanying Web site has a suggested layout template for your cover, while **Figure 6-27** shows a solution to a similar problem.

Goals and Objectives

Learn to apply gestalt unit-forming principles to multiple-panel layout design.

Learn to integrate text and display type with image while carefully orchestrating eye direction.

Practice integrating typography and image to express a mood.

Graphic Design Basics

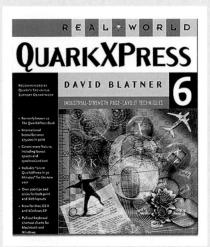

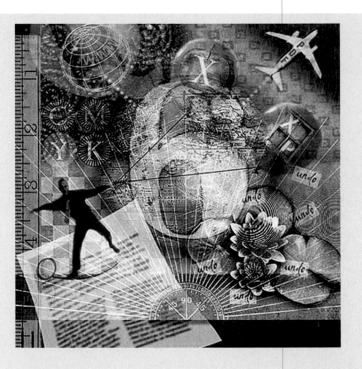

● **6-26** *Diane Fenster created the illustration for this cover in QuarkXPress.*
Courtesy of the artist.

Critique

Answer the following questions for your own design and for another from the class. What fonts were used in the solution to this design problem? Are they appropriate to the subject matter? How? Consider the characteristics of the chosen fonts. Is there any distinctive use of letterspacing?

Can the choice of point size be improved? Do you see any widows or orphans? How can they be avoided in this design? How is the image integrated with the choice and placement of the typography? How do the type and image contribute to establishing a mood appropriate to the book's content?

● **6-27** *Tiffany Dorner created this cover design for her student portfolio by using Photoshop and Illustrator. Her personal logo is included on the spine.*

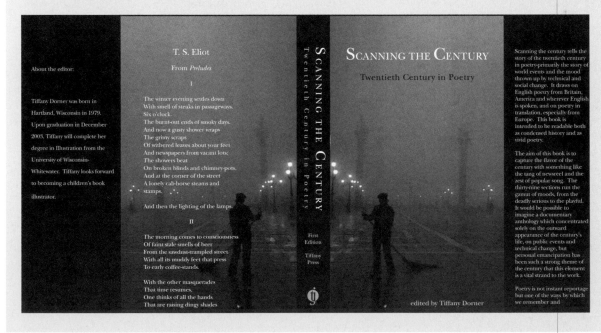

TERMINOLOGY

CHAPTER 7

See glossary
for
definitions.

Layout Design	Alternating Rhythm	Path Layout
Symmetrical Layout	Progressive Rhythm	Focal Point
Asymmetrical Layout	Grid Layout	Cropping
Proportion	Visual Weight	Resizing
Golden Section	Visual Design Theme	Resolution
Visual Rhythm	Editorial Content Theme	Interpolation

Layout

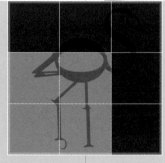

KEY POINTS Page layout, whether in print or Web format, calls for a skillful balancing of diverse visual elements throughout the design. Multiple pages, and sometimes multiple documents, must be integrated with one another through the repetition and variation of visual (and related conceptual) themes. This chapter discusses how to use grid and path layouts to achieve a dynamic, unified design between pages. Everything you have studied in previous chapters about visual gestalt is relevant here.

THE BALANCING ACT

Layout design is a balancing act in two senses. First, it relates the diverse elements on a printed page in a way that communicates and has aesthetic appeal. Ideally, the form enhances the communication, no matter what style is being used. **Figure 7-1** uses type placement to illustrate the fear of flying. Second, as in all design, every element on the page affects how the other elements are perceived. Layout is not simply the addition of photographs, text type, display type, or artwork. It is a carefully balanced integration of elements.

The layout artist must select an appropriate typeface from the vast array available. The format, size, and value contrast of the typographical elements must be closely related to accompanying photographs and illustrations. Layout may be the most difficult balancing act a designer is ever called on to perform.

Everything you have studied so far about creating a balanced visual gestalt holds true for layout design. A good relationship between figure and ground is essential. The careful shaping of the white ground of the page gives cohesion and unity to the figures or elements placed on it. No leftover space should be unshaped, undersigned, because open white space functions as an active, participating part of the whole design. Page design can be *symmetrically* or *asymmetrically*

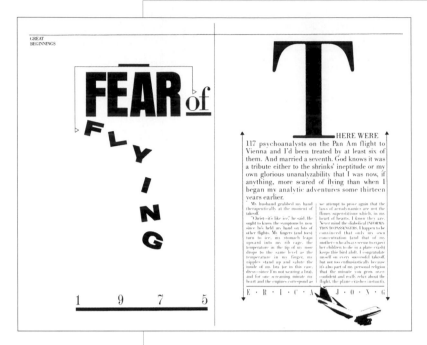

7-1 *Terry Koppel. (Koppel & Scher, New York.) Layout for* Fear of Flying *in brochure for Great Beginnings series.*
Courtesy of the designer.

7-2 *Albrecht Dürer. Fifteenth-century type designs based on the golden section.*

A careful balancing of contrast can give the page dynamic, unpredictable energy that will draw the reader's eyes. Chapter 4 discussed contrasts in size, shape, value, and texture, showing how a combination of similarity and contrast creates a balanced and successful layout. Chapter 6 discussed the use of typography and design elements in a single-page layout. This chapter discusses the balancing of multiple pages.

SIZE AND PROPORTION

This difficult balancing act calls for sensitivity to *proportion*—the organization of several things into a relationship of size, quantity, or degree. Artists have understood the importance of size relationships for centuries. The Parthenon expressed the Greeks' sense of proportion. It was based on a mathematical principle that came to be known as the *golden section*. The fifteenth-century painter and printmaker Albrecht Dürer used the golden section to analyze and construct his alphabet (**Figure 7-2**). The 20th-century architect Le Corbusier applied the propor-

balanced. Figure 7-1 uses asymmetry on the left page and symmetry on the right page to achieve its overall design. In either case, sensitivity to figure/ground grouping and white space will enhance the readability and beauty of the page.

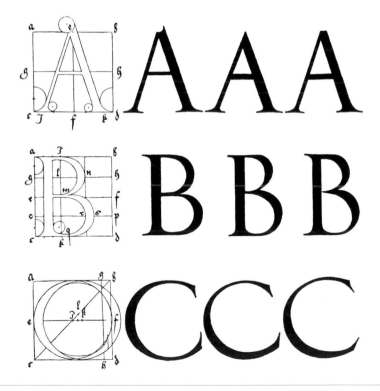

tions of the golden mean, or section, to architectural design. It is based on a rectangle that can be subdivided into a square. The square can be divided into two rectangles with the same proportions as the original. Each resulting small rectangle can be subdivided to produce the same results. **Figure 7-3** shows a diagram of those proportions. Ultimately, however, no mathematical system can take the place of an intuitive feeling for proportion or a sense of tension and energy in contrast. When the contrast between elements is too great, harmony and balance are lost.

The division of a page into areas in harmony with one another is at the heart of all layout design. **Figure 7-4** shows how Emil Ruder, an influential 20th-century Swiss

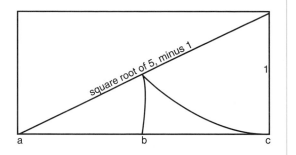

designer of the International Typographic Style, worked at bringing a page and its elements into harmony. He felt the relationships between type sizes, between printed and unprinted areas, between type and image, and between various values of gray must all be harmoniously proportionate.

● **7-3** *The golden section is believed to generate harmonious proportions.*

● **7-4** *Emil Ruder.*
Page areas in harmonious proportion.
Diagrams courtesy of Arthur Niggli Ltd., Niederteufen, Switzerland.

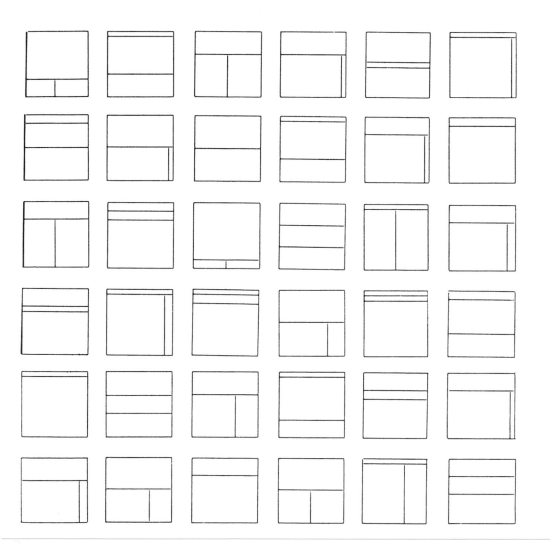

Chapter 7 Layout

When we refer to size, we usually use words like *big* or *small*. These terms are meaningless, however, unless we have two objects to compare. A 36-point word in a page with a lot of text type will seem large. On a spread with a 72-point headline, it will seem relatively small. An element large or bold in proportion to other elements on the page makes an obvious visual impact and a potentially strong focal point. Do not be afraid to use an element really LARGE, as in Figure 7-1, where the letter *T* makes a bold graphic statement. Several magazines use a larger format than is standard. This is another example of size contrast. Next to other magazines on the news racks, they have the impact of a comparatively large and impressive display.

Another way of determining size is to have a standard expected size in mind. If we refer to a large house cat, "large" might mean over 12 inches (30 cm) high. If we refer to a large horse, we have a different size in mind. Deliberately violating this expectation can create a dynamic, unusual effect. Mixing up standard relative sizes creates strong tension and compelling interest.

Another approach to confusing our sense of size and scale is showing objects larger than life. On the printed page, viewers have come to expect things to be shown smaller than they really are. We have no problem accepting a photograph in which the Empire State Building appears 3" (8 cm) high; but magnify a relatively tiny object, and we get a visual jolt that makes us pay attention. Imagine a photograph of a common housefly twenty times its actual size. **Figure 7-5** shows a wonderful play on portfolio size by designer Karen Roehr. This tiny portfolio, when mailed to a potential client, draws attention because it is so much smaller than expected.

VISUAL RHYTHM

Another important consideration in layout design is *visual rhythm*. Life itself is based

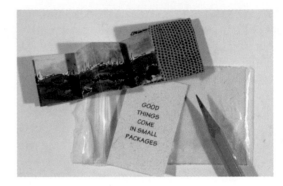

● **7-5** *Karen Roehr: "Good Things Come in Small Packages," a direct mail self promotional design. The accompanying note suggests that the recipient call to see the "bigger book" of this contemporary freelance designer.*

on rhythm. There is a rhythm to the passing days and seasons. The tempo of our days may be fast or slow. The growth and gradual decline of all natural life forms has a rhythm. Cities have particular pulsing rhythms. Different periods in our history have seemed to move to various beats. Our current age has an eclectic/quickened tempo compared with a hundred years ago.

Visual rhythm is based on repetition of shapes, values, colors, and textures. Recurrence of shapes and the spacing between them set up a pattern or rhythm. It can be lively and lyrical or solemn and dignified. Rhythm is crucial in many visual artists' work, including the London subway illustration in **Figure 7-6**, in which repeated shapes in water, woods, and sky vibrate with energy. The bird and boat reinforce each other, carrying our eyes in a race toward the lower right of the composition, while the rounded triangles of sailboats (in primary colors) set up a counterpoint to the primary rhythm.

There are many ways to use rhythm in typography. Within a single word, a rhythmic pattern of ascenders and descenders and curves and straights is created. The rhythm might be symmetrical or asymmetrical. Letter and word spacing can set up a typographical movement of varying tempos, as can changes in value and size (**Figure 7-7**).

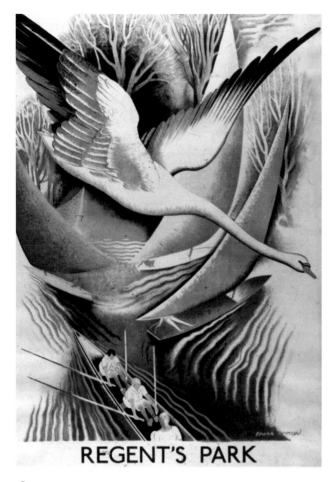

7-6 Regent's Park *by **Frank Ormrod**, created in 1937 for the London Underground. 40 × 25". This illustration for the London subway system uses rhythm and repetition of line and shape to unify its design.*
London Transport Museum

The total layout of the page is another opportunity to form a rhythmic pattern. The lines of type can form a rhythm of silent pauses, of leaps, of slow ascents and descents. An endless variety of rhythms can be created this way (**Figure 7-8**).

The spacing and size of photographs can intermingle with typography. An *alternating rhythm* may reserve every left page for a full-page photograph while the right page is textured with smaller units of text and other elements.

Another form of rhythm is *progressive rhythm*. The repeated element changes in a regular fashion. Text type might be used in changing values from regular to bold to

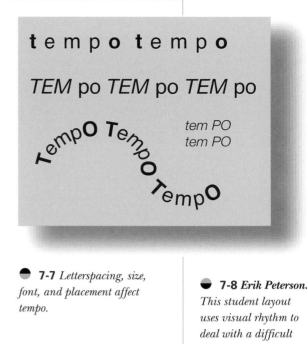

7-7 *Letterspacing, size, font, and placement affect tempo.*

7-8 *Erik Peterson. This student layout uses visual rhythm to deal with a difficult topic.*

extra bold and back again. A photograph might be repeated on successive pages, each time with more of the image displayed. Change in a regular manner is at the heart of a progressive rhythm.

GRID LAYOUT

A sense of pacing and rhythm can be set up throughout an entire publication with the aid of a grid. A *grid* is an invisible structure that underlies the page and functions as a guide for the placement of layout elements.

When and why is it appropriate to use a grid? Large publications usually require one to keep order. Grids may also be used in single-page designs, such as advertisements and posters, as in **Figure 7-9**, created by the 20th-century American modernist designer Herb Lubalin. In addition, grids are used to bring continuity to the separate pieces of a design series (**Figure 7-10**). A grid is most useful when it brings an organized unity not only to a single page but also to facing pages, an entire publication, or a series of publications.

Layout design that utilizes a grid is as flexible and creative as its designer is. The grid has been accused of bringing a boring conformity to page design. Grids, however, can help generate distinctive, dynamic images. They allow for experimentation with all the forms of contrast. A grid functions like a musical instrument. A piano, for instance, has a limited number of keys of fixed tone and position. It is possible, however, to play many different musical compositions through placement, rhythm, and emphasis. **Figure 7-11** by Herb Lubalin brings many different elements into harmony by using a grid.

Keeping the Beat

A musical composition has timing or a beat that pulses beneath all the long and short

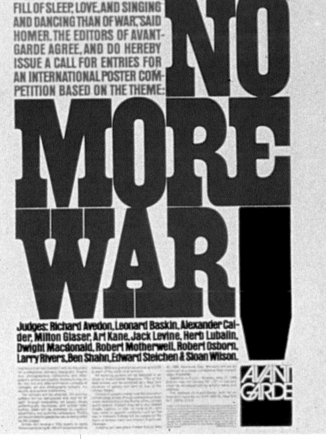

● *7-9 Herb Lubalin. Advertisement for the magazine* Avant Garde's *antiwar poster competition, 1967. An underlying grid and play on size contrast give a tight structure to this design.*

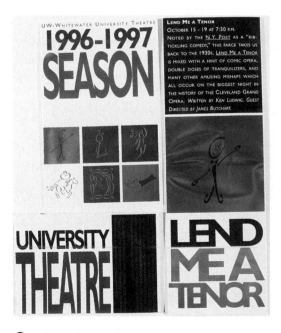

● *7-10 Design Studio 45, a student design agency at UW-Whitewater, created this series of publications promoting an upcoming theater season. A grid layout integrates the various pieces.*

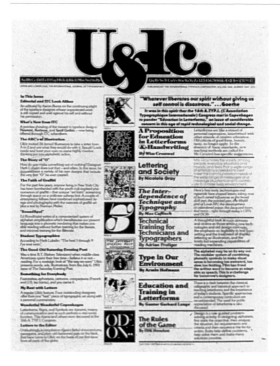

● **7-11 Herb Lubalin.** *Cover for* U&lc *magazine.*
1974. An underlying grid gives a clear structure to the
many diverse elements in this layout design.

notes. In a visual composition, a grid often
keeps this beat. Just as a four-beats-to-the-
measure musical score would not be cut
off at 3.5 beats, a grid layout that has four
sections across will not end at 3.5. Whether
the fourth unit is filled with an element or
left as a white ground, it gets its full count
and full *visual weight*. Within these four
musical counts might be a mixture of quar-
ter notes, half notes, and whole notes. The
four-unit grid might hold one large four-unit
element, two half-unit elements, or four
quarter-unit elements. The beauty in any
composition, whether visual or auditory,
comes once the structure is set up and the
variations in pacing, timing, and emphasis
begin.

Playing the Theme

An underlying musical theme, as in
Beethoven's Sixth Symphony (the "Pas-
toral"), will appear over and over in different guises, tying the symphony together

into a whole. An underlying visual theme
will accomplish the same for a visual composition. A layout for a publication unfolds
through time, just as a musical concert
does. Each page must be turned before
the next is revealed. It cannot be seen and
grasped at one viewing like a painting, an
advertisement, or a poster. Unifying it
requires a theme. Often this theme will
include both a purely visual *design* theme
and an editorial *content* theme (**Figures
7-12** and **7-13**).

The editorial theme could be the repetition of quotations on a particular topic. It
could be a contrast of "then and now," a
set of interviews—anything that seems to
tell an interesting story related to a common topic. Advertising campaigns are usually based on an editorial theme. Specialty
publications such as annual reports, which
revolve around one company, may also
use an editorial approach.

A visual theme almost always accompanies the editorial theme. It might be the
repeated use of a single thematic photograph on several pages throughout the
publication. It might be a particular
repeated arrangement of typography—or
of the grid itself. **Figure 7-14** shows two
two-page spreads that make sensitive use
of an underlying structure to bring unity to
the pages.

Grids in History

The grid is by no means a new invention. It
has been used for centuries by various cultures to design ornamental screens and
textiles (**Figure 7-15**). It has formed the
basis for quilt design, architecture, and
navigation. Pakistanis, Native Americans,
Africans, contemporary designers, and a
host of others have used it. The squared
grid, in which each of the four sides of a
unit is equal to the others, is the simplest
variation, but it is capable of yielding sophisticated results, whether used in quilts or
layout design (**Figure 7-16**).

Renaissance artists developed a method
of examining a subject through a network

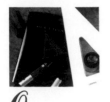

*O*verture. *An instrumental composition intended especially as an introduction to a complete work.*

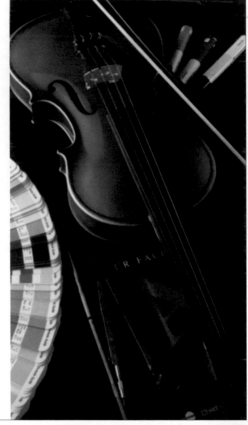

Our overture is an arrangement of artistic talents.
Ranging from the design of a single piece . . . to
the development of an entire corporate identity
program, our creativity is always conducted by your
instruction.

● **7-12, 7-13** *Layouts for self-promotional brochure by 12Twelve Design, a division of Terry Printing.* **Mary Hakala,** *art director;* **Dennis Dooley,** *photographer.*
Courtesy of the artist.

*C*rescendo. *A gradual increase in volume or intensity.*

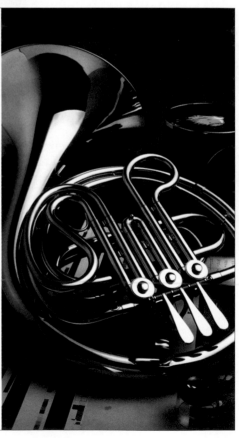

Through the crescendo, our printing professionals
continually strive to create new scales of printing
excellence so that your composition reflects the
tone of your company.

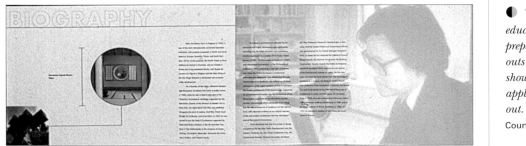

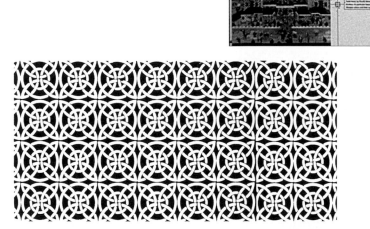

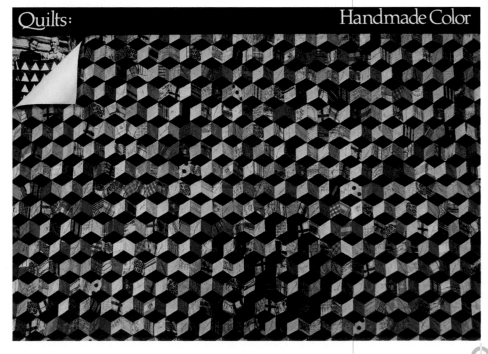

● **7-14** *Designer and educator* **Daniel Kim** *prepared these comp layouts for his portfolio, showing a creative application of grid layout.*
Courtesy of the artist.

● **7-16** *Julius Friedman* and **Walter McCord**, *designers;* **Craig Guyon,** *photographer. Quilts: Handmade Color.*
Courtesy of the artist.

● **7-15** *An ornamental grid design.*

Quilts: Handmade Color

of strings and then drawing on paper similarly divided into sections. In the 20th century, the grid became interesting to artists as a shape in itself. Frequently drawings, illustrations, and paintings allow the grid structure to show through, just as Bauhaus architects insisted that the structure of their buildings show through.

Today many layouts that have a strong grid structure trace their origins to the de Stijl movement. By 1918 both Van Doesburg and Mondrian were using dark lines to divide their canvases into asymmetrical patterns (Figures 2-23, 4-2).

A more recent figure associated with the grid layout is Swiss designer Josef Müller-Brockmann. He had tremendous influence on the structure and definition of graphic design. "The tauter the composition of elements in the space available," he stated, "the more effectively can the thematic idea be formulated." Copy, photographs, drawings, and trade names are all subservient to the underlying grid structure in this modernist approach, which continues to have relevance (Figure 4-3).

Grid design is incorporated into our current technology. Dedicated page layout programs like Quark and InDesign do an excellent job of accommodating a grid-based layout. They allow the designer to construct a grid or use a pre-packaged one and specify type to fill the columns.

Choosing a Grid

Grids differ from one another as much as the minds that create them. They vary from the familiar three-column format to a Swiss grid, based on overlapping squares, to an original creation.

The first consideration when choosing a grid is the elements it will contain. Consider the copy. How long is it, how long are the individual segments, and how many inserts and subheads does it contain? If the copy is composed of many independent paragraphs, the underlying grid should break the page area up into small units. If the copy is a textbook of long unbroken

chapters with few visuals, however, a complex grid is wasted; most of its divisions will seldom be used.

Now consider the art. A publication that uses many photographs will call for a grid different from that of a publication that is copy-heavy. Whenever many elements need to be incorporated into a layout, a more complex grid, broken down into many small units, is the most useful. It will give more possibilities for placing and sizing photographs.

You can create your own grid that corresponds to the number of elements and the size of your page. The tinier the grid units, the more choices you will need to make about placement. The more placement options there are, the greater the chance that the underlying unity will be lost. In other words, sometimes a simple grid is the best choice.

Both the vertical and the horizontal divisions in a grid are important. The vertical dividers determine the line length of the copy. Both the vertical and horizontal lines determine the size of photographs or artwork. Remember to relate line length and type size to make it easy for the eye to read and keep its place. Forcing large type into small grid units makes for slow, difficult reading.

Constructing the Grid

The vertical divisions of the grid are usually expressed in picas or in inches, as is the line length of copy measured for typesetting. The horizontal divisions are most frequently measured in points, as is leading. A 10-point type, for example, with 2 points of leading between lines would be set on 12-point leading. This type could be specified at a 21-pica or $3\frac{1}{2}$-inch line length. The column width would correspond. The structure is usually sounder if the elements themselves align with the grid edges and merely suggest the presence of the grid. With precise alignment, our eyes will draw an invisible line of continuation between elements that forms a much stronger bond

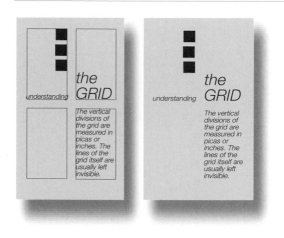

7-17 *The invisible line of continuation between elements on a grid helps create a unified composition.*

than a physical inked line, as shown in **Figure 7-17**.

Grid structure and the path layout are both used to bring balance and harmony to page design. Both depend on the eye and mind detecting such unit-forming factors as repetition and continuation, tempered with a deliberate contrast or variation for effect.

PATH LAYOUT

The *path layout* assumes no underlying, unifying grid structure. Rather, the designer begins with a blank sheet of paper and attempts to visualize the elements on it in various arrangements. This complex approach can yield tremendously varied results. The unity comes from a direct reliance on unit-forming factors. This reliance is sometimes unconscious, but beginning designers should learn and practice it on a conscious level. It can lead to excellent results.

The word *path* describes this less structured, more spontaneous approach because the designer is attempting to set up a path for the eye. The goal is to guide the eye skillfully through the various elements. To do so, there must usually be a clear entry point, or focal point, and a clear

path to the next element and the next. A simple symmetrical and centered path layout is used effectively in **Figure 7-18**, a poster for the Louisville Ballet by designer Julius Friedman.

Focal Point

The *focal point,* or the point of entry into a design, is the first area that attracts attention

7-18 *Julius Friedman,* designer; *John Lair,* photographer. *Poster for the Louisville Ballet.*

Courtesy of the artist.

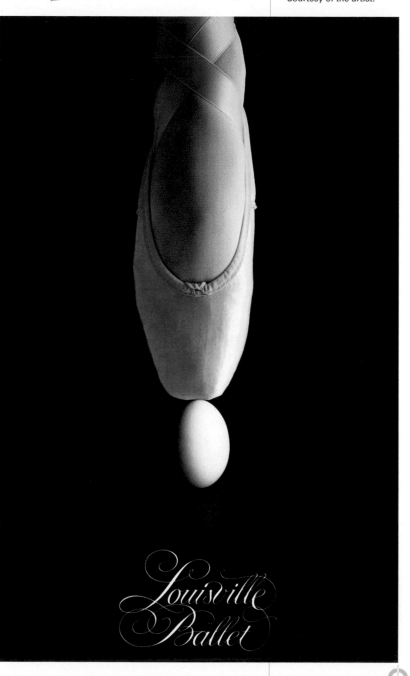

and encourages the viewer to look further. If at first glance, our eyes are drawn equally to several different areas, visual chaos results and interest is lost. A focal point can be set up in many different ways, but they all have to do with creating difference or variety. Whatever disrupts an overall visual field will draw the eye. The focal point should not be so overwhelming that the eye misses the rest of the composition.

These differences could become the focal point:

- A heavy black value set down in a field of gray and white.
- A small isolated element set next to several larger elements near one another.
- An irregular, organically shaped element set next to geometric ones.
- A textured element set next to solid areas. Text type can often function in this manner.
- An image or word that is emotionally loaded.

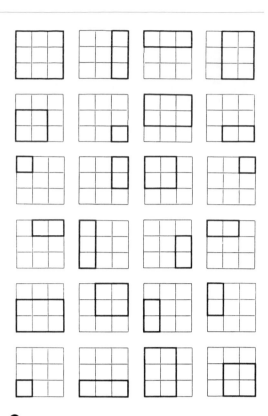

● **7-19** *Emil Ruder. Photo placements on a grid.*
Design courtesy Arthur Niggli Ltd.

PHOTOGRAPHY IN A LAYOUT

An important element in layout design is the photograph. A designer must learn what makes a good photograph and how to use it to best advantage. Copywriters, photographers, and designers depend on one another's skills. Poor page design can make a beautiful photograph lose all its impact and appeal. Conversely, a poor photograph can be strengthened by a good design.

Dynamic photos, strong in design and human interest, can be made to look lifeless with certain design mistakes. One problem can be the paper choice. If it is too absorbent for the reproduction method, it will ink poorly, so the value contrast in the reproduced photos will be muddy. Another common mistake is lack of size contrast. When photos of similar sizes compete for attention, the eye will be drawn to none. Other elements on the page may also point away or detract from the photographic image.

Figure 7-19 by Emil Ruder shows different ways of placing a photograph on a grid layout. Practice some variations yourself, attempting to establish a visual pacing. A similar grid and photographs for placement can be found on this book's accompanying Web site. You will need to crop and resize these photographs in Photoshop.

Cropping

Many photographs can be improved by the designer's careful cropping. *Cropping* is eliminating part of the vertical or horizontal dimension of a photograph to focus attention on the remaining portion. Cropping is also used to fit a photograph into an available space by altering its proportions. When cropping to fit a space, use discretion. Cropping too tightly will destroy the mood of the image.

Sometimes a photograph, like an overwritten paragraph, can be improved by deleting excess information. The format is fixed in a camera, but the action being photographed might be taking place within a compact square area or a long, thin vertical. Trimming away the meaningless part of the image on the sides will improve the impact, as in the newspaper image shown in **Figure 7-20**. It can also enhance a feeling of motion, as shown in the same photograph.

Cropping a photograph can make it dramatic. If you wish to emphasize the height of a tall building, for example, cropping the sides to make a long, thin rectangle will increase the sense of height. Cropping the top and bottom of a long horizontal shot will increase the sense of an endless horizon.

Cropping causes us to focus on the dramatic part of the image in **Figure 7-21**, a poster for the Cincinnati Ballet Company. The feet present a theme of repetition and variation and set up a wonderful visual rhythm.

Resizing

All the traditional resizing methods are becoming less important, as designers usually resize, crop, and experiment with the results on the computer. The important thing to understand is the concept of ratio. You must maintain the integrity of the original photograph, without expanding or distorting the image to fit a space. Always maintain the original height-to-width ratio when rescaling a photograph. The software can help with that if you check the retain-proportion box or hold down the shift key when resizing.

Selecting

A designer may receive the photographs to work with or have the opportunity to order specific photos shot. You might also elect

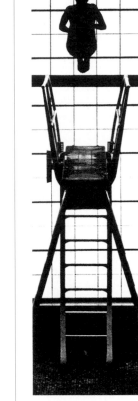

◗ **7-20** *Gordon Baer (Cincinnati, OH). Pepsi-Cola Diving Competition.* Courtesy of the artist.

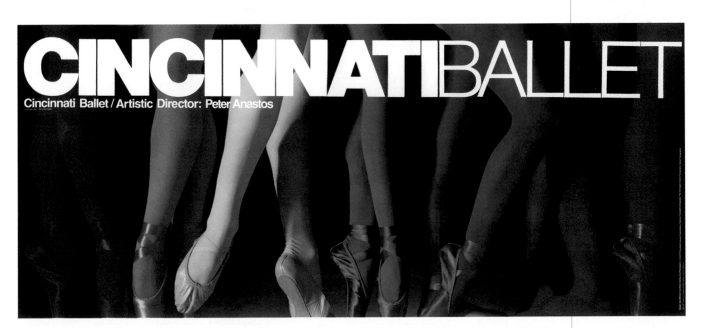

● **7-21** *Dan Bittman, designer; Corson Hirschfeld, photographer; and the Hennegan Company, lithography. Poster for the Cincinnati Ballet Company.*

to shoot them personally. It is a wise idea for anyone considering a career in graphic design to take a course in photography.

Choose photographs for your layout on three grounds: *the quality of the print or digital file, the merit of the design, and the strength of the communication.*

Photo retouching programs make it easier to correct problems with print quality. It is helpful to understand what good reproduction qualities in a photograph are in

order to recognize and achieve them. Watch for good contrast between darks and lights, a full tonal range, sharp focus (where appropriate), and lack of scratches, dust spots, and other imperfections. The Digital Focus feature discusses the relationship between digital resolution and resizing.

● **7-22a** *The digital relationship between resizing and resolution.*
Adobe Product screenshots reprinted with permission from Adobe Systems Incorporated.

Digital Focus

When resizing a digital image it is important to pay attention to the resolution. *Resolution* refers to the fineness or sharpness of an image, based on the number of pixels per inch (ppi). Plan on 72 ppi for screen images and 300 dots per inch (dpi) for most print applications. When an image is resized, the resolution changes. As the image gets larger, the resolution decreases, because the same number of pixels are covering a larger area. To fill the space, the pixels get larger and coarser.

If you need to change the resolution or size of your digital image, open it in Photoshop and select Image>Image Size. Look at the resolution and document size. Check the constrain-proportions box to keep the horizontal and vertical dimensions proportionally true. Unclick the resample-image box to make the resolution increase and decrease with changes in the file's physical size, as shown in **Figure 7-22a**. Clicking the box will let you maintain a resolution while changing the physical size, and vice versa. If you enlarge the image size significantly, however, it will not stay a clear image, because the increased pixels are *interpolated,* or generated by the program, and do not reflect actual data. Locking in a resolution while reducing size will produce crisp results.

Multipanel Design

Folders and brochures present a layout problem slightly different from that of magazines, newspapers, and books. A brochure is actually more a three-dimensional construction than a two-dimensional layout. Nevertheless, a grid may be used. Contrasting size and visual rhythm to achieve harmonious proportions remains important.

The additional element of the fold complicates matters. Brochures may fold and unfold into unusual shapes (**Figure 7-22b**). They may unfold several times and at each successive unfolding present a new facet of the design. Use this opportunity to tell a story. Each panel can give additional information, with the front panel acting as a teaser. Never give your punch line on the front panel. Lead up to it. A successful front panel will lure the reader inside. The succeeding panels will build interest and develop a theme. The panels in **Figure 7-23** gradually unfold to reveal the message "Imagine." If the brochure is a self-mailer, address and stamp are placed directly on the back.

Other special decisions go into a multi-panel design: the size of the piece, the number of folds and their direction, and the flexibility of the paper. Usually, when preparing a comprehensive, the designer will try to use a paper similar to the one on which the brochure will finally be printed. Then the client can hold and unfold the design.

The brochure or flyer will often be part of a unified publication series. Then you must sustain the visual and intellectual theme of the series (**Figures 7-24a, b**).

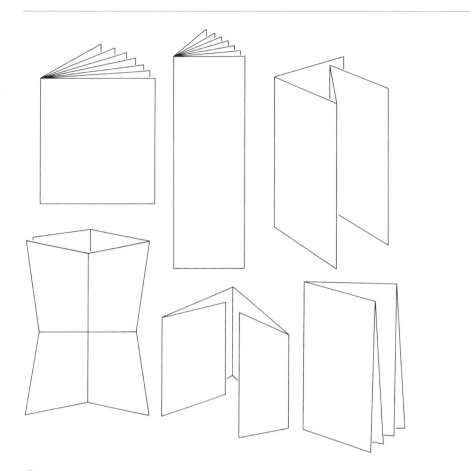

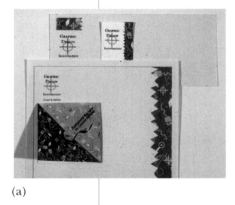

7-24a, b *Connie McNish.* *This unified series, designed while McNish was a student, includes a letterhead, an envelope, a business card, and a promotional brochure with an unusual and creative fold.*

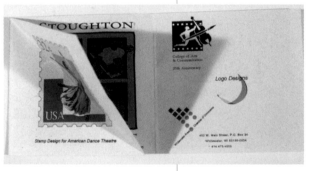

(a)

(b)

● **7-22b** *Brochure construction calls for a design unified across multiple panels.*

● **7-23** **Anita Syverson** *created this multipanel design for Cummings Advertising, making creative use of stock photography.*

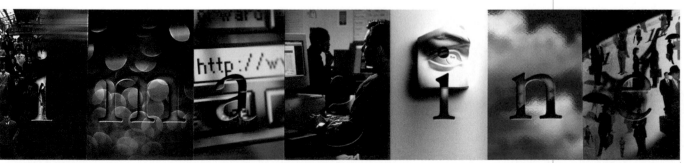

Layout Styles

During the discussion of design history presented in Chapter 2, you learned that the European-influenced modern style was exported to the United States during the 1940s. Characterized by sans-serif typography and the belief in a universally shared aesthetic, the modern style saw order as the spirit of a modern, rational, technological civilization. The development of the grid system seen in the work of Swiss designers Josef Müller-Brockmann, Emil Ruder, and others fit into this perception of design as a wedding of science and aesthetics in a rational world.

Design in the 1960s became more eclectic and inclusive. The 1970s saw a questioning of the rational Swiss Design approach that led to the development of New Wave or postmodern graphic design. The designs of the International Typographic Style and modernism were seen as too reductive. A new interest in complex, layered forms and meaning developed. April Greiman's work shows the exuberance of this inclusive, eclectic style, which celebrates complexity and diversity. Greiman's work retains a strong sense of underlying structure (see **Figure 7-25a**). As postmodernism has grown, art and design history has become a great visual resource for inspiration, a resource in which all styles are potentially meaningful. Art nouveau, art deco, pop art, Swiss modernism, and personal intuition may all be combined to generate the postmodern design.

Katherine McCoy is another important figure in postmodern design who, as an educator and designer, articulates and defines the nature of the multiple layers of communication possible in the contemporary visual design. She writes about design criticism and consults in graphic design, marketing, and interior design for cultural, educational, and corporate clients. Her Web site at **www.highgrounddesign .com** contains an excellent discussion of contemporary issues.

Technological innovations contribute greatly to the changing face of design. The IBM PC and Apple Macintosh dominated the widespread use of computers in design that began in the 1980s. The computer brought a great deal of flexibility and made easy shifts of type size, shape, and style accessible to designers. **Figure 7-25b** shows this flexibility and rich visual texturing of typography by a contemporary design group from the former East Ger-

● **7-25a** *April Greiman. Poster. Objects in Space, Selby Gallery. American Institute of Graphic Arts, Orange County. Four-color offset, fluorescent process, 24 × 36", 1999.*

Courtesy of the artist and Made in Space, Inc.

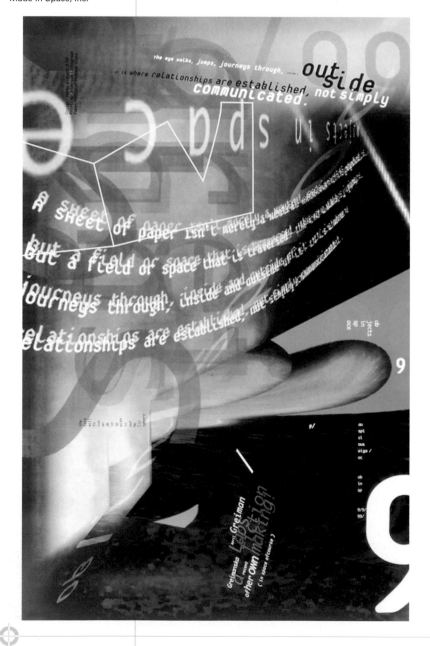

many. They gained access to computer technology after the fall of the Berlin Wall in 1989. Much of their work is created for German cultural institutions.

Figure 7-26 by contemporary illustrator Diane Fenster shows an integration of type and image made possible by current technology. The ability to create such a powerful aesthetic, however, is ultimately in the eye and mind of the designer/illustrator.

Graphics are now generated and prepared for prepress with software that encourages complexity and reflects our society's complex structure and informational mix. Electronic mail, facsimile transmissions, and low-volume desktop publishing decentralize information processing.

The Internet is a great experiment in democracy, because information can be disseminated and accessed on personal computers beyond anything previously possible.

CONCLUSION

Layout is a balancing act that creates unity among the diverse elements on a page. An underlying grid can unite the many pages of a large publication. When combining copy, illustration, and photography, unity can also be established by finding similar shapes, angles, values, and typestyles. Like a musical composition, a layout needs

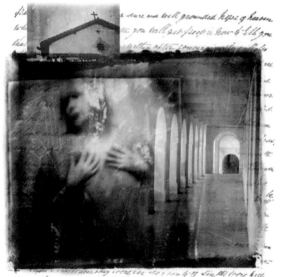

7-26 *Diane Fenster. 1999. Illustration for Simon & Schuster using a visually rich integration of text and image.*
Courtesy of the artist.

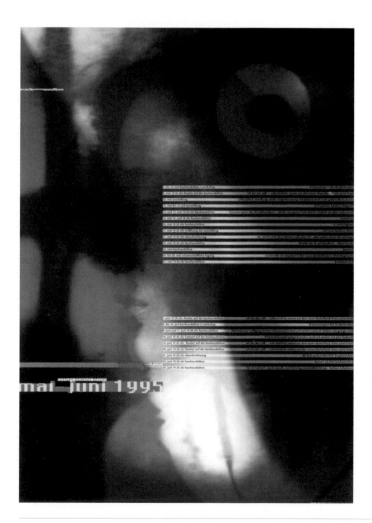

7-25b *Cyan. Sophie Alex, Wilhelm Ebentreich, Detlef Fiedler, Daniela Haufe, Siegfried Jablonsky.* Stiftung Bauhaus Dessau, May–June 1995. *1995. Offset lithograph, printed in color, 33 × 23³/₈" (83.8 × 59.4 cm).* The Museum of Modern Art, New York. Gift of the designers.
Photograph © 2001 The Museum of Modern Art, New York/Art Resource, NY.

pacing, rhythm, and theme. This problem-solving approach stems from an understanding of visual language developed by 20th-century modernism.

Variety or contrast is important too. Many kinds of contrast—in visual texture, value, shape, typestyle, and size—can create a focal point or visual path in a layout. A combination of contrasting historical styles is currently used to provide a rich, visually complex design. Multiple layers of communication created with this approach are a feature of postmodern style. Whatever the historical style, it is more than merely an affectation. Movements in art and design reflect the structure and values of society and help disseminate those values. Both modernism and postmodernism have been informed and enriched by an understanding of how visual information is processed and meaning is derived. This understanding is fundamental to all forms of graphic design.

Finally, whatever the style, your layout should strive to do justice to the intentions of the copywriter, photographer, illustrator, client, and yourself.

EXERCISES

1. Enlarge the sample grids in **Figure 7-27** to design several rhythmic layouts. See the accompanying Web site for a template. If you choose to use collage or paste-up, use old magazines and cut out photographs, cropping where necessary and adding some version of comped type blocks. If you use a computer, refer to the accompanying Web site to access photos and sample layout grids. You will be asked to paste the cropped, resized raster image into a vector type program.

2. Select several magazines or annual reports and figure out their grid structure. Can you find one with an interesting complexity and nuance? Look for stylistic influences. Bring one publication in for class discussion of strengths and weaknesses.

3. Save samples of brochure designs that appeal to you and study them for future inspiration. Look for interesting multi-panel samples that unfold the message in sequential steps. Plan to keep a file of such samples throughout your career. Share what you've found with others in the class.

◗ **7-27** *Sample grids.*

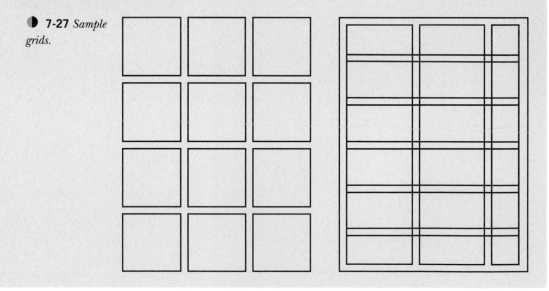

PROJECT

Two-Page Layout

In consultation with your instructor, choose a short story, myth, or fable. Select a visual and conceptual theme appropriate to your story. Incorporate original imagery and create a two-page layout with a grid structure. After doing several roughs by experimenting with at least two different grids, choose the most successful. Prepare a final polished version using any method you prefer. **Figure 7-28** uses shaped type in an area to create a visual-path layout with a good figure/ground relationship. "Nymph" (**Figure 7-29**) is a well-integrated grid layout with an excellent airbrush illustration that makes a strong use of figure/ground relationships.

Goals and Objectives

Learn to choose an appropriate grid and fit layout elements into it.

Practice cropping and resizing photographs without distortion and integrating them with typography.

Use all the information studied so far on balance, rhythm, figure/ground relationships, unity, and contrast to create a dynamic, integrated multi-page layout.

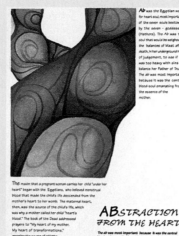

ABSTRACTION FROM THE HEART

Critique

Be prepared to present your work in class and to discuss the following questions:

What is your grid structure? Why did you choose it? What decisions did you make related to it?

Describe your choice of typestyle, point size, line length, leading, and format. Did you make any variations in letterspacing?

How does the eye move through your layout?

Select your favorite design from the class and be prepared to talk about why it works.

● **7-28** *Natalie Krug. "Heart" is a path layout integrated with a water-color illustration that addresses the multiple meanings of the word* heart.

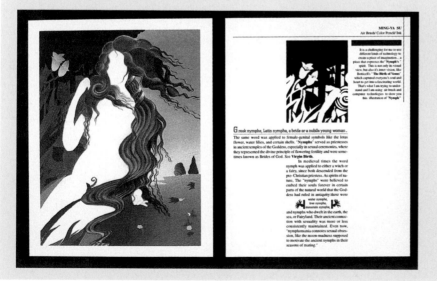

◐ **7-29** *Ming Ya Su. "Nymph." A grid layout in which both illustration and layout show a sensitivity to figure/ground relationships.*

TERMINOLOGY

CHAPTER 8

See glossary
for
definitions.

Light Waves

Additive Primaries

Subtractive Primaries

Process Colors

Hue

Value

Intensity

Color Schemes

Complementary

Split Comple-

mentary

Analogous

Monochromatic

Simultaneous Contrast

Pixels

RGB

CMYK

HSL

Tint Screen

Moiré

Halftone

Duotone

Tritone

Local Color

Arbitrary Color

The Dynamics of Color

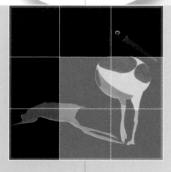

KEY POINTS Color for the designer and color for the fine artist are similar at the creative stage. A fundamental knowledge of color theory is vital to both designer and fine artist. Later, in preparing art on the computer for the Web or for the printing process, the designer needs to be familiar with how color is influenced by its intended publication venue. A great deal of new terminology and concepts will be introduced. First we'll brush up on color as a creative, pigment-based, and artistic communication. Then we will consider color from the computer and printing perspectives.

DESIGNING WITH COLOR

Every student who has completed an elementary course in art has heard that color is a property of light. Many people do not fully understand those words, however, until years after their art degree is completed. A young painter several years past her B.F.A. tells a story of looking around her living room for a composition to paint. "I considered the objects in the room and the space they occupied; the corners of the ceiling and the negative spaces in the staircase. I looked at the carpet and saw the standard 'landlord green.' And then I looked at the carpet again and realized that my mind was processing 'landlord green,' but my eyes were actually looking at black geometric shapes swimming beside a shining pastel/fluorescent color of fresh spring leaves. The sun was shining in the window of my dark living room and transforming my carpet. Color is a property of light, I thought. Oh!"

Color has been accurately described as both "the way an object absorbs or reflects light" and "the kind of light that strikes an object." The painter's carpet would have appeared to have a different color had it had a deep shag texture or a slick, shiny surface. It would have appeared to have a different color under an incandescent or fluorescent light, under bright natural sunlight or light overcast by cloud cover. Even the angle from which it was viewed would have had an effect.

Isaac Newton first passed a beam of white light through a prism and saw it divide into several colors. The colors of the light-wave spectrum are red, orange, yellow, green, blue, and indigo (**Figure 8-1**). In physics, mixing the colors of the light wave together produces pure white light. It is such *light waves,* bouncing off or being absorbed by the objects around us, that give the objects color.

The three primary colors in white light are red, green, and blue (RGB). They are called *additive primaries* because together they can produce white light. The eye contains three different types of color receptors, each sensitive to one of the primary colors of the light spectrum. This seems to suggest an active connection between our physiological makeup and the world in which we live.

The designer should understand that color depends on light. *Color is not an unchanging, absolute property of the object. It is dynamic and affected by its environment.* We'll learn more about RGB as it applies to computer monitors, photography, and the Web later.

The Color Wheel

For the artist and print designer, mixing pigments will never produce white. Black is the sum of all pigment colors. Several color wheels have been developed to help us understand the effects of combining pigments.

The traditional pigment-based color wheel, developed by Herbert Ives, begins with the *subtractive primary* colors red, yellow, and blue. Mixing these hues produces secondary colors. Mixing the secondary colored pigments with the primaries produces a tertiary color. The term *subtractive* means that a pigment absorbs, or "subtracts," a segment of white light in order to reflect back its particular hue. The visual effect produced by combining such pigments is actually the sum of their subtractions. For the artist and print designer, that means a less brilliant result than is produced by a single pigment.

The Munsell color wheel is based on five key hues: red, yellow, blue, green, and purple. Mixing these primaries forms secondaries. Although these two classification systems differ, the basic look of the resulting colors is similar. The color wheel is only a workable system, not an absolute. **Figures 8-2a** and **8-2b** show the traditional and the Munsell color wheels. The cyan, magenta, yellow, and black (CMYK) *process colors* used in offset printing are also a pigment-based subtractive gamut that we'll discuss later in this chapter.

Properties of Color

Every color has three properties: hue, value, and intensity. *Hue* is the name by which we identify a color. The color wheel is set up according to hue.

Value is the degree of lightness or darkness in a hue. It is easiest to understand value when looking at a black and white image. The darkest value will be close to black, the lightest close to white, with a range of grays in between. Value also plays an important role in all color images. Every hue has its own value range. Yellow, for example, is normally lighter than purple. Its normal value in the middle of a yellow value scale will be lighter than purple. In a value scale, the color values lighter than normal value are called _tints;_ those darker than normal value are called _shades._ When working with pigments, the addition of white lightens a value, whereas the addition of black darkens it. **Figure 8-3** shows a value scale.

The third property of color is *intensity,* or saturation. It is a measure of a color's purity and brightness. In pigments there are two ways of reducing the intensity of a color: mix it with a gray of the same value, or mix it with its complement (the

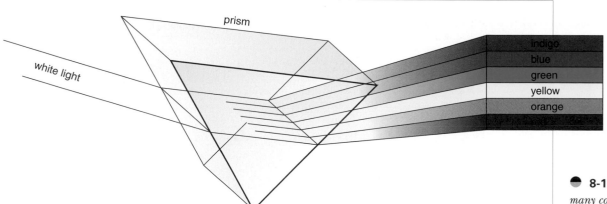

indigo
blue
green
yellow
orange

8-1 *Light waves of many colors join to make white light.*

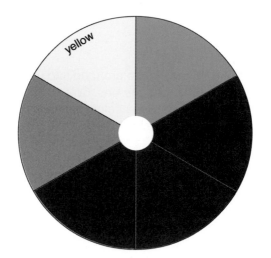

yellow

8-2a *The traditional pigment-based color wheel, developed by Herbert Ives, shows the three primary colors red, yellow, and blue with their secondary colors.*

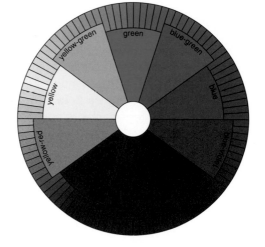

yellow-green • green • blue-green • yellow • blue • yellow-red • red-violet

8-2b *The Munsell color wheel is based on five key hues with secondaries formed by mixing these primaries.*

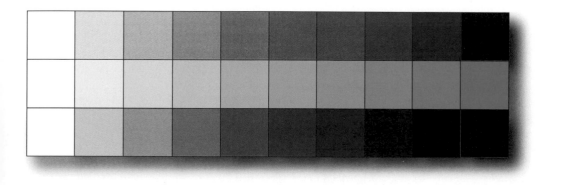

8-3 *Changes in value within a single hue create a wide range of "colors."*

● **8-4b** *Tim Girvin,*
art director, designer;
Anton Kimball, *illustrator;* **Mary Radosevich,**
production. Bright Blocks
is a package design by
Tom Girvin Design, Inc.
It uses highly saturated
color to target its young
audience. The colorful
design was credited with
increasing sales
dramatically.
Courtesy of the artist.

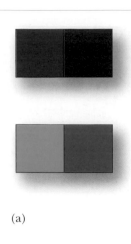

(a)

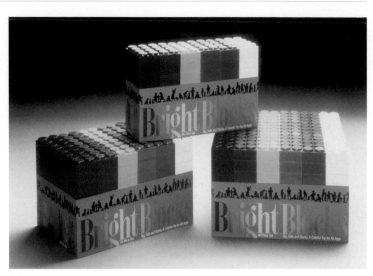

(b)

● **8-5a** *Linda Godfrey. While she was still a*
student, this freelance
illustrator created a
whimsical collage using
photographic textures.
The strong use of blue is
accented with complements, and repetition is
used throughout this creative design.

color opposite on the color wheel). Low-intensity colors have been toned down and are often referred to as *tones.* Colors not grayed are at their most vivid at full intensity, as shown in **Figure 8-4a**. **Figure 8-4b** shows high-intensity colors applied to children's toys.

Color Schemes

Color combinations are grouped into categories called *color schemes.* Colors opposite one another on the color wheel are called *complements.* Art that combines these colors is said to be using a complementary color scheme. The artwork in **Figure 8-5a** uses a range between blue and gold/brown/orange. Complements heighten and accent one another. They are often used to produce a bold, exciting effect. A *split complementary* scheme includes one hue and the hue on either side of its direct

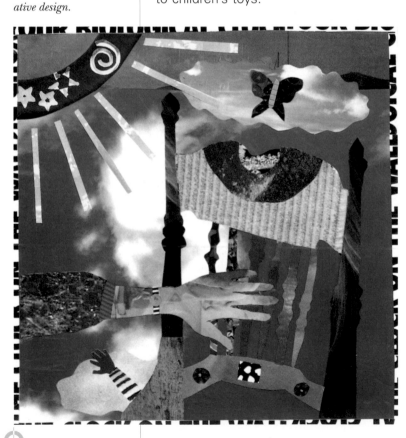

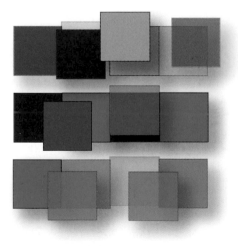

● **8-5b** *Complementary, split-complementary, analogous, and monochromatic color schemes.*

complement. Colors next to one another on the color wheel are called *analogous.* An analogous color scheme is generally considered soothing and restful. A *monochromatic* color scheme is composed of one hue in several values. These color schemes are shown in **Figure 8-5b**.

In color there are no real absolutes. That is why this information is often called *color theory.* It is unusual, but quite possible, to produce a tense, dramatic effect using analogous colors or a soothing, harmonious effect using complementary colors. Remember, these principles are not rules but useful guidelines. An artist or a designer may choose to violate them for effect.

THE RELATIVITY OF COLOR

Our perception of color is colored by many considerations. For example, the way each color looks to us is strongly affected by what surrounds it. This phenomenon is known as *simultaneous contrast.* We automatically compare colors that sit side by side. When complements (such as red and green) are placed side by side, they seem to become more intense. They complement one another. A gray placed beside a color appears to have a tinge of that color's complement in it because our eye automatically searches for it. Therefore a neutral gray beside a red will appear to be a greenish gray; the same neutral gray beside a green will appear to have a reddish cast.

Simultaneous contrast also affects value. A gray placed against a black ground will appear to have a lighter value than the same gray placed against a white ground (**Figure 8-6**). Our eyes make a comparison between the black and gray and judge the gray as much lighter. In the other sample, our eyes look at the white and judge the gray as much darker.

One designer first experienced this effect when she was a child visiting her aunt for dinner. Butter in her own home was a yellow stick brought home from the

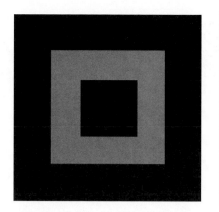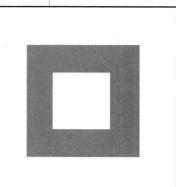

● **8-6** *Simultaneous contrast makes the center rectangles, which are the same color, appear to be different.*

store. On the aunt's farm it came straight from the cows, after a little churning. This fresh butter did not have yellow food coloring added to it. When her aunt placed it on the table on a yellow plate, the niece would not eat it. It looked white and could not be the real thing. Who would eat white butter? The aunt, however, knew about simultaneous contrast, although not by that name. She whisked the butter plate away and returned with the same butter, this time on a white plate. The young girl was delighted with the "new" butter. This time, compared with the white plate it sat on, the fresh butter looked yellow.

Simultaneous contrast means that color is relative to the colors surrounding it. This fact was first discovered in the 19th century when a French chemist named Michel-Eugène Chevreul, also a merchant who dyed fabric, was disturbed by apparent inconsistencies in his bolts of cloth. He discovered that his dye remained consistent, but the viewing conditions did not. Bolts of the same color appeared to be different colors, depending on the color of the fiber samples around them. He went on to research and document color properties. In the 20th century, Josef Albers made a further intensive study of color. Albers experimented with simultaneous contrast and contributed greatly to our

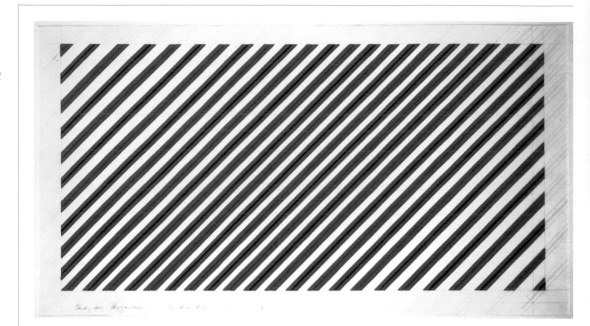

● **8-7** *Bridget Riley.*
1969. Gouache study.
H 62 cm W 98 cm.
Each red stripe is altered
by the band it encloses.
Victoria and Albert
Museum, London/Art
Resource, NY, copyright
2005 Bridget Riley.

understanding of that effect. **Figure 8-7** by British artist Bridget Riley uses the optical effects of color and rhythm in her painting. See the accompanying Web site for additional information.

THE PSYCHOLOGY OF COLOR

Relativity also holds true in the psychology of color. Colors have the power to evoke specific emotional responses in the viewer—some personal and some more universal. In general, for example, warm colors stimulate people, whereas cool colors relax them. Interior designers pay close attention to this relationship when they consider the color schemes for a dentist's waiting room or the newsroom of a daily paper. Imagine sitting in a dentist's chair, staring at a bright red wall!

Red, yellow, and their variations are referred to as warm colors, perhaps because we associate them with fire and the sun. Blue and green are considered cool colors. They also happen to be the colors of sky, water, and forests. The difference in the wavelengths of these colors may also account for our reactions to them.

Associations

Personal memories play a part in color perception as well. If your mother usually wore a particular shade of blue, and you loved your mother (and she loved you), that shade of blue has good associations for you. It seems a warm, friendly color, although to other eyes it might look cool.

Along with personal associations, we have cultural associations with color. They often appear in the English language in the United States as "black anger," "yellow-bellied coward," "feeling blue," and "seeing red". To her wedding a bride in this culture wears white, the color of purity. Black is a funeral color, and the color of mourning. These are not absolute associations; they change from culture to culture. For example, people in India wear white to a funeral. For a wedding, they favor yellow. These cultural differences continue to blend together with our increasing sense of a global community.

We can describe our culture's general color associations. It is by no means a description to be memorized and taken as gospel. Color psychology is complex, affected by many considerations, but if you can combine this information with a light hand and a sensitive eye, it may prove useful.

RED Red is a dramatic, highly visible hue. It is associated with sexuality and aggression, with passion and violence. It is also an official hue found in most national colors. Red is often the favored color of a sports car or a sports team. A dignified, conservative executive, however, is unlikely to choose red for a car or a corporate logo unless its intensity is toned down or its value darkened toward black.

BLUE In its darker values, blue is associated with authority. Our executive might likely favor a navy blue car, suit, and logo. A middle-value blue is generally associated with cleanliness and honesty and has a cooling, soothing effect. It is used as a background color in package design because of its quiet, positive associations. Even at full intensity, blue retains a calm quality.

YELLOW Yellow is used in food packaging a great deal because it is associated with warmth, good health, and optimism. There still are reminders in the English language that yellow also has been associated with cowardliness and weakness. That does not appear to be the case currently, however. Even cultural associations are subject to change.

GREEN Green is associated with the environment, cleanliness, and naturalness. Soothing and cooling, it is consequently a favored color among manufacturers of such products as menthol cigarettes and non-cola beverages. These products benefit from a visual association with a healthy environment.

Selecting Color

When choosing a color, consider the psychology of the audience. A game or toy intended to appeal to children should have colors different from one intended to reach adults considering retirement plans. Our color preferences change as we grow older. In general, youth prefers a more intense color that signals urgency and excitement. The subtle color preferences of age are associated with restraint and dignity.

The institution you are designing for should also affect the selection of color. Banks tend to prefer the darker values and the blues and grays associated with authority and stability. A physical fitness club would probably want more vibrant and intense colors. A restaurant may choose complementary colors that are toned down to an attractive and intimate level (**Figure 8-8**).

Personal color preference is not the only, or even the primary, consideration for a designer. Choice of color should reflect five psychological factors:

1. Cultural associations with color.
2. The profile of the audience and its color preferences.

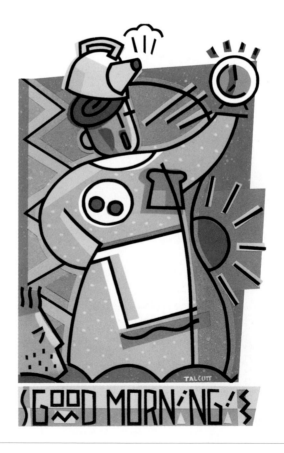

 8-8 *Julie Talcott. Freelance illustrator. This computer-generated illustration uses complementary colors and strong repetition of line and shape to create an integrated design.* Courtesy of the artist.

3. The character and personality of the organization represented.

4. The designer's personal relationship with color.

5. An awareness of current color trends.

UNDERSTANDING ELECTRONIC COLOR

Color on a computer monitor is created in a manner much like a pointillist painting by Georges Seurat. Computer images are composed of individual dots called *pixels*. The pixel is a rectangle of light on the computer screen that can be set to different colors. The more pixels, the better the resolution and clarity of the image. The resolution is determined by the hardware (**Figure 8-9**).

Many designers work with a 24-bit system. In such a system, each pixel is represented by 24 bits of color information: 8 for red, 8 for green, and 8 for blue. There

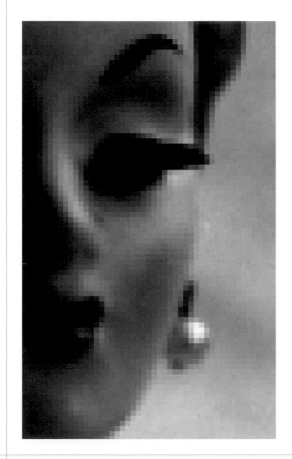

are 256 possible values for each of these three colors. These differing values of red, green, and blue can be combined to produce more than 16.7 million colors.

Color Models

Designers study color theory in order to use it effectively. Color theory remains the same whether it is applied to a traditional design or an electronic one. But when using electronic color, it can be helpful to study its practical differences. We must understand the various ways color is created in order to see the final design printed and looking the way we intended. The previous section of this chapter discussed creating color using pigment-based subtractive primaries. There are three color models you need to be familiar with when using computer graphics. These are the most prevalent color models.

RGB Unlike a pointillist painting, an image on the computer monitor is displayed in the additive primaries *RGB* (red, green, blue). It is a backlit image made by adding light. An image on the monitor may display colors in RGB that cannot be duplicated in the reflective copy of CMYK printing. Be prepared if the image on a printout does not match the image on the computer screen. The images are displayed in different color *gamuts,* or models. Calibrating the monitor will help. Web design is produced and viewed in RGB and is discussed in Chapter 12. **Figure 8-10** shows how RGB overlaps to form the CMY process color gamut. *K* stands for the black ink that is added for density.

CMYK All of this electronic color is quite different from mixing and blending paint or colored pencils. When the monitor's colors are transferred to paper or the file is ripped for offset reproduction, it is printed in the subtractive model of CMYK. The *CMYK* model is the basis for four-color process printing composed of cyan, magenta, yellow, and black inks. Remem-

● **8-9** *This enlargement shows the pixel structure of a digital image.*

144

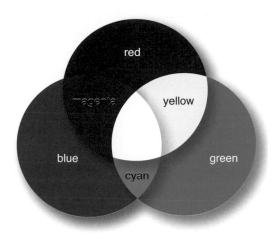

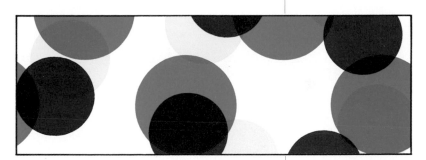

8-10 *Red, green, and blue are the primary colors in the additive system. Red, green, and blue together produce white. In this light-based system, cyan, magenta, and yellow are secondary colors.*

ber, the *K* stands for black, which is added to give density to the final print. For additional information on CMYK, see "Process Colors" later in this chapter. **Figure 8-11** shows the overlapping CMY of transparent printing inks producing a variety of colors.

HSL *Hue, saturation,* and *lightness* (*HSL*) are terms familiar to us from the world of color theory and a discussion of the properties of color. Photoshop allows the user to manipulate colors using this model and other models, by moving pop-up menu sliders. The intensity of a color diminishes when its saturation slider is moved (**Figure 8-12**). The lightness control varies a color from white to black (this corresponds to value in pigment-based color models). This can be a satisfying color model to use, because it is the most intuitive and closest to the way mixed pigment color is used in painting and drawing. You can switch to CMYK to prepare the pre-press file.

Another Color Wheel

The RGB/CMY color model positions the two sets of primaries equidistant from one another. Each secondary color is between two primary colors; each color on the wheel is between two colors that are used to create it; and each color is directly opposite its complement. This is a helpful model to study in order to understand what is happening on the computer monitor.

Red and blue make magenta. In order to decrease magenta in an image, the red and blue must be decreased. Whatever is done to a color, it has the opposite effect on that color's complement. In other words, decreasing red will increase cyan (**Figure 8-13**).

Various computer programs that allow designers to do color correction have pop-up menus allowing this kind of manipulation. Photoshop is an effective color correction software in common usage by designers, although there are other dedicated color management programs. Its sliders allow the user to manipulate color

8-11 *In four-color offset printing, cyan, magenta, and yellow are the primary colors, and their overlapping produces the look of full color. Although the overlap of cyan, magenta, and yellow produces a black effect, black ink is added for density.*

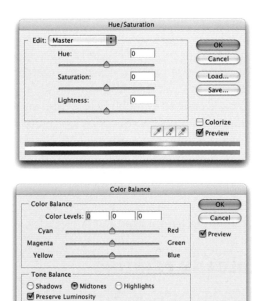

8-12 *Photoshop sliders allow careful control of hue, saturation, and lightness (value).*

Adobe Product screenshot reprinted with permission from Adobe Systems Incorporated.

8-13 *Photoshop sliders control and demonstrate the relationship between RGB and CMY color systems.*

Adobe Product screenshot reprinted with permission from Adobe Systems Incorporated.

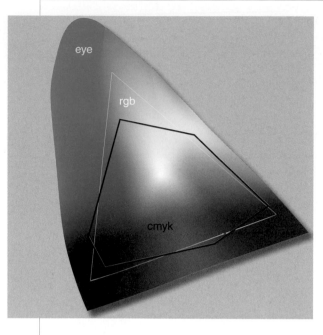

8-14 *The outer shape represents the colors the eye can see. The black triangle represents the colors that can be shown on the monitor. The dotted line represents colors that can be printed on coated paper.*

quickly and see the resulting effects. It also allows the user to work from numbered percentages in order to specify colors that will match a CMYK print. And, finally, it allows the user to switch between color models, specifying that an image be created in RGB, CMYK, spot color, black-and-white, or duotone modes.

Color Gamuts

The visible color range of a color model is called a *gamut*. As **Figure 8-14** shows, the eye can see more colors than can be created in either the RGB or CMYK color models. The gamut of RGB, however, is larger than that of CMYK. This means that if a design is created with the RGB mode, some of its colors probably cannot be printed using CMYK process colors. Photoshop will give you an alert symbol (a triangle with an exclamation mark inside it) in the picker palette if your color is not printable. This allows you to substitute a printable color before sending the file for reproduction.

COLOR IN PRINTING

In addition to applying the psychology of color theory to design work, you must stay within restrictions imposed by the technology of mass reproduction. Designs must be created within the limitation of the budget, equipment, expertise, and time available for a particular project. *The designer's use of color must be not only creative and appropriate but also practical and printable.*

Tint Screens

In mixed pigments, adding a different pigment-based hue creates color changes. White is altered to gray by the addition of black; red is altered to a light pink by the addition of white; and mixing blue and yellow creates green.

Additive color on the RGB computer monitor is created though varying intensities of light, as just discussed. When the file is sent to press, in order to create a tint or a light value of a hue, the printer cuts back on the density of the ink through varying screens. Screens are available in gradients from 10 to 90 percent. There is a similarity between the tint screens of printing inks and the application of transparent watercolor. In both cases, white is made by allowing the white of the paper to show through, and applying less pigment or ink makes lighter values.

In appearance, the value scale of printer's screens is similar to a value scale mixed by an artist combining pigments. However, if you look at the printer's scale under a magnifying glass, the screened dots will show up (**Figure 8-15**). All commercial

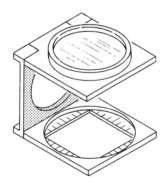

8-15 *A linen tester magnifies screened dots.*

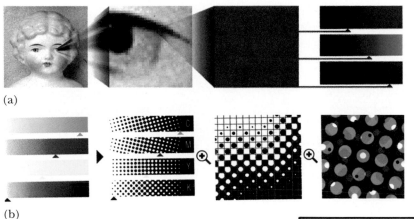

(a)

(b)

8-16a, b *This illustration documents the process of converting an original image into pixels, converting from RGB to CMYK halftones, and finally to the four-color printed piece.*

Courtesy of Apple Computer.

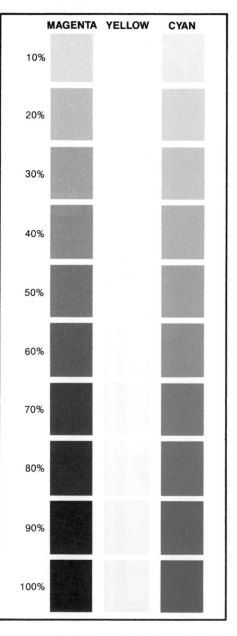

	MAGENTA	YELLOW	CYAN
10%			
20%			
30%			
40%			
50%			
60%			
70%			
80%			
90%			
100%			

printing is a form of optical illusion achieved not by sleight of hand, but by dot screens. The same black ink is applied to paper for a 90-percent gray or a 10-percent gray, but the dot screen fools the eye into believing it is different. Where there are more dots, the ink looks blacker. Solid ink is not screened but printed at 100 percent.

There is an analogy here with the computer screen. The image on-screen is composed of dots, or pixels, of varying colors. The image the printer creates is also composed of dots, this time of solid colors of ink. The monitor uses varying intensities of light to create (additive) color, and the printer uses varying densities of ink (subtractive pigment) (**Figures 8-16a, b**).

Figure 8-17 shows 10- to 100-percent tint screens of the three process colors: yellow, magenta, and cyan. Try looking at them with a magnifier. Changing the hue or making an ink appear darker is done by combining screened percentages of different colors. To change a cyan to purple, for example, a tint screen of magenta could be laid over it. The new color effects generated

8-17 *Changing tint values with screens. Material furnished by Hammermill Papers Group for plates 4 and 5.*

by using overlapping screens of process colors are referred to as *fake colors* (**Figure 8-18**). **Figure 8-19a** is a Pantone guide that shows process color combinations; **Figure 8-19b** shows an array of solid spot colors. When creating such colors electronically, use reference guides like these charts and specify ink percentages or numbers rather than only "going by eye." The colors you see on the monitor may

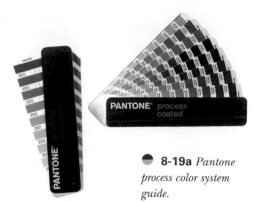

8-18 *Tint screen percentages of the four process colors were combined to create this illustration.*

8-19a *Pantone process color system guide.*

8-19b *Pantone color formula guide.*

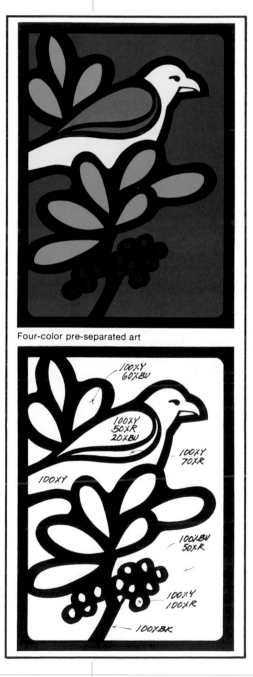

Four-color pre-separated art

100%Y
60%BU

100%Y
50%R
20%BU

100%Y
70%R

100%Y

100%BU
50%R

100%Y
100%R

100%BK

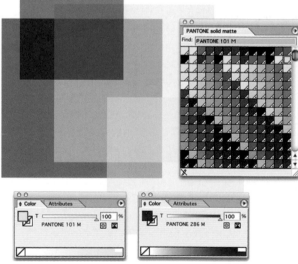

PANTONE solid matte
Find: PANTONE 101 M

Color Attributes
PANTONE 101 M

Color Attributes
PANTONE 286 M

8-19c *Overlapping two screened "spot" colors can produce a wide variety of color effects when you can't afford four-color reproduction.*

not be the colors you'll get on the printing press. **Figure 8-19c** shows the overlap of two spot colors specified by the Pantone color formula guide.

When overlapping screened percentages of color, or halftone screens of photographic images, you may encounter a moiré effect. A *moiré* pattern occurs when two sets of parallel lines or screens are crossed. It looks like a set of window screens stacked together and creating odd patterns. Watch for this problem and avoid it by changing the angle of your screens or by not overlapping different halftone screens.

It is important to visualize screened color combinations correctly before sending them to the printer. The "comp" may have been generated on the computer and shown on-screen, or it may be output as a proof print to show the client and the printer. The goal is to arrive at a printed piece that matches your expectations.

Spot Color or Process Color?

If you are using one to three spot colors, several numbered guides are available to assist you. The most complete, the Pantone matching system, consists of a full line of color specification books coordinated by numbers. These formula guides, first developed in 1963, enable you to specify a color number that the printer can match by using a reference guide. This is much more scientific than specifying a logo be printed in a bright cool red. Each ink color has its own number.

Choose the ink color from the guide and enter it on your computer, or tell the printer its number. The printer then prepares the ink you have specified. To get the desired blue for a two-color design, you might specify a spot color of Pantone 313 with a 20-percent screen of black. Various reference books show screened percentages of these ink colors. They also show what happens when you combine two different ink colors in screened percentages. Using spot colors is usually less expensive than using full process colors.

Process Color Separations

The offset reproduction of a full range of color, rather than just two or three colors, is done with CMYK process color. The three primary colors in process printing are yellow, magenta, and cyan, as we have discovered. The addition of black as a fourth color gives depth and solidity to the image. These four printer's inks produce the visual effect of full color (**Figure 8-20**).

Once the designer has given the printer a full-color illustration or photograph to reproduce, either traditionally or electronically transferred, the printer separates out the process colors. Artwork is separated into three color exposures from which the final prints are made. A black separation is also made. When the press is inked with

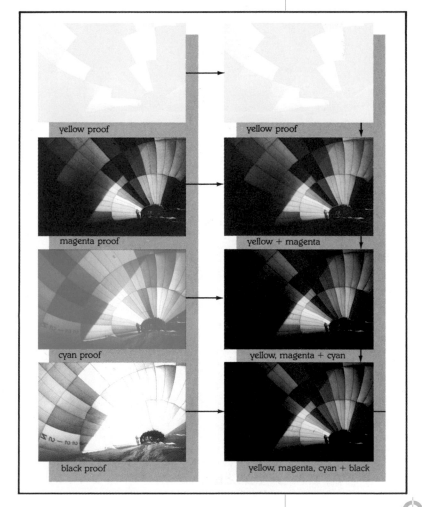

● **8-20** *Yellow, magenta, cyan, and black inks and their combinations.*

yellow proof

yellow proof

magenta proof

yellow + magenta

cyan proof

yellow, magenta + cyan

black proof

yellow, magenta, cyan + black

each of these four colors, and the color is laid down onto the paper, an illusion of full color results. The varying densities of halftone dots overlap and lie beside one another, mixing optically. It is a truly effective illusion.

As with spot color tint screens, the mixing happens not within the pigment, but within the eye of the viewer. Unlike the even dot coverage of tint screens, a process color separation is made of dots of varying densities that correspond to the color density in the original image. This variation is why such a complex range of colors can be produced from only four process colors. Examine the full-color images in this book with a linen tester (see Figure 8-15).

Cutting Costs

Each additional ink used in a design means the printer must do additional work preparing plates, ripping files, and inking the press. The more ink colors you use, the more printing the design will cost. Combining screened percentages of inks will enable you to get the most out of each color and can decrease the cost of the job.

Another way to get more color into a job without increasing the cost is by printing on colored paper. Excellent reference books (many free from paper companies) deal with using colored inks on colored papers. The color of the paper will show through, subtly altering the look of the ink. White ink is seldom used in the printing industry, because opaque white is difficult to achieve. A study of the way tint screens, ink, and paper interact will help achieve the desired effect at a minimum cost.

Halftones, Duotones, and Tritones

Photographic prints used for *halftones* should have an extended tonal range with good contrast. If your negative has good detail, it can be converted to a good halftone. Although a poor negative or print with loss of detail can be improved, it cannot be converted into a high-quality halftone.

Duotones and tritones are commonly used techniques for printing black-and-white photography by using spot colors. Although these halftones are limited in color, there are many options to consider (**Figure 8-21**). Electronic scanning can selectively enhance the tonal range, and different line screens can be employed from coarse to very fine. A halftone can be printed over a solid color or over a screened color to create a fake duotone effect.

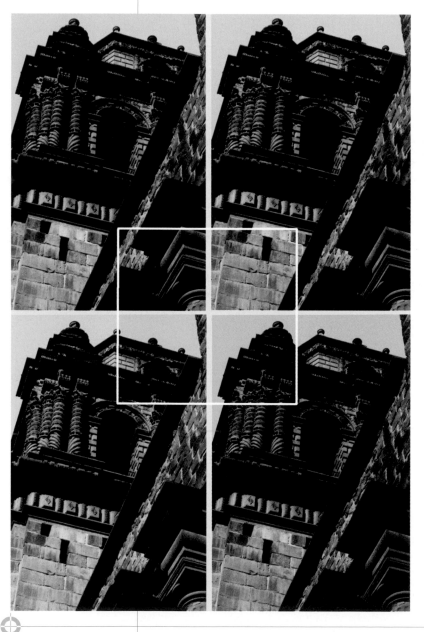

● **8-21** *Duotone and tritone combinations.*

Graphic Design Basics

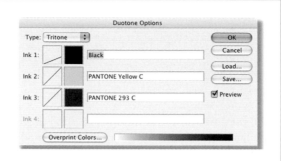

● **8-22a** *Photoshop pop-up menu showing a duotone curve on one of the colors that will be used to create a duotone. This curve controls the distribution of color throughout the darks and lights of the image.*
Adobe Product screenshot reprinted with permission from Adobe Systems Incorporated.

● **8-22b** *Photoshop pop-up menu showing a tritone combination of inks.*
Adobe Product screenshot reprinted with permission from Adobe Systems Incorporated.

Generating two halftone negatives from the same image creates a *duotone*. By printing these negatives in various colors, you can achieve various effects (**Figure 8-22a**). Duotone effects depend as much on how you use the two colors as on what colors you specify. For example, a black-and-violet duotone can be run with the black dominant or the violet dominant. The density range of each plate can be extended or compressed, producing shadow detail in one color while accenting the highlights in the other color.

The *tritone* uses three colors for still more creative options. Black combined with two colors yields a new effect, as does printing with a warm black instead of a true black. A tritone can also be created during printing by using varnishes as a third color (**Figure 8-22b**).

Whereas designers used to depend on reference guides and their instincts to specify these techniques, now it is possible to simulate them quite accurately on the computer. The effects of varnishes and various paper surfaces on ink color, however, are still difficult to visualize before printing.

Technology is changing fast in the design and printing industry, but many principles stay the same. A good design sense and a working knowledge of color theory, coupled with a basic foundation in computer graphics, will see you through.

PROCESS COLOR SEPARATION SUMMARY

When a computer is used to generate four process color separations, a scanner first digitizes your photo into a fine grid of rectangles called pixels (see Figure 8-9). A high-quality scanner gives a fine grid with a high resolution and more pixels. Each pixel is assigned a value for each of the three additive primaries (red, green, blue, or RGB).

The scanned image can be previewed on a color monitor. This display also uses RGB colors, but the final image is converted and printed with subtractive primary colors (cyan, magenta, yellow, or CMY), with the addition of black (K).

Translating the three RGB values into four CMYK values results in variations caused by switching from an additive (RGB) system to a subtractive (CMYK) system. This entire translation process can be done on a personal computer as well as on higher-end systems.

The final step is to turn the CMYK values (which are continuous tone separations) into four halftone films. The halftones are translated into film for making printing plates. In the halftone film, various sizes of halftone dots simulate color shades. In a digital press environment the film step is skipped. Files are sent directly from computer to press.

Chapter 8   The Dynamics of Color

1. Find printed samples of monochromatic, analogous, and complementary color schemes. Search for samples of color used in graphic design, advertising, or packaging that convey a particular mood and reach a particular audience.

2. Find an example of a two-color design that uses tint screens to achieve a multi-color effect. Analyze how this design was prepared for printing. Make notes and discuss them with your instructor.

3. Find a duotone or tritone and use a magnifying lens to compare it with a traditional process color photograph. Then compare these halftone effects with the tint screen you analyzed.

4. Using a program such as Photoshop, practice converting from RGB to CMYK to HSL and manipulating the colors by using slider controls (see Figures 8-22a and 8-22b).

PROJECT

Word and Image Poster

Prepare two full-color posters that combine the image of a famous person, place, or thing with a related word. The word related to each image can be a name or an association the image brings to mind. Pay close attention to integrating the typography with the image through various gestalt unit-forming techniques and color choices (see **Figure 8-23**).

Choose a complementary, split-complementary, monochromatic, or analogous color scheme, and create two color versions of the poster. Use tint, tone, and shade to give your color schemes different personalities. Be creative with color choices. *Local color* designs try to keep realistic color (the sky is blue), but there are other choices. The use of *arbitrary color* frees you to assign whatever color seems desirable. The sky may become yellow to enhance the purple backlit tree trunks (as in Figure 8-23), or a man's hair may become dark blue in an analogous color scheme of cool hues (see Figure 9-12b).

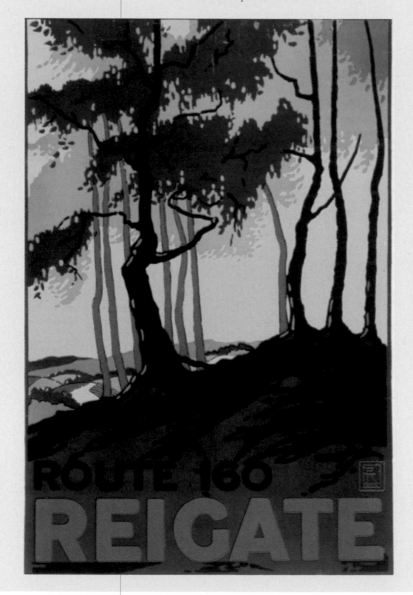

◖ **8-23** *E. McKnight Kauffer.* Reigate, *1916. 24.4 × 20" (62 × 50.8 cm). London's Transport Museum. This well-known painter and designer used complementary colors to create this striking poster for Britain's public transport system.*

Goals and Objectives

Practice using color to express a mood appropriate to an image.

Practice integrating word and image from the standpoint of design, concept, and content.

Control color and learn more about it by using different models and creating variants of tint, tone, and shade.

Critique

Your instructor may choose to have you display your work in print or do the initial critique on the monitor.

Present your work to the class. Discuss the following attributes of your final solution:

Why did you choose this particular subject?

What is the color scheme and why is it appropriate to the subject?

Did you use local or arbitrary color? Why?

How is the typography integrated with the image?

Discuss the process you followed to produce this image, and discuss any problems you encountered.

Ask the class and the instructor how your work could be improved. Based on the discussion, make any changes that seem wise.

TERMINOLOGY

CHAPTER 9

Illustration and Photography in Design

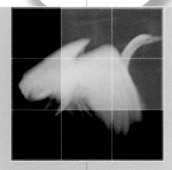

KEY POINTS Graphic designers work with illustrators and photographers. Often they also create illustration and photography themselves. This chapter describes the various types of illustration and photography that appear in print and on the Web. It also discusses methods for creating and critiquing your own images.

Often the graphic designer is called on to create or to acquire illustration and photography. The boundaries between design, illustration, and photography are less rigid than in the past, especially as electronic media make photographic manipulation, drawing tools, and typography available to a broad range of professionals. It is advisable for every graphic designer to be familiar with the basics of image generation and utilization.

THE DESIGNER-ILLUSTRATOR

Illustration is a specialized area of art that uses images, usually representational or expressionist, to make a visual statement. Illustration is created for commercial reproduction, either in print form or as animation or motion graphics for various venues, including Web delivery. Many drawings and paintings done as illustrations look and function like fine art and are exhibited and collected as such. Many painters have worked as illustrators at some point in their careers, and vice versa. The 20th-century painter Edward Hopper earned his living as an illustrator for the first half of his career; Pablo Picasso and William Blake illustrated books.

Some designers never actually do an illustration themselves; instead, they purchase freelance illustrations. Many illustrators are freelance artists who maintain their own studios and work for a variety of clients (**Figure 9-1**). Some studios have illustrators who do nothing but illustration, working with designers who are in charge of typography, photography, layout, and art direction. But often the field has a need for illustrators who design and designers who illustrate.

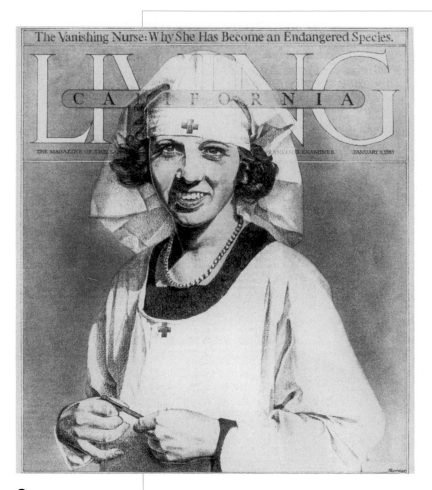

The Vanishing Nurse: Why She Has Become an Endangered Species.

LIVING
CALIFORNIA
THE MAGAZINE OF THE SAN FRANCISCO EXAMINER · JANUARY 9, 1983

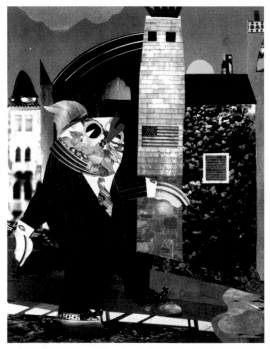

Also, by enhancing details, illustration can demonstrate certain particulars more clearly than a photograph can. For example, it can enlarge tiny engine parts that are difficult to see or photograph, and it can label them. Illustration can also eliminate misleading or unnecessary details that confuse an image, thereby forcing the eye to focus on important characteristics. An illustrator may be allowed where a photographer and camera are prohibited, as in a courtroom. Finally, illustration is a very effective way to present highly emotional or fantasy-based material.

Although photography is capable of creating surreal and strongly emotive images, illustration is still more flexible. It is capable of turning out images of pure fantasy, both by computer and by hand techniques. **Figure 9-2** is a collage construction. The hand-generated quality of illustration is considered by many to have a warmer, more intimate quality than other forms of illustration and photography. But the field

● **9-1** *Dugald Stermer. This illustration by a renowned illustrator integrates hand-drawn typography with a drawn and painted image.*
Courtesy of the artist.

Some people feel that editorial illustration is the highest and most artistic form of design. Nevertheless, however much an illustration created for print reproduction may resemble a painting, the restrictions an illustrator works under are similar to those in other areas of graphic design. The illustrator works with the guidance of an art director, must be concerned about how the work will be reproduced, has to meet a deadline, and is responsible for satisfying a client and achieving a defined purpose.

WHY ILLUSTRATION?

Illustration may be chosen instead of photography for several reasons. It can show something about the subject that cannot be photographed, such as detailed information about how photosynthesis works.

● **9-2** *Linda Godfrey.* Fish Out of Water. *This playful illustration, created by a freelance illustrator for her student portfolio, is constructed with collaged photographic textures cut from magazines.*

of electronic illustration is growing as it continues to branch into animation and images for the Web.

Many examples of both contemporary and historical illustration appear throughout this book. Illustration has a variety of looks, depending on the medium, the style of the illustrator, and the purpose of the illustration. The artwork can be drawn, painted, constructed through mixed-media collage, or computer generated. It can be three-dimensional or a combination of 2-D and 3-D imagery. The illustrator may use a revived art deco style, a New Wave or postmodern look, a highly personalized style, or an informational, descriptive rendering technique. Professionals usually concentrate on a consistent personal style. **Figures 9-3** and **9-4** show powerful sources

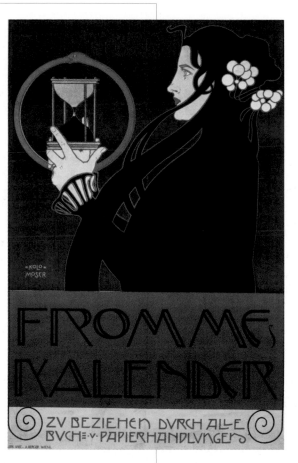

◗ **9-4** *Koloman Moser.* Frommes Kalender. *1903. Lithograph, printed in color, 37³/₈ × 24 ⁹/₁₆" (94.9 × 62.4 cm). The Museum of Modern Art, New York. Given anonymously.*

Photograph © 2001 The Museum of Modern Art, New York/Art Resource, NY.

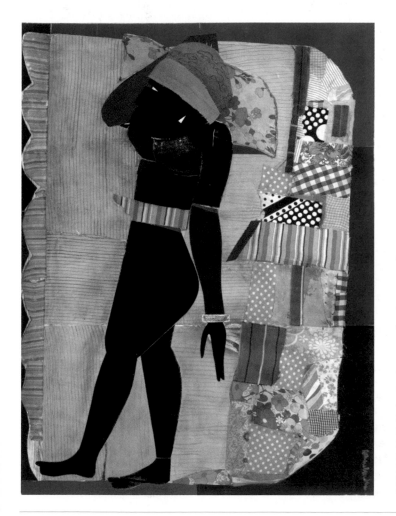

◗ **9-3** *Romare Bearden.* Patchwork Quilt. *1970. Cut-and-pasted cloth and paper with synthetic paint on composition board, 35³/₄ × 47⁷/₈" (90.9 × 121.6 cm). The Museum of Modern Art, New York. Blanchette Rockefeller Fund.*

Photograph © 2001 The Museum of Modern Art, New York/Art Resource, NY, copyright Romare Bearden Foundation. Licensed by VAGA, New York.

of inspiration that can be found in the history of both fine art and design.

If the field of illustration varies in medium and style, it also varies in intent. The purpose for an illustration may be to present a product, tell a story, clarify a concept, or demonstrate a service. The following section lists these varied purposes. For detailed information about contracts, trade practices, and pricing, consult the *Graphic Artists Guild Handbook: Pricing and Ethical Guidelines.* It is a valuable reference updated yearly with information for illustrators as well as designers.

ADVERTISING AND EDITORIAL ILLUSTRATION

Advertising and editorial illustration are two important divisions in the field with quite different focuses. *Advertising illustration* is intended to sell a product or a service—almost anything that can be offered to a consumer. **Figure 9-5a** is a poster design that encourages the public to use the London subway system, called the Tube, to visit interesting places such as the Tate Gallery. The paint mimics a subway map that Londoners are familiar with.

In advertising illustration commonplace objects must be shown with style and often be enhanced with dramatic highlights and textures. Sometimes a creative concept leads to delightful artwork that goes beyond simple product presentations, as in **Figure 9-5b**. In the field of advertising illustration, illustrators work with art directors, account executives, and copywriters. Their work may need to please many people of various opinions. The best prices for illustration are paid in the advertising field.

In *editorial illustration,* the artist may concentrate on the communication of emotion through an expressive treatment of line, shape, and placement. Editorial illustration can offer the freedom to experiment with media and to obscure details in favor of mood. Most importantly, edito-

rial illustration can convey a concept or story by using a purely visual language. The following sections discuss various uses for editorial and advertising illustration.

Recording and Book Illustration

Illustrators are used extensively to make creative packaging for recordings. Many record covers have become collector's items, and several books have been published on them. CD and DVD covers have also become a creative avenue for illustration. Although smaller in format than record covers, they provide an opportunity to integrate type and image over multiple pages. Payment varies widely, depending on the recording company, the recording artist, the complexity of the job, and the renown of the illustrator.

The book-jacket illustration is vital to the promotion and sale of a book. Some

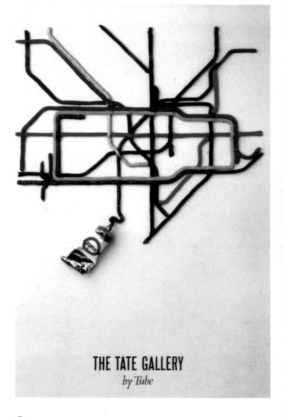

THE TATE GALLERY
by Tube

● **9-5a** *David Booth. 1987. 30 × 20″. A photo illustration commissioned by the London Underground subway for traveling to the Tate Gallery.*

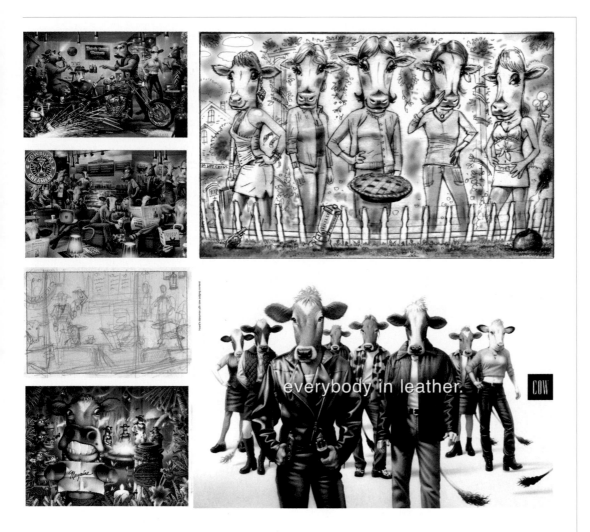

● **9-5b** *Professional illustrator **Matt Zumbo** created these posters for Hoard's Dairyman's yearly Wisconsin cow-judging contest. The pencil sketch at the top right is Matt's 2006 poster concept inspired by the TV program* Desperate Housewives. *His process includes thumbnails, pencils, and color studies. His finished illustrations are done with a traditional underdrawing on illustration board, scanned, and then value and all color added with Photoshop tools. The delightful humor behind these poster concepts joins with Matt's amazing skill to create an unexpected and powerful result.*
Courtesy of the artist.

book publishers give the illustrator very specific instructions, along with detailed notes from the art director. The illustrator may be asked to read a lengthy manuscript. Pricing depends on these considerations as well as on whether the work is done for a trade book or a textbook, in paperback or in hardcover. **Figure 9-6** is a cover by the well-known illustrator and educator Dugald Stermer, who incorporated hand-drawn and airbrushed letterforms.

When the illustrator handles the type as well as the artwork for a book cover, these elements are often well integrated.

Artists who illustrate a book's interior add an important ingredient to the value of the book. Children's books, depending on the age of the target audience, often require illustration throughout. Payment for illustration varies from a flat fee for books in which the illustrator contributes but is not the author to a royalty contract

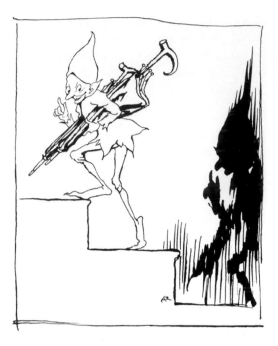

● **9-8** *Arthur Rackham. A children's book illustration from the period at the turn of the 20th century known as the golden age of illustration.*

for books in which the illustrator is responsible for a major part of the impact and content. Children's book illustration is a rewarding field, because, unlike most adult books, children's books are commonly illustrated throughout. In books for young children, artwork must tell much of the story, with little reliance on the text. It is responsible for generating excitement and advancing the plot (**Figure 9-7**). Some of the best current illustration appears in beautifully designed and illustrated children's books. One of the many excellent children's book illustrators from the turn of the 20th century was Arthur Rackham (**Figure 9-8**).

Magazine and Newspaper Illustration

Magazines depend on illustration to set a tone and pique a reader's interest. A single full-page image will often be expected to carry all the visual information for the accompanying story. The designer responsible for layout must integrate the illustration into the overall layout without detracting from the artwork. Ideally, treatment of the headline and text will reinforce the art through repetition and careful placement.

Sometimes small spot illustrations are dropped into a page of text to enliven the visual presence. They are often black and white and executed in pen and ink.

Newspapers often use black-and-white spot art in editorial sections. Many different kinds of illustration can be found as you search through the sections of a newspaper. Fashion, sports, editorial, product, and technical illustration of charts and graphs are all there. The newspaper will often use color only on the front pages of each section or for special feature articles. Newsprint does not reproduce details and nuances in tonal quality well, and the newspaper industry does not pay as well as some other fields of illustration, such as corporate work for annual reports.

Often payment is not the driving reason people become artists and illustrators. The illustration in **Figure 9-9a** by artist David McLimans accompanies an article in *The Progressive* magazine. This publication and its contributors are concerned with political activism. **Figure 9-9b** by McLimans was created for an annual report.

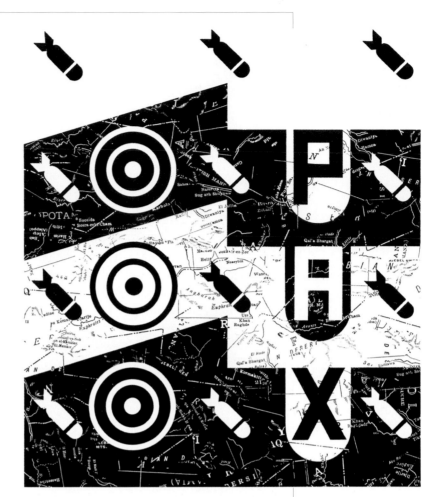

● **9-9a** *David McLimans. Line-art illustration for the March 1991 issue of* The Progressive *magazine, accompanying an article on American political policy during the war in the Persian Gulf.*
Courtesy of the artist.

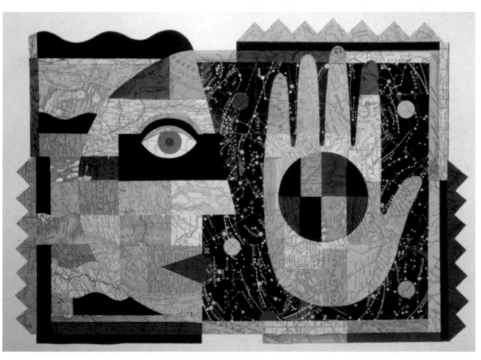

◐ **9-9b** *David McLimans applied the same strong figure/ground and shape relationships in this annual report illustration.*

Fashion Illustration

Fashion illustration is a specialized area of advertising. A strictly literal drawing lacks the appeal of a drawing that presents the garment in a romantic, stylized manner. As a result, fashion illustration does not always simply convey information about the garment. It often attempts to persuade the viewer with the mood of the illustration. An important and interesting drape or texture of the garment or accessory, as well as the model's height, pose, and curves, is often emphasized for effect. Fashion photography shows a similar concern. A fashion illustrator draws from either a live model or a photograph of a model wearing clothes furnished by the client. The growth in the beauty and cosmetic areas, including related package illustration, has kept this field alive (**Figure 9-10**).

Illustration for In-House Projects

Educational institutions, government agencies, corporations and businesses, and not-for-profit entities hire illustrators to generate material targeted at internal audiences. The assignment often calls for editorial illustration—that is, the communication of a concept. Annual reports, corporate calendars, brochures, posters, and an array of other materials are produced to communicate the nature of the institution to its employees and constituents. Fees for illustration are relative to the size of the institution and the complexity of the job. Depending on the company, in-house staff designers may be asked to provide illustrations as a part of their regular job. **Figure 9-11a** is a highly creative piece done by an in-house department for UCLA. It uses a combination of photography and drawing to give it a 2-D/3-D appeal.

Greeting cards as well as medical and technical illustration are other markets that call for illustration, both freelance and in-house. The *Artist's and Graphic Designer's Market,* published by F+W Publications, lists over 2,500 companies that hire freelance designers and illustrators.

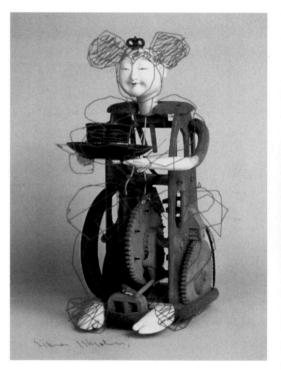

● **9-11a** *UCLA Extension summer 1991 catalog. Art director:* **Inju Sturgeon,** *UCLA Extension Marketing Department. Designer:* **Eiko Ishioka.** *A playful and highly skilled integration of 2-D and 3-D enlivens this in-house illustration.*
Courtesy of the artist.

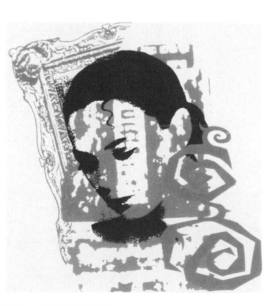

◗ **9-10** *Margo Chase. This logo/icon for hair care products signifies modern beauty.*
Courtesy of the artist.

Graphic Design Basics

Greeting Card and Retail Illustration

Illustration in this category involves retail products such as apparel, toys, greeting cards, calendars, and posters. The major greeting card companies publish cards created by staff artists, but they do commission some outside work as well. Major kinds of greeting cards include seasonal cards, special-occasion cards, and everyday cards. A new direction for growth is cards targeted at specific lifestyle audiences, such as working women and seniors. Illustration for cards and retail goods may be paid as flat fees or royalties.

Medical and Technical Illustration

Medical illustrators are specially trained artists who often have a master's degree in the field with a combined pre-med and art undergraduate degree. The accuracy of information as well as the clarity and effectiveness of presentation are vital in this field. The artist must be better than a camera in his or her ability to simplify, clarify, and select only what must be shown for complete communication. Illustrators should have knowledge of the human body and a background and interest in science and medicine.

Technical illustrators create highly accurate renderings of scientific or technological subjects, such as geological formations and chemical reactions as well as machinery and instruments. They often work closely with scientists or technicians in the field, and they produce art for a wide variety of publications, advertisements, and audiovisuals.

Animation and Motion Graphics

Expanding fields for illustration include Web graphics and various forms of motion graphics. These fields use illustration in the form of both scanned print-based artwork and artwork created electronically for online, CD-ROM, and film and video presentation.

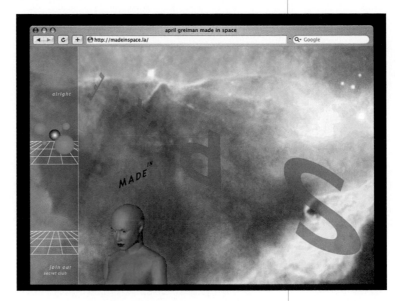

Another expanding field that requires illustrators is 3-D imaging.

The computer has made an important impact in the field of illustration, especially for the designer-illustrator. **Figure 9-11b** exemplifies the flexibility of digital illustration. Visit this site.

● **9-11b** *Animation for the Web is a new and growing area for illustrators. This page is from **April Greiman's** animated Made in Space Web site.*
Courtesy April Greiman and Made in Space, Inc.

Digital Focus

Illustrators use painting and drawing materials to create a wide range of subtly blended colors. Creating gradients enables you to enhance the blended color effects in your digital illustration. The gradient tool in raster and vector programs such as Photoshop and Illustrator can create multicolor linear and radial blends. You can find the existing gradients in the Swatches window, or construct your own custom gradient. Open the gradient window, and click a color gradient swatch to observe the change. In Photoshop the window opens when the gradient swatch in the Properties bar is clicked. To make a custom gradient, click the color tab on the bottom slider in the Gradient window. Then pick a color from the Color window. If the color isn't exactly what you want, it can be adjusted in the Color window. Adjust the color as many times as you want, moving the Gradient slider tabs. Save your custom gradient by clicking New in the Gradient Editor or by dragging the color to the Swatches window. You can create a more advanced look by placing semi-transparent gradients on top of each other. **Figure 9-11c** shows the tools you can use in each program.

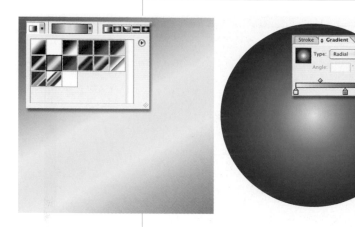

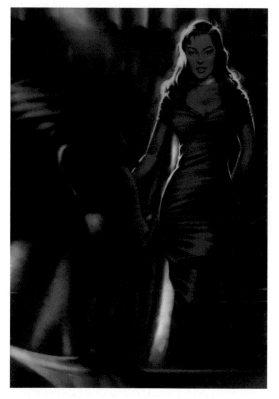

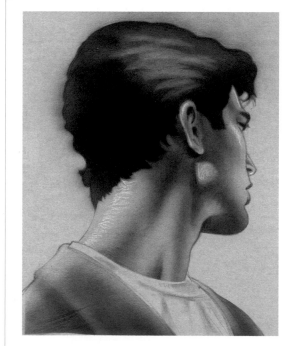

9-11c *Photoshop and Illustrator tools can be used to create your own radial and linear gradients.*

STYLE AND MEDIUM

Illustrators use a wide variety of techniques, such as mixed-media collage, cut paper, pen and ink, gouache and other painting media, sculptural construction, and computer generation. **Figures 9-12a, b** by Matt Zumbo show a skillful integration of hand and electronic techniques. His choice of a complementary color scheme enhances the drama in the final piece.

9-12a *Matt Zumbo,* illustrator, created this black-and-white graphite and colored pencil drawing on toned board.

Courtesy of the artist.

Illustrator, Photoshop, and Painter get a lot of use, and professional computer systems come with their own specialized software programs. Programs such as Free-hand and Illustrator are vector graphics (object-oriented) programs that allow the creation of clean, precise, editable images. Painter is a raster program that gives a more intuitive feeling to the process of creating an image. However the artwork is originally created, computer graphics allows an ease of editing that cannot be ignored. When the client asks, "Can you make this change?" it is a lot easier to say yes when working with a digital image—even one that started with traditional media, like Figure 9-12a, b, created by a contemporary Milwaukee illustrator who operates his own business.

Computer-generated and photographically based work will not replace hand-

9-12b *Matt Zumbo composited and colorized his original drawings on the computer to generate the final illustration. His use of a complementary color scheme enhances the dramatic quality.*

created illustration, however, because many people feel that hand-created images are appropriate when a warmer, more human touch is desired. Computer technology can always enhance, and aid the creation of, drawn and painted artwork. The artwork can be scanned, and then the final touches or revisions can be completed electronically. Computer technology is also helpful in archiving and transferring files. What is currently threatening illustrators is not computer-generated work but stock illustration that is readily and cheaply available electronically.

Whatever their artistic style, illustrators must be aware of all the technical information concerning color separations and printing methods. Die cuts, embossing techniques, and specialty inks may also play a part in the final product.

GETTING IDEAS

The illustrator goes through the same planning and visualizing procedures described in Chapter 1. The first step is getting to know the assignment. This research might call for reading a manuscript or understanding how a product functions.

Next comes the idea stage. Look at illustrations by other artists. Many annuals and periodicals show the most current illustrations. *Step-by-Step Graphics* and *How* present ideas and techniques in the field of illustration. The *CA Illustration Annual* and the many illustration sourcebooks such as the *Workbook* and the Graphic Artists Guild's *Directory of Illustration* are excellent sources to see the standards and styles in a particular field.

Classics from the history of illustration can also provide food for visual thought. Great artists from Dürer to Goya to Magritte have provided inspiration for illustrators. Look through books of both fine-art and simple descriptive photography for subjects related to your project. **Figures 9-13** and **9-14** show this process in reverse. Artist Roy Lichtenstein used art by DC

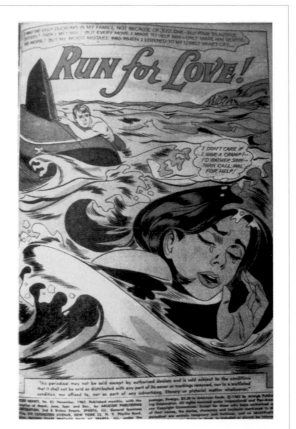

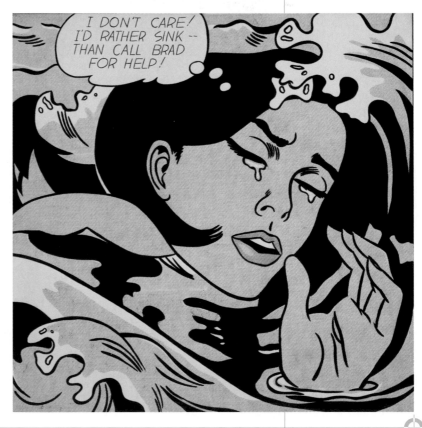

9-13 *Panel from "Run for Love," in* Secret Hearts, *83 (November 1962).* **Tony Abruzzo,** *artist;* **Ira Schnapp,** *lettering.*

9-14 **Roy Lichtenstein.** Drowning Girl. *1963. Oil and synthetic polymer paint on canvas, $67^5/_8 \times 66^3/_4$".*

Comics illustrators Tony Abruzzo and Bernard Sachs as material for his painting.

Thumbnail sketches should explore the subject from every angle—high and low, as well as tightly cropped and at a distance. Imagine different kinds of spatial treatment, from a Western perspective to isometric to surrealistic. Sketch these ideas, trying them in different media. Exploration is especially valuable to student illustrators who have not yet developed a particular style. As you progress from sketches to roughs, you may need additional reference materials.

Another approach is to use *semiotics*. Analyze your subject from the point of view of creating an icon, a symbol, and an index. Again, do several thumbnails of each. This method can lead to highly individual and creative problem solving. An *icon* is an image of a thing. A *symbol* shows cultural associations with the thing. An *index* indicates the presence of the thing. How would you illustrate America? Perhaps your choice of an icon is a field of wheat in the Midwest. Perhaps your choice of a symbol is an eagle. Perhaps your choice of an index is the shadow of an eagle on the field of wheat. This approach can lead to the creation of visual metaphors. Fig. 1-9 shows a cover proposal that takes a semiotic approach to illustrating a bird. The chapter openers use these.

REFERENCE MATERIALS

Drawing from life means drawing from an actual object, landscape, or human model. Such work is most practical when using a still-life setup or a landscape. Models can get tired, and they can also get expensive. Drawing from life, however, can give illustrations an immediacy and a vitality that drawing from photographs cannot.

Drawing from a photograph is convenient for many reasons. The camera has already converted the subject into a two-dimensional language. Cropping is easily visualized by placing a few pieces of paper

around the photo's edges. The subject never gets tired.

Reference materials can add authenticity to your work. An excellent source of photographs is the public library. Most major libraries keep photo collections. Once the source photos are obtained, adapt them to the particular situation. **Figure 9-15** is a portfolio piece that uses multiple photographic references. It is a good idea for all designers and illustrators to begin a clip file of their own with images of many different subjects. Old magazines are a great source. You may be able to organize magazines by categories instead of cutting out the photographs. *Life, People,* and *Newsweek* magazines would fit into a "people" category; *Smithsonian, National Geographic,* and *Audubon* would fit into a "nature" cat-

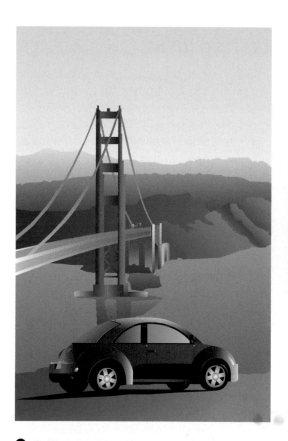

● **9-15** *Steve Hojnacki. This portfolio piece was created in Adobe Illustrator for a student portfolio by using the gradient function and a combination of photographic references.*

egory. The Internet is an excellent source for images. Its low-resolution files give vague visual data for any final file, but they are a helpful reference when creating your original.

When working with photographs, respect the photographer as an artist. Do not duplicate a photograph exactly unless it has been shot specifically for you or by you. Copyright infringement laws concerning the use of photographs have gotten increasingly tight in recent years. The source photograph must be substantially altered before it will be legal to reproduce it as your own artwork. *Clip art* denotes copyright-free images that can be used as is or altered to suit your needs. Books and CDs of electronic and traditional clip art are available from many publishing sources, such as Dynamic Graphics and EyeWire. Dover is the best print source for wonderful old line-art engravings on every subject (**Figure 9-16**). This book's Web site has copyright-free clip art for you to use.

There can be disadvantages to working with clip art or relying too closely on photos. The preexisting image makes many decisions about composition, lighting, and size. The photograph can also provide only one kind of spatial representation. These limitations can be overcome by remembering to use the clip art or photo as a source, not as an answer. Reference sources need not be taken literally; they should be interpreted creatively.

CONTEMPORARY VISION

The invention of offset lithography brought an explosion of illustration in the late 1800s. Coming into the 20th century as a vital force, and aided by new advances in printing technology, illustration retained its ability to draw inspiration from the fine arts. Painters in the early 20th century followed an investigation begun by Cézanne, and their art reflected the relativity of space, time, point of view, and emotional coloring. Discoveries in science, psychology, and technology supported their depiction of reality as changeable. It could shift, alter, and be processed by the brain in a variety of ways. The artist could interact with reality and help shape it.

Much of the art of the 20th century deals with *picture plane space*—the construction of a flat pattern on the flat surface of the

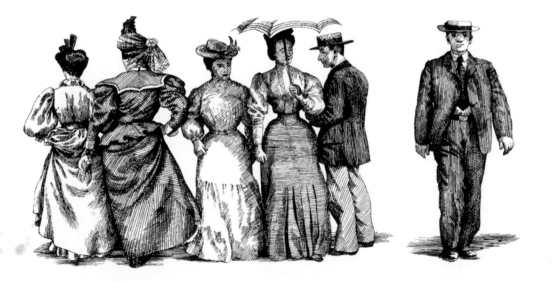

9-16 *Copyright-free clip art is available from a variety of sources for reference and reproduction, both in print and CD. Stock art can be purchased by individual image with controlled usage or by CD or book with all usage rights transferred to the purchaser.*

paper or canvas. There is less illusion to this work than to previous art; it does not attempt to deny the flat surface it exists on. Constructivism and the de Stijl movement worked with picture plane space. Cubism presented reality from multiple points of view within the same plane. An object might be portrayed simultaneously from the top, the front, and the sides. The concept and handling of picture plane space is a strong influence in contemporary illustration. Designers and illustrators have always been aware of the flat surface, because they have also worked with typography, which encourages flat patterning.

The representation of space is a varying cultural convention—a fact many contemporary illustrators play on (**Figures 9-17a–c**). These poster illustrations by Michael Vanderbyl, an important illustrator and designer, make good use of a bird's-eye view to render playful isometric forms.

The fauves and the German expressionists in the early 20th century also emphasized the flat patterning of the surface, using bright, flat colors to create images that were personal and highly emotional. This expressive quality currently takes various forms in editorial illustration. The emo-

tionally charged image in **Figure 9-18** by Alan E. Cober uses a visual pun to match the topic of tools of violence making up the face of violence. It becomes what it represents, thus exemplifying editorial illustration at its best.

An interest in other forms of spatial representation began to appear in the mid-20th century. Trompe l'oeil artists revived an interest in life-size images inside a space that looks only inches deep. A French term meaning "fool the eye," *trompe l'oeil* works extremely well as an illusion of spatial reality. Our culture will probably never lose its admiration for this sort of artistic reality.

There are more artists, designers, and illustrators now than ever before in history. We have the benefit of a mass-communications network to keep us informed of what is happening now in art. We have a documented history of previous art and design movements, and our influences are more numerous than ever. Designers and illustrators are combining many materials and styles, concepts, and technologies to produce a rich variety of images and techniques. This makes the 21st century a truly exciting time to be a designer and illustrator.

● **9-17a, b, c**
Michael Vanderbyl.
Three self-promotional posters in conjunction with the publication of Seven Graphic Designers *by Takenobu Igarashi. Printed in Japan by Mitsumura Printing Company.*
Courtesy of the artist.

(a)

(b)

(c)

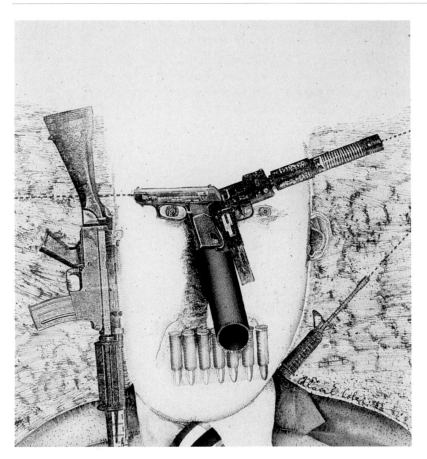

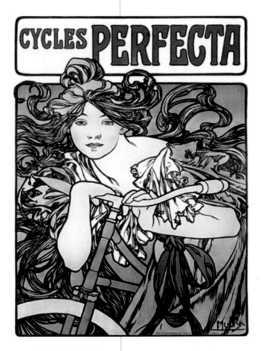

◗ **9-18** *Alan E. Cober.*
Illustration for the Dallas
Times Herald.
Courtesy of the artist.

◖ **9-19** *Alphonse*
Mucha. Art nouveau
poster design based on
the photographic refer-
ence shown in Figure
9-20.

THE IMPACT OF PHOTOGRAPHY

Paul Delaroche, a French painter com-
menting on the invention of photography,
exclaimed, "From today painting is dead!"
While some artists shared that fear, others
embraced the new medium as a tool and
an opportunity. From its beginning, illustrators have used photographs as aids. The
art nouveau illustrator Alphonse Mucha
carefully posed models amid studio props
and photographed them as a reference for
his poster designs (**Figures 9-19** and **9-20**).
Such well-known 20th-century illustrators
as Maxfield Parrish and Norman Rockwell
also relied heavily on posing and photographing models as a visual reference for
later paintings. Photographer Eadweard
Muybridge is well known in the design
community for his photographic series
documenting the movement of people and

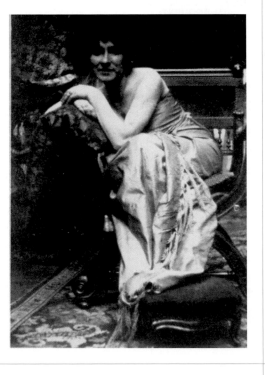

◗ **9-20** *Alphonse*
Mucha. Studio photo-
graph of model.

169

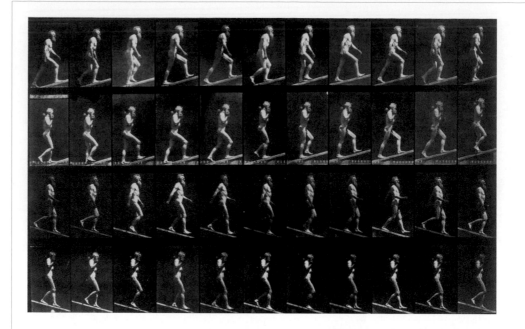

animals. His books remain a valuable resource for illustrators today (**Figure 9-21**).

THE DESIGNER-PHOTOGRAPHER

Often the designer is called on to create or locate, and then integrate, photography into a layout design. A working knowledge of how to evaluate photographs is very useful.

Photography is a strong, expressive tool with which to prove a point, explore a problem, or sell a product. Many people believe that the camera does not lie. They believe that an illustrator can change things around and make people or situations out to be better than they really are, but such people fail to realize that the camera also represents a point of view. It is this suspension of disbelief that makes the camera such an effective tool for persuasion and communication. It is also this belief in the "photograph as document" that is changing with the computer and the growth of photo illustration.

People want to know if they are looking at a manipulated image. The staff working on the cover for the February 1982 issue of *National Geographic* magazine had difficulty getting a photograph of Egyptian pyramids to fit the magazine's format. Because

the image was stored digitally on a computer, it was a simple matter to move one pyramid over. When that photo manipulation became public knowledge (it was widely reported), people's faith in photographic reality was badly shaken.

No photograph is truly candid. Its subject is selected, framed, and shot by an individual who is interacting with the environment. Moreover, a situation will change just because a camera is introduced. Another editing and selection process occurs when the contact prints are viewed. Darkroom and computer manipulation may influence the last stages. All of these processes place photography firmly in the camp of interpretative art. A photograph can tell the truth, but that truth is filtered through the eye and intent of the photographer. In the early 20th century, photomontage emerged as a precursor to the effects now possible with computer-mediated photography (**Figure 9-22**). John Heartfield's work is an inspiration to editorial illustrators everywhere.

Designers use photographs and work with photographers throughout their careers. A photograph may be needed to document an event, illustrate a story, sell a product, or put across a point of view. In

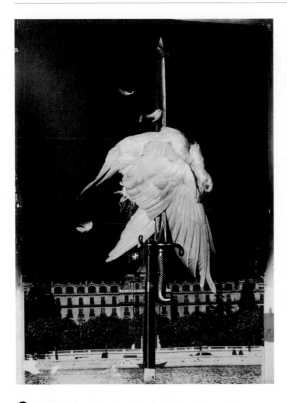

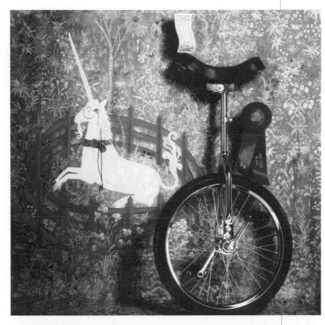

Nora Scarlett 212 741 2620

● **9-22** *John Heartfield.* The Meaning of Geneva. *Photomontage, 1932.*
Copyright 1998 Artists Rights Society (ARS), New York/VG Bild-Kunst, Bonn.

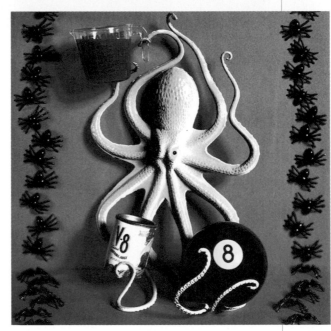

Nora Scarlett 212 741 2620

all cases, the photograph must be evaluated in terms of print quality, design quality, and ability to communicate. It is advisable to study and learn to appreciate good photos, and a class in darkroom work will help develop a feeling for print quality. Experimentation with digital photography can be an exciting and very accessible way to begin or to augment this learning process. A photograph communicates in a particular and powerful way. We have a special relationship with photography, based on history, memory, and the photograph's similarity to the retinal image.

The criteria for good design in a photograph are similar to good design in layout or illustration. **Figures 9-23a** and **9-23b** by Nora Scarlett show a highly creative and effective use of photography for self-promotion. The photographer-designer

mailed a sequential series of ten post-cards to clients around the country.

Digital Photography

Once an analog continuous-tone photograph is translated into digital data, it can be accessed, manipulated, and transformed with incredible speed and efficiency. Digital

● **9-23a, b,** *Nora Scarlett, New York photographer, created these self-promotional direct-mail pieces. She located or created all the necessary still-life props for this creative series.*
Courtesy of the artist.

171

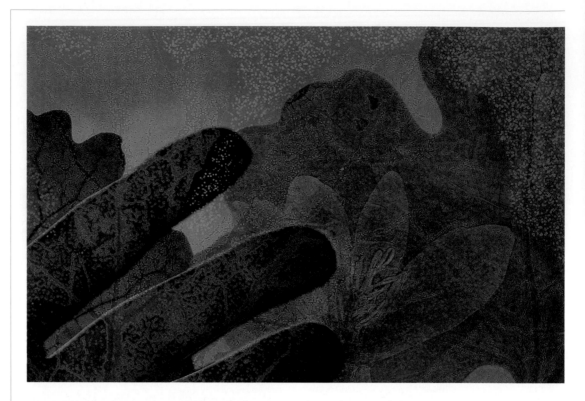

cameras skip the analog stage entirely. Artist-educator Susan Ressler created the fine art image in **Figure 9-24** by digitizing original objects for a complex and rich series of manipulations.

Multiple variations of a single image can be generated when the image is digital, and color editing and retouching can be easily accomplished. Mistakes are never fatal, because the original image is stored on disk. Materials intended for the offset press can be sent directly to film after retouching on a computer system. The impact of digital imaging on photography, especially on the growth of photo illustration, has been tremendous.

A video camera can be cabled to a desktop computer and the resulting image captured as still data or as a manipulated live recording that will later be edited. It is increasingly necessary to honor and understand copyright issues. Appropriating photographers' or illustrators' images without payment or authorization infringes on their livelihood.

The most important aspect of photography remains in the eye and mind (and perhaps heart) of the artist. The concept, the design, the element of communication, and finally, the output determine the quality of a photographic image.

SPECIALTIES

Photojournalism

Photographs fall into two general categories: candid and staged. Most photojournalism is candid. It is not shot in a studio or with hired models. *Photojournalism* attempts to capture a news event on location with immediacy and honesty. When a feature story is run in a newspaper, an art director or editor may ask for a photo essay that will illustrate a feature story with a sequence of images that give a sense of movement, establish a narrative, or set an emotional tone.

Staged photographs are often used in advertising and product photography. They are tightly directed and require elaborate studio lighting. Hired models can make shooting time expensive. Product photographers are usually less concerned with truth telling than photojournalists and more concerned with presenting a product in the most favorable light.

Product Photography

Whenever the intent of photography is to promote or sell a product, it is called *product photography*. The product may be food, automobiles, furniture, clothing, fine art, or a wide range of other items. The metal sculpture in **Figure 9-25** is captured in all of its surface texture and complexity through the art of the photographer. Still-life photographs enhance the beauty and desirability of many products. Often this sort of product is prepared for the camera with special gels and coatings that intensify lighting effects.

Whether the assignment comes from an art director at an advertising agency or directly from the client, the product photographer is often told what to shoot within very narrow specifications. The challenge in this form of photography is to help sell or present the product in a way that is personally and aesthetically satisfying. **Figure 9-26** shows successful product photography integrated into a poster for an exhibition at the Detroit Institute of Arts.

Most photographers doing this kind of work are freelancers, and many work

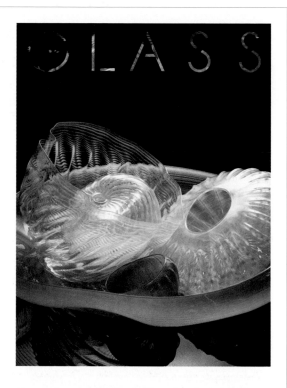

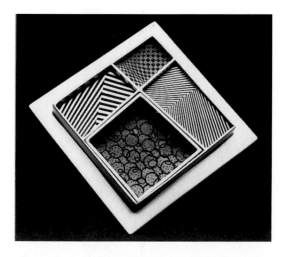

● **9-25** *Linda Threadgill, artist, and Jim Threadgill, photographer.* Patchwork Pin. *1984.*

● **9-26** *Poster by Chuck Byrne and Julius Friedman for the Detroit Institute of Arts.* Courtesy of the designer.

through an agent, or "rep," who solicits work from clients. The rep usually will get a 25 to 30 percent finder's fee from an assignment. Major catalog houses and department stores have their own in-house photographic staff and facilities. Many regional advertisers also use an in-house photographic staff. However, national advertisers usually hire dependable freelancers whose previous work suits the project at hand.

When shooting a fashion layout for a catalog, newspaper, or direct-mail piece that calls for a model, the photographer will work with an art director and with assistants who help with the details of clothing, makeup, props, and so on. All people at a shoot should show respect for one another's professional abilities.

Corporate Photography

Large corporations need a great deal of photography for annual reports, presentations, and other publications. The company's art director or designer often hires a photographer for an individual assignment and offers suggestions regarding the project.

A public-relations (PR) executive also may become involved in the considerations. Sometimes a staff photographer does the photographic work. This photographer is typically a generalist working out of the PR department and shooting everything from candid news release photos to carefully composed and lighted architectural interiors.

Architectural photography calls for special skill in handling building interiors and exteriors. Lighting an interior so that the bright chandeliers as well as the details in dark corners of the room are all properly exposed and not distorted calls for considerable expertise (Fig. 1-4). Photographing exteriors of tall buildings often requires special equipment that will correct for parallax.

Architectural photography is a specialty in itself, and those who specialize in it work for a variety of interior design firms, landscape designers, and corporate accounts.

Photo Illustration

Photography can illustrate an accompanying story—anything from fiction to a feature article on restaurant dining to a CD cover. Photographic illustrations are sometimes closely art directed by the designer. The necessary props and set may be provided, or the photographer may be asked to find or construct them.

This form of illustration leaves room for creative interpretation, but communication remains the primary objective. Digital pho-

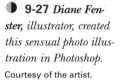 **9-27** *Diane Fenster, illustrator, created this sensual photo illustration in Photoshop.* Courtesy of the artist.

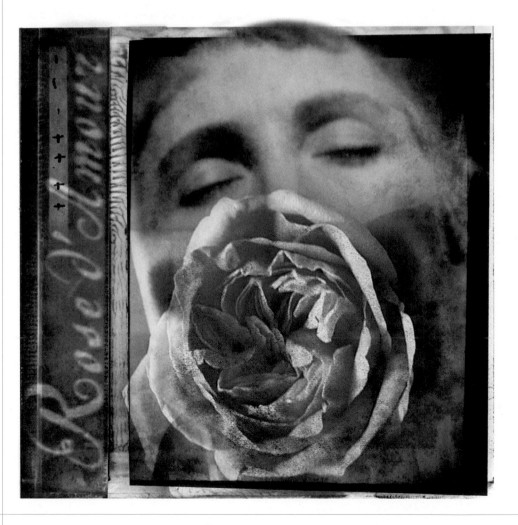

tography has made a great contribution to photo illustration (**Figure 9-27**).

FINDING PHOTOGRAPHS AND PHOTOGRAPHERS

Stock photography agencies sell photographs to freelancers, advertising agencies, and in-house design departments. They have thousands of images on file that are constantly updated. Any type of photograph is available by transparency or CD-ROM, and agencies specialize in everything from architecture to current events to the history of civilization.

The Bettmann Archive, Black Star Publishing Company, and Getty Images are three of hundreds of companies providing images and/or photographic services for use in editorial work, advertising, and television. *American Showcase: Illustration* is a full-color reference book used by advertising agencies, PR firms, and others who want to hire freelance photographers and illustrators. Each portfolio page of photos is accompanied by the name and address of the photographer who shot them. See the accompanying Web site for a showcase product overview.

Photographers specialize in a variety of areas, each of which calls for unique expertise. As a designer, you'll want to know how to communicate and work with a photographer.

Know how to locate and select stock images when these are appropriate. The designer whose work is shown in **Figure 9-28** used a combination of family and clip art images as part of her student portfolio. In **Figure 9-29**, stock photography was used to illustrate a proposed children's book.

When such a book is accepted for publication, the photographs may be acquired or replaced by other, similar stock photographs, depending on copyright availability.

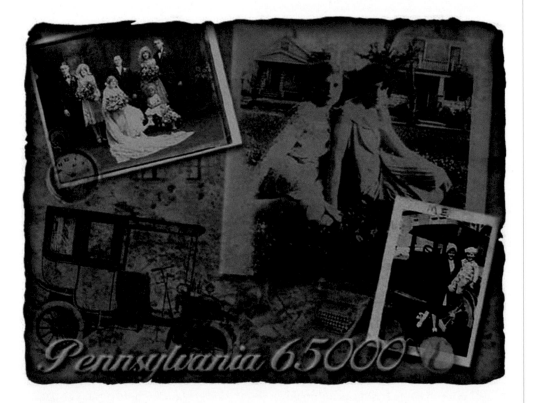

● **9-28** *Jackie Waylen* constructed this portfolio piece as a student, combining clip art and old family photos in Photoshop.

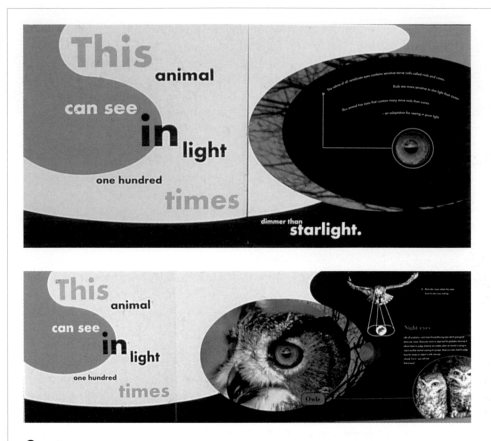

● **9-29** *Dan Kim,* *educator and designer, created this proposal for a children's book by using* *stock photography to complement his original design and editorial concept. Shown are two consecu-* *tive page spreads with a circular dye cut on the first spread revealing the eye of the owl.*
Courtesy of the artist.

PROJECT

Design the cover of a CD you enjoy, incorporating photography and/or illustration. Find several images that are appropriate. You may research and obtain authorized copies, shoot the images yourself, locate copyright-free art, generate the imagery through your own drawings, or look on the accompanying Web site. Do not appropriate a professional photographer's or illustrator's work from magazines or other printed sources. Choose the images you will work from, based on print quality, design quality, and visual information.

Combine the imagery with the title of the recording and the name of the artist. Prepare your piece to actual size. You may need to use traditional illustrator's mechanical enlarging and reducing aids, darkroom skills, or digitized images. Check with your instructor to see what combination of media you should pursue. Always keep your treatment appropriate to the subject matter, and remember to use the gestalt unit-forming techniques to integrate word and image. Complete the CD package, including all typography.

Graphic Design Basics

Goals and Objectives

Practice working with thumbnails to develop a variety of creative solutions.

Practice creating and integrating imagery in a layout design, making type and image work together.

Strive to create an illustration that communicates visually, without dependence on words.

Critique

How do type and image in your design reinforce and echo each other? Are there repeated shapes?

How does this solution relate *visually* to the content of the music? Consider tempo, type choice, and symmetrical or asymmetrical treatment of type and image.

How is figure/ground treated? Discuss these factors in your own design and in one other.

Request and recommend changes to improve this design for your portfolio.

TERMINOLOGY

CHAPTER 10

See glossary
for
definitions.

Advertising	Direct Mail
Retail Advertising	Point-of-Purchase Display
Market Research	Corporate Identity Program
Storyboard	Graphics Standard Manual

Advertising Design

10

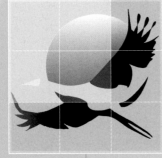

KEY POINTS   This chapter discusses the differences and similarities between advertising design and graphic design. Various areas of advertising design are presented, including 2-D and 3-D print applications, television, and the Web. The importance of design structure to a successful ad campaign is covered, as well as the importance of market research and working with a team.

THE PURPOSE OF ADVERTISING

Advertising differs from pure graphic design in intent. It primarily seeks to persuade, and the presentation of information is secondary to that intent.

The successful advertisement (1) attracts attention, (2) communicates a message, and (3) persuades an audience. Advertising can have many different looks. It may appear in television, newspapers, direct mail, magazines, billboards, outdoor displays, Web sites, and point-of-purchase displays. Whatever the medium, it is characterized by an attempt to persuade an audience, with the intent to boost sales, profits, and market share.

There are elements of information in an advertisement and elements of persuasion in pure graphic design. Those who believe "advertising is information" assume that the consumer initially buys a product based on information supplied by advertisements. Future purchases are based on firsthand assessment of the quality of the product. This theory states that the persuasive element in advertising is secondary to the information supplied.

To what extent is this view of advertising true? The ads most useful in informing consumers are probably regional ads announcing events such as plays, concerts, and meetings. Consumers might miss an opportunity to participate without an advertisement. Another example is advertisements for equipment, which typically come with information about specific attributes that are important in the decision to purchase.

Those who believe the function of advertising is persuasion maintain that advertisements exist to change perception. Advertising induces the consumer to believe that a product has certain desirable qualities or associations. Soda pop and blue jeans become associated with youth, zest, and popularity. Ads that use them "sell" an attitude and a lifestyle. Associated products have youth and zest "rubbed off" on them.

The purest example of advertising to persuade can be found in national advertising, especially of long-standing, leading products. Consumers no longer need a lot of basic information on these products. What sells such products are the associations consumers have with them. Many of these associations are generated by advertising and have nothing obvious to do with the actual products (**Figure 10-1**).

Many advertisements have both persuasive and informative qualities. The closer an advertisement comes to pure information, the closer it comes to pure graphic

design. The closer a graphic design such as a poster comes to not only announcing an event but also persuading ticket purchases, the closer it comes to pure advertising. **Figures 10-2** and **10-3** are part of an integrated campaign created for the Minnesota Zoo by Rapp Collins Communications, a well-known contemporary design firm in Minneapolis, Minnesota. Several examples of this wonderfully humorous and effective ad campaign are used throughout the chapter. An integrated advertising campaign crosses media boundaries, producing ads with a repeated visual and intellectual theme in various forms of print, on the Internet, and in other mass media.

TYPES OF ADVERTISING

Retail and national advertising are two major categories of advertising. Each can be divided into several major areas according to dollar volume: television, newspaper, direct mail, and the Internet.

Retail advertising is so named because a retail establishment often sponsors it. It tends to be informational, especially when announcing special discounts or availability. It often attempts to get people to go to sponsoring stores to buy items they have seen advertised nationally. Studies show that retail advertising encourages price competition.

National advertising is advertising run by manufacturers with a nationwide distribution network for their product. It tends to be persuasive. It began when manufacturers wanted to differentiate their brands from similar or identical brands, and when there was a national delivery system for advertisements. **Figure 10-4** shows the national TV presentation of the trademark designed by Paul Rand as part of the Westinghouse corporate identity system.

Television

A large percentage of total advertising dollars is spent on television commercials.

◗ **10-1** Ad layout courtesy of Apple Computer. *Gavin Milner* and *Bob Cockrell, art directors; Harold Einstein, writer; Ed Adler, producer; Tom Nelson, photographer. Prepared by BBDO, Los Angeles, California.*

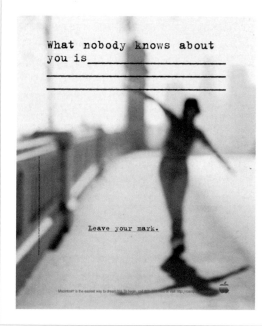

What nobody knows about you is_____
_____
_____

Leave your mark.

Graphic Design Basics

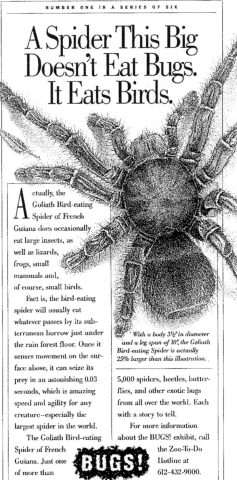

A Spider This Big Doesn't Eat Bugs. It Eats Birds.

Actually, the Goliath Bird-eating Spider of French Guiana does occasionally eat large insects, as well as lizards, frogs, small mammals and, of course, small birds.

Fact is, the bird-eating spider will usually eat whatever passes by its subterranean burrow just under the rain forest floor. Once it senses movement on the surface above, it can seize its prey in an astonishing 0.03 seconds, which is amazing speed and agility for any creature—especially the largest spider in the world.

The Goliath Bird-eating Spider of French Guiana. Just one of more than

With a body 3½" in diameter and a leg span of 10", the Goliath Bird-eating Spider is actually 25% larger than this illustration.

5,000 spiders, beetles, butterflies, and other exotic bugs from all over the world. Each with a story to tell.

For more information about the BUGS! exhibit, call the Zoo-To-Do Hotline at 612-432-9000.

BUGS!

At the Minnesota Zoo. Now through Labor Day.

Why The Red-eyed Assassin Is As Dangerous As It Sounds.

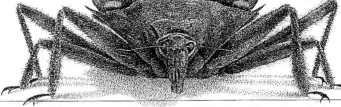

If you guessed that an insect named "the assassin" just might be dangerous, you're right. The red-eyed assassin possesses a powerful venom, which it can spray up to 18 inches to stun its victims. For survival, the red-eyed assassin injects this liquefying venom into its victims — and then sucks their insides out.

Ironically enough, even though the red-eyed assassin does have keen eyesight, it does not have red eyes. "Red-eyed" refers to the two red dots on its back that resemble eyes, which keep potential predators at bay.

The red-eyed assassin of West Africa. Just one of more than 5,000 spiders, beetles, butterflies, and other exotic bugs. Each with a story to tell.

For more information about the BUGS! exhibit, call the Zoo-To-Do Hotline at 612-432-9000.

BUGS!

At the Minnesota Zoo. Now through Labor Day.

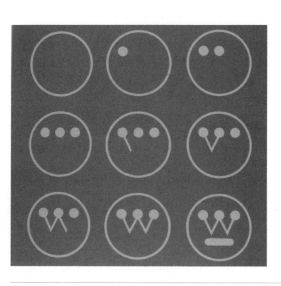

The content of national television advertising is strongly persuasive. Commercials may take the form of a network advertisement, shown on national shows; a spot advertisement, prepared nationally and shipped to local areas; or a local advertisement, prepared and shown locally.

Market research is important in all advertising, especially the heavily persuasive kind. It is a study of consumer groups and business competition used to define a projected market. Market researchers survey the area where a product or service will be offered, and use the results to determine the cost of doing business, assess the competition, estimate potential sales, and so on. The two primary marketing considerations in television advertising are program attentiveness and viewer volume.

● **10-2, 10-3** *Two advertisements created as part of the Bugs! ad campaign prepared for the Minnesota Zoo by Rapp Collins Communications. Creative director* **Bruce Edwards,** *art director* **Bruce Edwards,** *copywriter* **Chris Mihock.**

◑ **10-4** *TV storyboard of an animated logo designed for Westinghouse Electric Corporation by* **Paul Rand.** *1961.*

Program attentiveness is how strongly viewers concentrate on a show. Maximum attention ensures maximum recall. Unlike an ad on the Web or in print media such as newspapers and direct mail, a television ad occurs within a specific time and cannot usually be "reread."

The second marketing consideration in TV advertising is the number of persons viewing programs. Certain hours are considered peak viewing periods. These prime-time slots cost prime dollars. Because so much money is at stake, a great deal of research goes into ad effectiveness.

Usually a television advertisement is initially prepared in the form of a *storyboard*. When prepared two-dimensionally, it consists of two frames per scene, one carrying a visual depiction of the scene, the other carrying words to be spoken by an announcer or a cast. The storyboard depicts only key scenes (**Figure 10-5**).

10-5 *Storyboard of a TV advertisement created by Rapp Collins Communications for the Minnesota Zoo. Creative director* **Bruce Edwards**, *art director* **Bruce Edwards**, *copywriter* **Chris Mihock**.

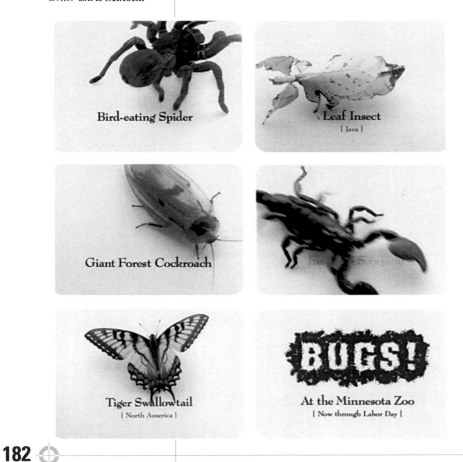

The visual is often prepared so it will carry the message even if the TV volume is muted. The product name is often superimposed over the scene at the end of the ad. The audio is written to carry the message alone, in case the viewer is temporarily out of the room or unable to see the screen.

Newspapers

Newspaper advertising carries both regional and national ads. National advertising often arrives as an "ad slick" or a file ready for insertion. The creative work has been done at the company's ad agency. Regional display advertising often requires designing by the newspaper's staff of artists and copywriters. Most newspapers now have a Web presence and hire designers to create and maintain the Web sites.

ADVANTAGES AND DISADVANTAGES Some challenges face the designer in newspaper advertising. First, the designer must often include diverse art elements and typefaces in a single ad. A logo and other elements relating to a national campaign must often be incorporated into an ad for a local sale. Often the cost of an advertisement will be shared by multiple companies if their logos appear in the ad. This diversity of elements can make creating a well-designed, attractive advertisement a real challenge. Second, the designer must create within the limitations of cheap, absorbent newsprint and hurried printing to meet daily, sometimes hourly, deadlines.

Single-item ads for large institutional clients such as banks may use a full page with room for white space. These ads allow more leeway for design. *No matter how many elements the advertisement contains, no matter whether it is national or local, and no matter whether it is reproduced on newsprint or expensive glossy paper, good design will always aid communication.* Given some creativity, it will also attract attention and help persuade the audience.

The advantages of newspaper advertising are many. Papers are widely read. Circulation rates are available to help advertisers anticipate the number of people their ads will reach. Moreover, the circulation is localized. It is therefore easy for a retail outlet to reach the people most likely to be interested in and able to travel to a sale. Finally, the copy can be changed daily, and the updated ad will still reach its audience within a day.

THE AUDIENCE The readership for a mainstream newspaper is diverse. People from nearly all age groups and from every socioeconomic group read the paper. When a product is of interest to a limited group, newspaper advertising is not advisable, because only a small percentage of readers would be potential buyers.

Newspaper advertising can be targeted to a limited extent, however, by considering the type of reader attracted to a certain type of paper. The readership of the *Wall Street Journal,* for example, differs from that of the *New York Post.*

Advertising rates are based on the size of the ad, the circulation of the paper, and the position of the ad within the paper. The sports, society, home, and financial sections are areas where advertisements allied to special subjects are likely to be seen by the desired group of readers. Advertisers pay extra dollars to ensure that the appropriate audience sees their ad. Other positions within the paper that are worth extra money are the outside pages, the top of a column, and next to reading material.

Direct Mail and Internet

Direct-mail advertising comes in many forms. It is an exciting and growing area of advertising that has boomed partly because of the credit card business and partly because of today's busy lifestyles. Direct mail accounts for most third-class mail and a considerable amount of first-class mail. Increasingly, the Internet is an

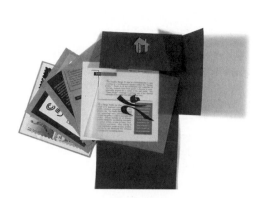

important way for advertisers to target specific audiences with tailored messages.

Direct mail is advertising in which the advertiser also acts as publisher. The advertiser produces a publication (rather than renting space in someone else's), selects the mailing list, and sends the publication directly to the prospects through the mail (**Figure 10-6**). A highly targeted form of direct mail includes printed communication to investors such as annual reports. Often these are very high-quality, high-dollar publications that carefully present an integrated corporate identity. **Figure 10-7a** shows the Westinghouse Electric annual report cover from 1971, utilizing the logo created by the 20th-century design leader Paul Rand.

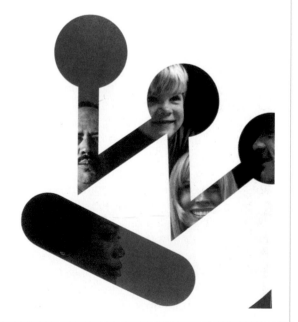

◗ **10-6** *Studio 45. A direct-mail piece created by the student design agency at the University of Wisconsin–Whitewater announcing an open house in their computer lab.*

◗ **10-7a** *Cover for an annual report designed for Westinghouse Electric Corporation by **Paul Rand** in 1971.*
Courtesy of Mrs. Marion Rand.

● **10-7b** *The Web is a new and important advertising venue. This on-line catalog site for Pearl art supplies makes shopping easy.*

ink color, and folding characteristics are all additional variables to be designed. A piece that folds is a three-dimensional problem. It must succeed visually from a variety of positions. The design develops from front to back, building interest and encouraging the reader to continue.

One disadvantage of direct mail is that people are often hostile to it. If the audience throws away the envelope or catalog without even opening it, communication has failed. Studies have shown that a mailing that requires participation, such as a lottery, will increase effectiveness. Copy and graphics that present specific offers and a clear, simple message succeed well.

Forms of direct mail include letters, flyers, folders and brochures of various dimensions and formats, catalogs, and booklets. A single mailing may consist of several pieces, such as an outside envelope, a letter, a brochure, and a business reply card. It might be part of a campaign of related pieces that are mailed out over a period of weeks.

Internet forms of advertising include Web sites for catalogs, e-mail messages alerting customers to sales opportunities, and banner ads that may feature movement and sound. **Figure 10-7b** shows the catalog site for a large art supply store.

Online delivery of sales material is a fast-growing market, as corporations increasingly find it appropriate to communicate with their audience via the Internet. This medium calls for an integration of the corporate identity program into the pages of Web sites and other forms of advertising. Notice the similarity between the print cover design in Figure 10-7a and the TV storyboard in Figure 10-4.

ADVANTAGES AND DISADVANTAGES The advantages of direct mail are substantial. First, the advertiser can use a mailing list that has been compiled to reach a specialized audience. Businesses sometimes develop their own mailing list. The primary sources of names, however, are mailing-list brokers. They are in the business of building and maintaining lists of individuals likely to have an interest in a given topic. Lists are usually rented for onetime use, because they go out of date quickly and must be constantly updated. Second, direct mail does not have to compete for attention with other ads on a newspaper page or on television. Third, it is flexible in format. This feature makes direct mail challenging to the designer. The size, paper,

Other Forms of Advertising

Magazines also offer a forum for advertising (**Figure 10-8**). A wide variety of magazines are published. There are general-interest magazines, such as *Newsweek* and *Life,* and specialty or "class" magazines, such as computer, religious, sports, and health publications. There are trade and professional magazines, such as *Print, Communication Arts,* and *ARTnews,* as well as professional publications for doctors, engineers, and so on. With magazines it is possible to target a specific interest group. If advertisers have a regional or national product to promote, they may choose magazine advertising because many magazines have a national circula-

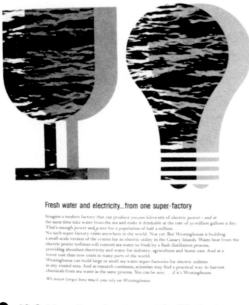

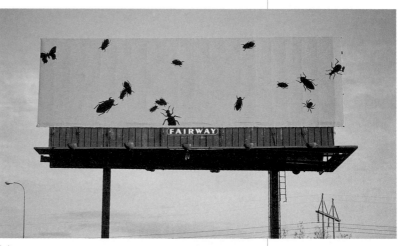

(a)

10-8 *Magazine advertisement for Westinghouse Electric Corporation designed in 1962 by* **Paul Rand.**
Courtesy of Mrs. Marion Rand.

tion. Some national magazines have regional versions, targeting different parts of the country.

Another form of advertising is billboard display (**Figures 10-9a, b, c**). When designing for billboards, remember that the message will be seen from a moving vehicle at a distance of at least 100 feet (30 m). The visual and the copy must be kept simple. It is surprising how many billboards violate this principle. Type for billboards should be more than 3 inches (8 cm) high at 100 feet (30 m) and over 12 inches (30 cm) high at 400 feet (120 m). A message of more than seven words is difficult to read. A single image is easiest to grasp. An easily recognizable silhouette makes a strong visual that can carry the message. A strong intellectual and visual unity is important. The problems presented by transit advertising and outdoor advertising in general are similar to those for

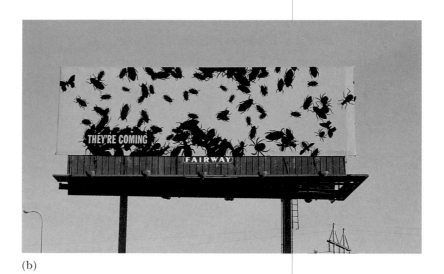

(b)

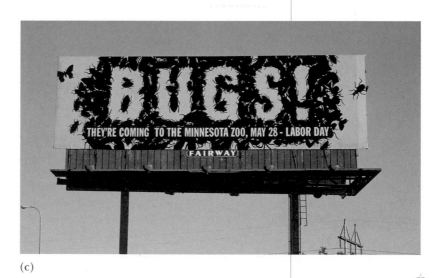

(c)

10-9a, b, c *Billboard ads created by Rapp Collins Communications as part of the Bugs! campaign for the Minnesota Zoo. Creative director* **Bruce Edwards,** *art director* **Bruce Edwards,** *copywriter* **Chris Mihock.**

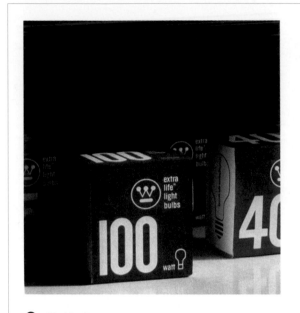

● **10-10** *Light bulb packaging designed by **Paul Rand** for Westinghouse Electric Corporation in 1968.* Courtesy of Mrs. Marion Rand.

billboards. The audience is always in motion. The form of the appeal must be bold and simple, eliminating details.

Point-of-purchase ads and package design are other important forms of advertising. Both are primarily three-dimensional and should present a look consistent with the other promotional materials established for a product. **Figure 10-10**, designed by Paul Rand, shows an integrated use of the Westinghouse "W." The term *point of purchase* describes the display that is pres-

ent along with the product in stores. Studies have shown that people frequently make purchases on impulse. More than one-third of purchases in department stores and almost two-thirds of purchases in supermarkets are influenced by the display of the product. The display in stores, especially supermarkets, consequently plays an important part in advertising products. Package design can be considered a form of point-of-purchase advertising and is an interesting area to investigate.

Personal Promotion

A special form of advertising that brings out the most creative and delightful work samples is personal promotion. This is the campaign an individual creates to advertise freelance services or to promote a small design firm. The goal is to design a creative sample that shows the best of concept development, illustration, and design skills. It must reach and appeal to the appropriate audience. **Figure 10-11a** shows one piece from a direct-mail print campaign designed by photographer Nora Scarlett.

CORPORATE IDENTITY

Companies have used trademarks to identify themselves since the early Renaissance, as discussed in Chapter 5. This practice grew and flourished with the Industrial Revolution and culminated in the 1950s with very complete visual identification systems. Names associated with this golden age of corporate identity include Paul Rand, Saul Bass, and Lester Beall.

Many large companies and institutions now have a master corporate identity plan that coordinates all their designs. This plan begins with the trademark and applies it to the layout of business cards, letterhead, advertisements, product identification, and packaging. Even the company uniforms and vehicles form part of this identity program. **Figures 10-12a, b, and c** show the J. I. Case Company's strong corporate logo

Digital Focus

Web design is growing in importance as a form of advertising. Modern businesses are searching for ways to cut overhead costs and target new market segments as well as improve communication and profit margins. Web-site design and Internet marketing strategies provide powerful applications that enable a company to achieve those goals. A design that reflects the corporate identity and unites a site from page to page is a vital part of this interactive advertising medium. **Figure 10-11b** shows four pages from the Richardson furniture company's Web site designed to reach potential clients. Among the company's products are yachting interiors.

10-11a *Personal promotional campaign designed by contemporary photographer* **Nora Scarlett** *for direct-mail delivery.*
Courtesy of the artist.

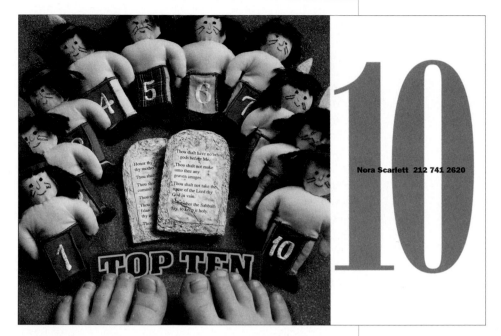

Nora Scarlett 212 741 2620

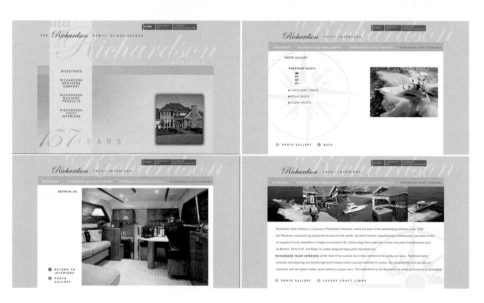

10-11b *Four pages from the Richardson furniture company's Web site. Among the company's products are yachting interiors.*

10-12a, b, c *J. I. Case Company corporate logo applied to signage, packaging, and vehicles.*
Courtesy of J. I. Case, Racine, Wisconsin.

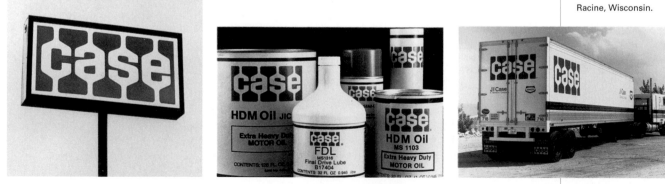

applied to signage, package design, and vehicles. *Corporate identity* is a specialized branch of advertising and design that creates a unified image of a corporation through a systematic application of constant design elements. Every aspect of typography and imagery and their application must be considered part of an integrated presentation.

This integrated presentation shows the corporation to the public in a positive and memorable light. It not only communicates an image, but it attempts to persuade the public that the corporation, and hence its products, is superior. A *graphics standard manual,* distributed to company personnel, details the appropriate use and placement of the trademark and related materials. The identity program must be flexible enough to be adapted to future needs. It is one of the most comprehensive applications of design and advertising.

WORKING WITH OTHERS

Advertising takes teamwork. You must communicate closely with copywriters, photographers, illustrators, clients, and market researchers. Either the visual or the verbal element may be the departure point for developing a message. An integration of form and content, of design and communication is at the heart of good advertising.

Work with others to establish key information. Who is the audience? What is the nature of the product? Where will the ad appear? What is the purpose of the ad? What is the budget? Once you have answered these questions, you can begin to translate this information into visual form.

A successful ad attracts attention, communicates through its unified arrangement of elements, and persuades through the interaction of strong and appropriate copy and layout.

EXERCISES

1. Find some persuasive ads in a magazine. How do they catch the attention of their intended audience? What associations with the product do the ads induce? How?

2. Find a product ad that targets different audiences by appearing in two different magazines in a different format. Try looking at "African American" and "senior" and "youth" magazines.

3. Turn off the sound on a TV set and watch some commercials. Does the visual convey a complete message? Now try listening without viewing commercials.

4. Scan your local newspaper. Which advertisements attract your attention? How do position and design affect their success?

PROJECT

Choose one of the following assignments:

Magazine Advertisements

Design two magazine advertisements in an $8^1/_2 \times 11$" (20 × 28 cm) format for a nonprofit public-service organization. Your task is to warn two different readerships of a hazard you are concerned about. Consider alcohol and drug abuse, smoking, and environmental and social problems. The primary audience for one ad is 18- to 24-year-olds; the primary audience for the other ad is up to you. Identify the magazines in which each ad will appear.

Research issues that might be targeted and discuss them in class.

Prepare one of the ads for black-and-white reproduction, including an image, a headline, and a few lines of body copy. Prepare the other ad for full-color reproduction. In your thumbnails, try various approaches, including a path layout, a grid layout, and a simple dominant image. For each ad write an accompanying explanation of your subject, your message, and how the message relates to the visual design choices you made. **Figure 10-13** is a student solution for a similar project.

Personal Promotion

Prepare a personal promotional campaign. Create a logo for yourself as an independent designer-illustrator, apply it to a business card and letterhead, and prepare a brochure for your promotional mailing. The research stage of this assignment primarily involves looking at other personal promotional campaigns. Set your standards very high. Try to top the professionals. Write an explanation of your message and how it relates to the visual design choices you made. What is your market? How are you addressing it?

Goals and Objectives

Experiment with researching an issue and targeting (or appealing to) a particular audience.

Practice both communicating a message and persuading an audience.

Critique

Present your solutions, discussing each topic, your relationship to it, and the research you conducted. How do your choices of type, image, and layout relate to the topic and the audience? Be as specific as possible.

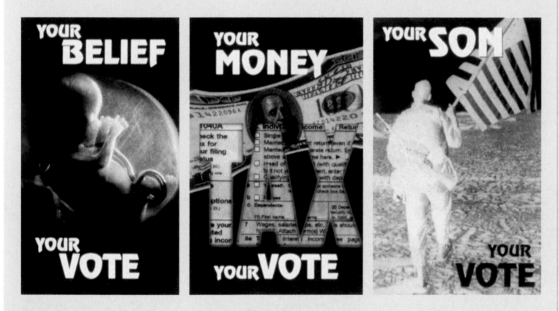

● **10-13** *Terri Breese. Integrated ad campaign created to encourage voter participation.*

TERMINOLOGY

CHAPTER 11

See glossary for definitions.

Analog	Software	Registration
Pixel	VDT	Dot Gain
Bitmap	CPU	LPI
Bit plane	Memory	RIP
Resolution	RAM	Printer Font
Object-oriented Graphics	ROM	Screen Font
Bitmapped Graphics	Postscript	DPI
Vector Graphics	Prepress Production	Link
Cartesian Coordinates	Camera ready	File Format
Raster Graphics	Line Art	
Hardware	Continuous Tone	

Production: The Tools and Process

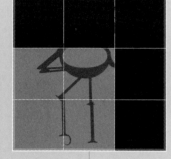

KEY POINTS   This chapter will introduce the structure of digital data and its application to print graphics. Computers are at the core of contemporary design and production. The design field is constantly expanding, as new avenues of non-print design and communication evolve with developing technology. This technology has the power to reshape our perception of ourselves and the world in which we live. Exciting as this electronic tool is, the greatest tool of all is a flexible, curious, open mind always ready to learn more. Education is a lifelong process—especially now, as changes come ever more quickly and challenge our understanding of the world and how we function in it.

A DESIGNER'S TOOL

There are many computer applications in design. These include CAD/CAM (computer-aided design and manufacturing) systems through which a designer can generate three-dimensional models of a new automobile without touching anything but the computer. Other print applications allow designs to go from the designer's computer to the offset press, all as digital files. Beyond print applications, the World Wide Web knits us together with an exchange of visual information and other data sharing like never before. Readily available multimedia and animation programs, such as Premiere, Director, Flash, and After Effects, allow the designer to generate animation, interactive environments, and presentation graphics in a desktop environment, as shown at the end of chapter 2.

The flexibility and convenience of this powerful tool are revolutionary. A designer can create multiple variations of an image or a page layout, experimenting with color, shape, or grid effects. Changes from the client can be accommodated quickly. Special effects in overlapping, tint screens, and collaged, manipulated, and drawn imagery can be readily

The development of desktop computer graphics has been a vital part of the computer revolution for the field of graphic design. Just as the invention of the printing press and movable type made the printed word accessible to a newly emerging middle class, desktop computers took computer graphics beyond the domain of the scientific and technological elite.

Apple Computer introduced the first Macintosh in 1984. The screen presented a black-and-white visual display at a resolution of 72 ppi (pixels per inch). The opportunity to integrate text and graphics was very limited. In 1985 Aldus introduced PageMaker software for the Macintosh, and desktop publishing began. Adobe Systems developed the PostScript programming language, which enabled printers to output a combination of text and images on a page, and Apple introduced a laser printer that used PostScript fonts. Technological developments continue at a rapid pace, giving individual designers increasing control over their product in a desktop environment, whether that product is a print, Web, or multimedia design.

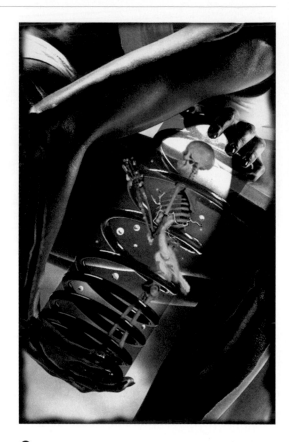

● **11-1** *Patrick McDonough.* SpringMan. *This portfolio piece created in 2000 is part of a series exploring a metaphor that compares humans and their creations.*

achieved (**Figures 11-1** and **11-2**). *Now, more than ever, there is a need for a designer's eye that is well educated and highly discriminating.*

Keep experimenting and asking yourself, "What is the relationship between the elements of the design? Special effects can be seductive, but are they also good design? Does the form of the design succeed in conveying the message?"

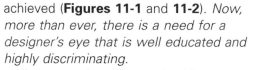

● **11-2** *Tammy Roemer.* Wine Calendar. *2003. Created in Painter, this series of four digitally drawn images reflects the four seasons.*

ANALOG AND DIGITAL DATA

Many users are unaware of the structure of the hardware they are manipulating. A basic knowledge of what makes it all work will help you prepare your files most effectively, and a knowledge of the terminology will help you communicate clearly about projects.

What is it that sets computers apart? They deal in digital information. The *analog* world is full of continuous-tone photo-

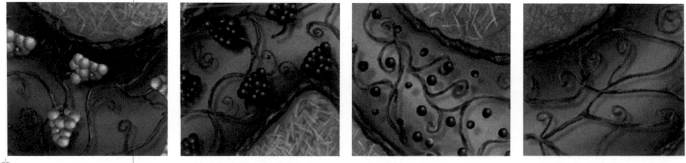

graphs, long-playing records (remember?), and clocks with smoothly moving hands. We ourselves live in an analog world, with time flowing smoothly past, as day fades to night, as we grow up and gradually age.

The digital world, however, is full of discrete units of information, like the music on CDs and the data on digital clocks. Each digitized piece of music and unit of time is a discrete entity that can be accessed and manipulated. When a black-and-white *continuous-tone* photograph is examined under a magnifier, all that can be seen are continuously changing gray values. When a digitized photograph is examined up close on a monitor, what can be seen are individual picture elements, or pixels, which give the illusion of continuous gray or color tones (**Figure 11-3**). Each of those pixels can be manipulated—adjusting value, hue, and luminosity—thus giving the designer, photographer, or photo retoucher total control over the image.

Analog to Digital Conversions

In a scanner or a digital camera, analog-to-digital converters (ADC) change analog voltage signals to digital RGB values. In a flatbed scanner, for example, a page is placed facedown on the scanner, and a scan head moves along the page, illuminating it. The light reflected from the page strikes a series of mirrors, which redirect the light to a lens. This lens focuses the beam of light into a prism that splits the beam into red, green, and blue components. The red, green, and blue light beams strike rows of photosensitive CCD cells, where they are converted into an analog voltage level. Finally, the analog-to-digital converter changes these voltage levels to digital information, storing the RGB levels for all the individual pixels in the image that appears on the screen.

The Screen Image

Raster graphics creates the video display the same way a traditional home television set does. A raster beam shot from electron guns illuminates the display line by line. As it moves across the screen, the raster beam's brightness and color are determined by instructions from the computer hardware.

Each spot on the screen, called a *pixel* (the basic unit that makes up a digital image), represents a location in memory. A digital image is composed of pixels, each of which can be individually accessed and manipulated. Each pixel location in memory consists of a *bitmap* that has an on or off command stored several *bit planes* (layers) deep. All of computer graphics comes down to on and off commands (**Figure 11-4**).

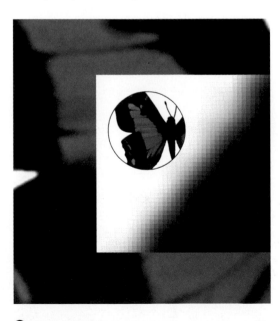

11-3 *Enlarging a raster image on a monitor will reveal its pixel structure.*

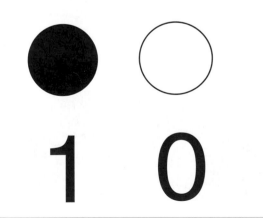

11-4 *All computer graphics are created by on and off commands, represented here as black and white and 1 and 0.*

The *resolution* of the screen controls the sharpness and clarity of the image. You may have noticed the jagged edges on some computer displays. Because each spot on the visual display is a pixel corresponding to a spot in memory, the number of individual pixels in the file determines the resolution of the image (**Figures 11-5a** and **11-5b**). The screen, the file, and the printer may all have different resolutions. For print graphics, a high-resolution file and output are mandatory. For online viewing, however, a lower resolution is adequate.

11-5a, b *This bitmap shows the on-and-off commands represented on the monitor as pixels forming a simple X.*

1	0	0	0	1
0	1	0	1	0
0	0	1	0	0
0	1	0	1	0
1	0	0	0	1

(a)

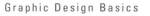

(b)

Object-Oriented and Bitmapped Graphics

There are two kinds of image files in computer graphics: vector, or *object-oriented,* graphics and raster, or *bitmapped,* graphics. Quark, InDesign, Illustrator, and Freehand are *vector graphics* programs. Images are created by lines drawn between coordinate points rather than being composed of pixels. These images can be selected and moved separately from other objects. Vector graphics programs create images with clean, sharp edges. Remember René Descartes? He was a 17th-century philosopher whose most famous words were, "I think, therefore I am." Descartes created the *Cartesian coordinate* system that vector graphics is based on. In this coordinate system, X and Y represent a two-dimensional graphic, and X, Y, and Z represent three dimensions (**Figure 11-6**). It is amazing to realize that computers use information developed that long ago. Objects created in vector graphics, such as the Illustrator image in **Figure 11-7**, are easily selected and manipulated through pushing, pulling, adding, and deleting points.

Bitmapped programs use *raster graphics* to create images. This means that each pixel is individually manipulated in terms of color and size to create a "map"

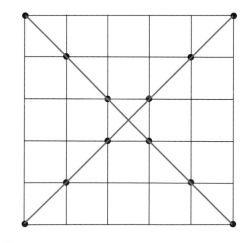

11-6 *Vector graphics consist of lines drawn between coordinate points.*

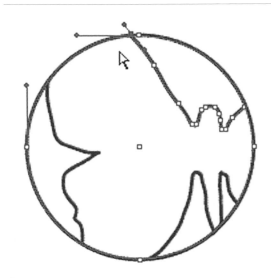

● **11-7** *The selection points in this vector graphic are easily manipulated to rescale or reshape the object.*

of an image. This is done by accessing the individual bits in each pixel. Photoshop and Painter are both bitmapped graphics programs. These programs seem to have a more intuitive feel than vector graphics programs, operating much like painting or drawing materials. Bitmapped images lose data when changed in size, unlike vector graphics, which retain their clarity as they are scaled up or down.

Page layout programs accept both forms of graphics. Such programs are usually where type, illustrations, and photographs are compiled for printing. QuarkXPress and Adobe InDesign work with outline vector graphics fonts to give sharp, clear, resizable typography.

Hardware and Software

Hardware components are the physical objects that make up a computer graphics system. *Software* programs are sets of instructions that tell the system what to do

and drive this hardware. The monitor we view images on is also known as a visual display terminal (VDT). The central processing unit (CPU), the main part of the system, houses the hard drive. This hard drive, along with CD-ROM, Zip, and DVD drives, gives access to personal file storage. Various forms of external storage can be added to your computer to provide greater portability and space for files.

Memory

All of a computer's ability to store, recall, and display images is based on the simple notion of on or off. A single piece of information equivalent to the choice of on or off is called a *bit.* It can represent a black or a white pixel. Hence the term *bitmapped graphics.* A group of bits can handle grays and even complex colors (**Figure 11-8a**). Eight bits are called a *byte* and can store 256 different grays or colors per pixel. Three bytes (24 bits) make it possible to render 16.7 million colors. Full-color effects are achieved when 8 or more bits represent each pixel within an image. A full-color image will take up more memory than a gray-scale image, because it uses more bits of information. Bitmaps are stacked several bit planes (layers) deep to achieve the number of on and off options necessary to achieve full color. **Figure 11-8b** shows two stacked bitplanes creating four possible numerical combinations per pixel. As shown, three stacked bitplanes give eight possible combinations per location. If there are eight stacked bitplanes in the bitmap, each pixel is one byte and can have 255 possible combinations, providing a full color effect.

◗ **11-8a** *A bit of information is organized into groups called a byte. A group of bytes make up a "word."*

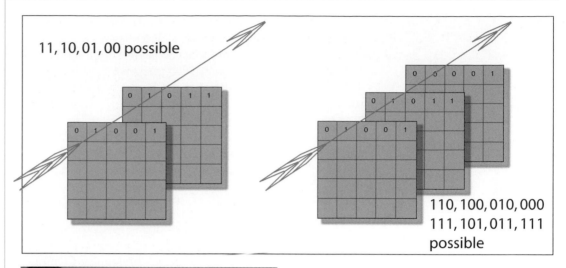

11, 10, 01, 00 possible

0 1 0 1 1

0 1 0 0 1

0 0 0 0 1

0 1 0 1 1

0 1 0 0 1

110, 100, 010, 000
111, 101, 011, 111
possible

11-8b *When each pixel has two bits, as shown on the left, four numerical possibilities exist per location. If there are three stacked bitplanes, then eight possibilities exist for each bit, providing eight color variations per pixel.*

11-8c *The many storage devices available on the market include highly portable minis as well as backup drives that regularly archive your computer's hard drive files.*

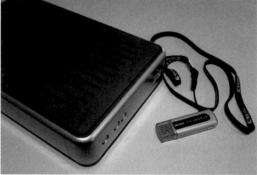

RAM and ROM

A computer has two kinds of memory. An integrated circuit chip on the computer's motherboard has a permanent memory called *ROM* (read-only memory). It holds the computer's essential operating instructions. The other kind of memory, called *RAM* (random-access memory), is used to actively create your files. When you launch an application or open a document, it is loaded into RAM and stored there while you work. Enough RAM is needed to hold the software you are using and the data you generate. RAM needs are constantly escalating. Buy as much as you can. RAM chips also range in speed (measured in ns, or nanoseconds). Be sure to buy the RAM chips specified for your computer.

Most RAM chips are soldered onto memory module boards. They are fairly easy to plug in and can be added to your system to increase its memory capacity. Each system has a particular configuration of SIMM (single in-line memory module) or DIMM (dual in-line memory module) boards. Make sure RAM chips will fit your particular board.

Storage Devices

Where do you store the large files you have created? Hard-drive space is always too small, but a few gigabytes are a good base unless you're planning to work on animation and multimedia. You can add an internal drive to most machines. Designers resort to a wide array of external portable storage devices to get their images to the prepress service bureau or to archive files. Obviously, whatever device you choose, the vendors you deal with must be able to support it. Current options include CD, DVD, and tiny portable storage drives (**Figure 11-8c**). Electronic file transfer via e-mail is a valuable timesaving method for sending graphics files to a client or reproduction house.

INPUT/OUTPUT DEVICES

Data In

Many peripheral devices are capable of capturing data for a computer. Scanners come in many varieties, from flatbed to transparency to drum scanners. Their operation is discussed later in this chapter, under Digital Prepress. The higher the resolution a scanner can produce, the more it will cost to purchase and the better the scan data will be.

Digital cameras and video cameras are two other forms of input. A digital camera captures a continuous-tone analog image and converts it to digital data, saving it to a hard drive as bits and bytes. Digital video is now commonly available at the consumer level in the United States, complete with simple editing programs. High-end digital video cameras are often used in the field by news organizations. A transceiver allows images to be transmitted anywhere in the world.

A tremendous variety of input devices are available, and careful background research will help determine which will meet your particular needs and budget.

Data Out

Will you want a print of your design for a portfolio? That image on the screen needs to be output in a usable manner, unless you plan to use it for a Web site or to download to a digital CD portfolio for viewing. It is wise to plan on a print portfolio as well as an electronic one.

A variety of printing technologies are available for your studio or computer lab, and each creates a slightly different kind of image. A basic description follows.

A PostScript-equipped printer that can read EPS (encapsulated PostScript) files is an important piece of equipment for a professional design studio that uses various software to create type and image files. *PostScript* is a device-independent format that means the file will print out at whatever dpi (dots per inch) the printer is capable of delivering.

The inkjet printer sprays ink drops onto paper, where they form characters or shapes. Epson sells archival ink sets for some of its product lines, producing a high-quality, long-lasting image. Inkjets are very cost-effective printers, and they are suit-

able for most color proofing and student portfolio prints.

Dye sublimation printers heat up colored ribbons until the pigments turn into gas, which is absorbed by the polyester coating on the paper. The output from these printers is continuous tone and thus can simulate a traditional photograph.

An imagesetter is a high-resolution device found at service bureaus and commercial print shops. It uses lasers to expose an image onto film in preparation for offset reproduction. It is increasingly common for imagesetters to generate output without using the wet chemical process of traditional film. A dry, chemical-free process can now produce positive or negative film separations direct from a PC compatible or Mac. The high resolutions (up to 3,000 dpi) of the imagesetter combined with the high quality of film provide high-quality printing for photographs and halftones.

A wide array of digital print options are available at Walgreens, Wal-Mart, and professional photo studios. These produce analog, chemical prints from your digital files for a portfolio.

PREPARING FOR PRESS

The Process

The first step in preparing art for the offset commercial printer is the job of the graphic designer. You are responsible for decisions about the placement of elements, the location of color, the choice of imagery, and the typographic treatment. Once the design is approved, the job is sometimes turned over to a prepress artist who prepares the design for printing. Many entry-level jobs for designers are in *prepress production,* although many designers who generate their own electronic designs also prepare their own files for press.

Preparing art for the printing process has changed a lot in recent years. In the United States, this preparation is done primarily with electronic techniques. An understanding of the terminology involved will provide a strong foundation for the new designer. It is possible to better understand the computer terminology and printing process when we begin with a historical knowledge of prepress production. Much of the terminology from the traditional hand techniques has carried over to the electronic techniques.

An Overview

Before computers, the traditional paste-up artist prepared a black-and-white version of the design that was *camera ready.* All the components of the design were assembled in black and white, and colors were specified before sending the job to a process camera to have film shot and plates burned. If any artwork was to be reproduced in full (process) color, it was sent separately to be color separated by a camera. All black-and-white photographs were also sent separately to be screened into halftones.

A process camera produced negatives of the black-and-white artwork, including all text and image materials. These nega-

tives were prepared for plate making by a technician called a *stripper.* He or she would cut, trim, and tape the negatives into position on a carrier sheet. The plate would then be exposed and put on the printing press, and the final printed copies of the original layout would be produced on specified paper in specified colors.

In the current digital prepress version, all scans, whether done by the designer or at a high-quality professional bureau, are placed on the computer file to be sent to the printer. There the final composite file can be created by *ripping* that data onto a negative and then *burning* (photographically exposing) it to a plate. In desktop publishing, **RIP** (raster image processing) is the process of turning vector information into a high-resolution raster image. The RIP takes the digital information about fonts and graphics and translates it into an image composed of individual dots that the imaging device (such as your desktop printer or an imagesetter) can output. If the press is digital, the file goes directly to press (**Figure 11-9**). The inking process on the offset press remains essentially the same as it was before digital file creation. Spot

11-9 *From concept to printed piece.*

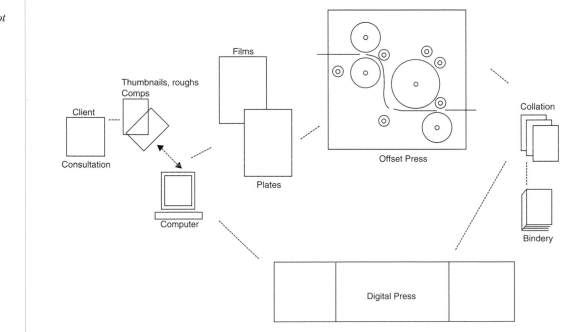

Graphic Design Basics

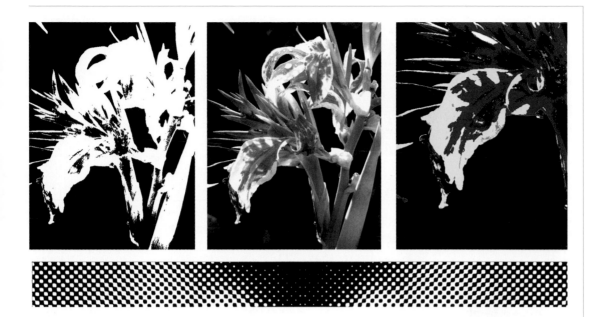

● **11-10** From left to right, *line art, grayscale, and three-color image, underlined with an enlarged halftone dot pattern.*

or process color inks are put on the press rollers, and the color is printed onto paper.

The prepress and printing process requires high standards and good communication from everyone involved. Often the printer can answer a designer's questions about the equipment a job will be run on, which will influence preparation of the artwork. This chapter discusses the preparation of artwork for the offset press, the most common method of reproduction.

Terminology

To the printer, the terms *art* and *copy* refer to all material to be reproduced. The copy is the typeset material; the art is everything else. All photographs, illustrations, and diagrams are called art. In general, they fall into two classifications: line art and continuous-tone images.

LINE ART   *Line art* consists of a black-and-white image with no variation in grays except those created by optical mixing. In the traditional prepress process, any line art could be pasted up directly onto a board and it was ready to be photographed for

reproduction. Anything not line art was handled separately, because it needed to be converted at the printer's or via electronic prepress into line art dots called screens or halftones. The printing press would only reproduce line art. **Figure 11-10** shows line art, gray-scale, and spot color images with an enlarged dot screen pattern beneath.

Typography, India ink drawings, one-color vector diagrams, high-contrast black-and-white photography, and line art scans are all forms of art and copy that contain only black-and-white data with no shades of gray. These are printed as one-color designs, as shown in **Figures 11-11a, b, d**.

CONTINUOUS-TONE ART   Art that produces a graduated or blended variety of values is called *continuous-tone* art. It includes photographs, art, and illustration done with pencil, paint, or any other method that produces a variety of values. When transferring such art to computer, the image is scanned or photographed digitally to capture the range of values.

The electronic prepress artist sends a file with line art or continuous-tone art in

11-11a *Line art reversed.*

11-11b *Line art with a tint screen.*

11-11c *Gray-scale art with Photoshop special effects.*

11-11d *Line art with two colors.*

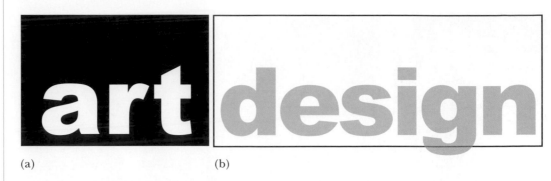

(a)   (b)

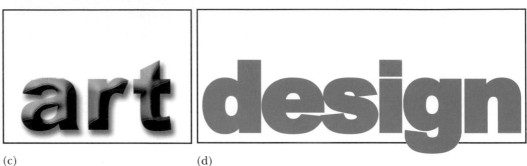

(c)   (d)

place and ink color specified. The final offset color printing on a non-digital press is created by making a separate negative and plate for each necessary color. The different inks are laid on the paper by the press in succession. As mentioned earlier, direct digital imaging can skip the negative and plate stages and go directly to press.

SPOT COLOR VARIATIONS   Reversals and tint screens are line art variations that can add interest to your one- or two-color art (also called spot color). This topic is discussed in Chapter 8. Such variations should be planned at the design stage. Figures 11-11a–d show various ways to enrich a one-color design. Crop marks indicated on the file show where the end of the page should be, and they tell the printer where to trim the sheet. Registration marks indicate how the layers of color should overprint (**Figure 11-12**).

REGISTRATION   There are three types of color register: nonregistered, commercial register, and hairline register. *Nonregistered colors* do not abut. *Commercial register* (sometimes called *lap register*) means

slight variations in placement of color, of about one row of screen dots, are not important. *Hairline register* is a term for extremely tight registration, where the tolerance is not greater than half a row of dots. When preparing an electronic file, trapping becomes an important consideration to ensure successful tight registration of colors that lie side by side. Otherwise,

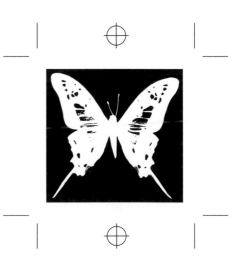

11-12 *Accurate registration and crop marks are vital for a file going to offset reproduction.*

a thin outline of white or dark can surround inked shapes. Some software programs, such as Quark, do automatic trapping, inserting *choaks* and *bleeds* to slightly reduce or enlarge the overlap of inked outlines. Such registration issues are easier to handle now than they were before computers. In most cases the printer or prepress service bureau will trap your file for you if your software program hasn't. It is important to clarify expectations.

Quality Issues

Careful consideration of dot gain, LPI (lines per inch), and paper quality is necessary to ensure quality output.

Dot gain occurs when halftone dots print larger than intended. It causes a printed piece to look very dark and full of high contrast. When examined under a magnifier (a linen tester or loupe), the halftone dots appear to be bleeding into the white spaces. An absorbent paper can cause dot gain, as can problems with the press itself.

LPI refers to the screen frequency of the actual printed piece. Again, your printer is a good source of information about the recommended LPI for your job. The higher the LPI, the finer the printed image, because the rows of halftone dots are closer together and are very small. However, the higher the LPI, the greater the tendency toward a clogging of halftone dots, or dot gain. Coated paper will handle higher screen frequencies than uncoated paper or newsprint:

133–175 LPI for coated paper stock
85–133 LPI for uncoated paper stock
60–80 LPI for newsprint

DIGITAL PREPRESS

Computer technology is continually changing how images are created and reproduced. The design and production stages are much more integrated now than before desktop computers became available to designers. Designs are previewed on the computer screen (or in a proof stage), changes are suggested by the client, adjustments are made by the designer, and the final design is sent to the production people as electronic files. Color correction, photo retouching, and color separations can be done on a desktop system before sending the files to a service bureau or printer for a high-resolution output to film or to press. Once the design is in digital form, there are vast possibilities for archiving and reutilization.

All this may sound simple, but it is actually quite complex. There are many ways to corrupt a digital file and confuse the printer. Clear communication between designer, prepress technician, and printer is a must.

The RIP

The designer may generate all the elements of an electronic file or may hire a service bureau to create high-resolution scans for images. Once the publication file is assembled, the designer, or someone he or she designates, needs to verify that the file is ready for *RIP* (raster image processing) on an imagesetter. A typical computer monitor has a resolution of 72 dpi; a typical laser printer has a resolution of several hundred dpi. The imagesetter that will send a file to film has a resolution of 2,400 dpi or higher. The pages might print fine on a laser printer, but fail to print on an imagesetter, because it calculates pixels by a different method. It is a safe bet that if the pages do not print on a laser printer, they will not print on an imagesetter either. How do you ensure that those pages are ready to RIP? Such considerations are especially important when using imported elements and multiple programs.

SOME DO'S AND DON'TS

■ It is important to keep an electronic file clean and neat. If you do not need something in a file, delete it. Do not cover it with a white rectangle or leave it on a hidden layer.
■ Avoid putting files into files and then putting these files into yet more files. This

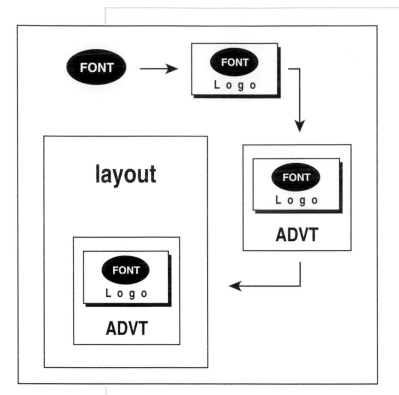

process is referred to as *nesting,* and it can snarl the RIP by requiring many unnecessary steps of electronic memory (**Figure 11-13**).

■ When using multiple programs, it is best to assemble all the elements in your final output program.

■ Finish any manipulation of those elements in the original file before importing. Rotate and resize an image in Photoshop, for example, before sending it to Quark or

InDesign. Do not plan to resize or rotate an imported graphic. They make the RIP work much harder.

■ Avoid scaling graphics up or down by large amounts. The data may stay the same, and you can end up with a very tiny, very high-resolution image, or a very large, relatively low-resolution image.

■ Scan an image at approximately the size it will be in the final publication. If it is necessary to drastically reduce the size of an image, plan to also use the software program to reduce the resolution (dpi). If you are planning to enlarge the image, watch what happens to the resolution. It will decrease as the image size increases.

Fonts

Fonts are composed of a *printer font* and a *screen font.* The printer (PostScript) font allows typography to output to print; the screen font is a cruder version that shows up on the monitor. The RIP needs to find and use exactly the font used to create the document. The font cannot be some other vendor's version of Helvetica. It has to be the exact one used in your publication for the line breaks to work out correctly. Send all printer and screen fonts along with your document. Otherwise, plan to convert vector files such as Illustrator to "Outline" and rasterize (convert to raster graphics) typographic files in Photoshop (**Figure 11-14**).

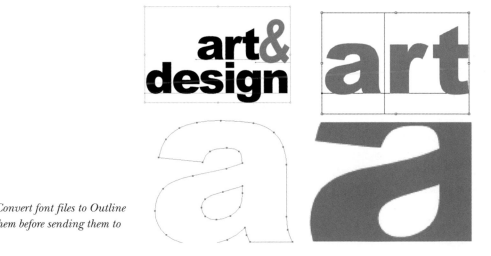

◗ **11-14** *Convert font files to Outline or rasterize them before sending them to print.*

Graphic Design Basics

Do not rely on pop-up menu styles to create bold, italic, or condensed versions of your font. These variations are not specially designed typography. They are computer-generated distortions and will not RIP well. Use the real fonts in the font menu.

Scanning

In the pre-computer days of offset reproduction, the designer sent a continuous-tone photograph or transparency along with the paste-up or mechanical and specified where the image should be inserted and resized. The printer then created a halftone negative at the correct LPI for the press and the paper choice. The primary tool for creating a halftone today is the computer.

When a designer creates a publication electronically, a photo is usually scanned on a desktop scanner and sent to a service bureau for a high-end drum scan, or the designer receives the photo in a digital format. The designer still needs to be familiar with terms such as *LPI* (discussed earlier) and *dpi* and to understand their relationship to ensure good results.

The higher the resolution an image has, the more *dpi* (dots per inch) it has. The term *dpi* refers to how many dots fit within each inch to recreate the image. More dpi produces more data and potentially a finer reproduction of the image or typography. A 72-dpi, or *low-res*, scan will show jagged edges of pixelation when printed. Many consumer-level digital cameras can now shoot a file that converts to 300-dpi print quality at 8 × 10".

LPI and DPI

When a continuous-tone, chemically processed photograph is scanned, it is converted into dots on an electronic file. The more dots, the higher the resolution, or dpi.

There is a relationship between the resolution of your scan and the lines per inch of the final printed piece. For a good-quality printed piece, pay attention to this relationship.

Do you know the optimum LPI of your printed piece? If not, ask the printer and look at the LPI list on page 201. LPI will vary depending on the paper used for printing. LPI is sometimes called *screen frequency* or *screen ruling.* For halftones, a final dpi resolution of 1.5 or 2 times the LPI usually works well. The formula is LPI × 1.5 = dpi scanning resolution. Remember that resizing the image can change the dpi, so plan accordingly.

SCANNING SUGGESTIONS

■ Using a retouching program to sharpen an image will produce a cleaner looking file. A blurry scan may not be improved with higher resolution, but it will look better when software sharpening filters, such as Photoshop's unsharp mask filter, are applied.

■ When scanning, crop away the white borders. They create data that adds to the file size. If any cropping is desirable, do it in the scanning stage.

■ A line-art image will not need to be screened when it is scanned. When creating a line-art scan, use very high resolution and use sharpening. Image resolution does not need to be higher than the output resolution, but if the file is going to an imagesetter for a RIP, try for at least 800 dpi on a line-art scan.

■ Every time photographic material is duplicated in a compressed JPEGfile format, image degeneration, or loss of information, occurs. Do not resave JPEG files. (See the section on File Formats.)

File Links

To insert scans or other graphics files into a layout program, the computer must find those files. To find a file, the computer searches along a path established when the graphic was imported into the layout program. This path is known as a *link.*

There are several reasons why this link may not be found. If the graphic was renamed or moved to another folder, the link could be broken. All graphics files should be sent to the printer along with the job if the job has various software graphics assembled in a page layout program. These files should be in the same folder that uses the graphics.

File Formats

The way an image is stored on a disk determines which programs can open, read, and edit that image. Two of the primary formats for storing graphic images on disk are TIFF and EPS, although there are many more formats. If an image is not stored in the proper format, it will not appear as an option to open or import into another program.

TIFF (tagged image file format) is a widely used bitmapped file format. It is appropriate for scanned images. Almost every program that works with bitmaps can use the TIFF format.

EPS (encapsulated PostScript) is an object-oriented file format that is excellent for storing graphics of any kind. A PostScript file consists of a series of text commands in a page-description language. This programming language was created to put type and graphics on paper. EPS is a refined form of PostScript that will allow an object-oriented *or* bitmapped program to open the file for editing.

JPEG (Joint Photographic Experts Group) is a compressed file format that produces graphics with a small file size. It is used for graduations or photographic images and is especially useful for Web elements and e-mail.

GIF (graphics interchange format) supports 256 indexed colors; most image editing programs can read and write GIF image files, but this format is not compatible with page-layout or illustration programs. It is useful for multimedia and Web page design, because a special plug-in is not needed to view its animation.

PICT is a Mac object-oriented file format. It handles bitmap and vector images well. Files should be converted to TIFF or EPS before placing in a page layout program such as InDesign, PageMaker, or QuarkXPress.

Once you understand the basic concept of file links and file formats, it clears up a lot of questions about why an image may not appear correctly on-screen when imported into another program. At a more advanced level, you will learn more about this topic.

Compression

Sometimes a file is simply too large for a storage device. In that case, data can be compressed to shrink the number of bytes needed for storage. Two methods are used to compress bitmapped data: *lossless compression* and *lossy compression*. Lossless methods give less compression but preserve the original image. Lossy methods give high compression but lose information in the original file. For example, JPEG is a lossy compression method that throws away some high-frequency variations in color. RLE (run-length encoding) is a lossless method that depends on batch-processing adjacent pixels with identical values.

CONCLUSION

There is a great deal to know about preparing artwork for reproduction. The better you as a beginning designer understand the tools and procedures of offset reproduction, the better you will be at reproducing your original designs in print. **Figure 11-15** was created at a high dpi and corresponding LPI for a large glossy poster.

All digital files prepared for offset reproduction must be clean and accurate. Next we'll summarize how to achieve accurate files.

Preparing Electronic Files for a Service Bureau

■ Assemble your file in a page layout program. It is easier to RIP files from a layout program than from an image manipulation program.

- Bring all your images from Illustrator, Freehand, and Photoshop into the final document as EPS files.
- Select the automatic trapping option in your layout program, and ask the service bureau to check your trapping.
- All files must be CMYK if you are doing full-color output.
- If you are using Photoshop, check the color picker menu for an alert symbol. If the triangle has an exclamation point in it, the selected screen color will not print accurately in printer's inks.

- Include all your original scans and vector graphics files.
- Be sure all documents are linked. Check the links menu in Quark, Illustrator, or the like. If files are missing, locate and include them.
- Supply all fonts used in your document or convert them to Outline or rasterize them.
- Organize and label all these files on a disk. Select Print Window from the desktop menu and make a print of your file folders on the disk. Send this print, along with a proof print of your file, to the service bureau or printing firm.

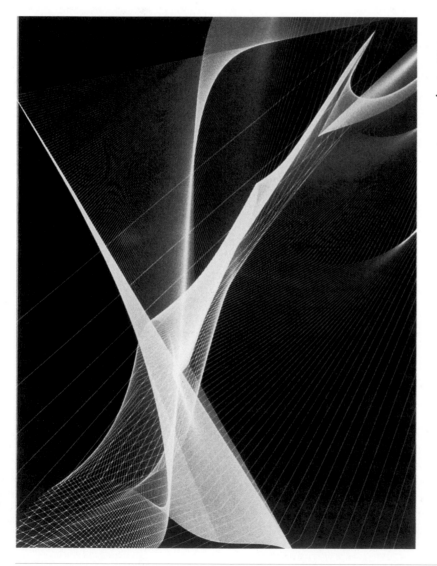

● **11-15** No Hope Can Exist Without Reason. *Melvin Pruett, computer artist; Julius Friedman, art director/ designer. This image was used as a poster for Brown Cancer Center.*

TERMINOLOGY

See glossary
for
definitions.

HTML	GIF	Indexed Color
URL	Lossless	Hyperlink
Protocol	JPEG	Tables
Domain Name	Lossy	Frames
Pathname	Dithering	

Web Design

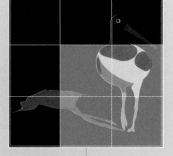

KEY POINTS There are many similarities between print design and
Web design. There are also a number of differences between production
for print and production for the Web. This chapter discusses these similarities and differences. It also introduces the basic structure of designing and
creating files for the Web.

INTRODUCTION

The Web has quickly become one of the most powerful and
exciting tools for designers today. The first Web sites were
created by computer scientists using an early, relatively limited version of *HTML* (hypertext markup language). These
sites were linear, text based, and unhampered by fine distinctions in typography because users set their font viewing
preferences on their own computers.

In the 21st century, Web and motion graphics takes us
beyond both text and image. As we know, human perception is a blend of sensory input from sight, hearing, touch,
taste, and smell—all shaped by memory. Increasingly, new
media can involve the senses of the human body by including sound and movement. They can help us develop new
ways of visualizing reality and sharing data. The Web is an
interactive medium with few geographic boundaries.

GLOBAL VILLAGE

New mass-media technologies are linked to changes in
social structure. Increasingly, as the medium of the World
Wide Web allows ease of international communication, our
communication and design issues become a shared world-

wide experience. The new media are vitally linked to the actualization of Canadian media theorist Marshall McLuhan's concept of a global village (see this text's accompanying Web site). These media are also linked to the establishment and redefinition of cultural and personal identity.

The telephone, the microscope, and the telescope are examples of earlier technologies that extended the range of our senses. Now we can see inside storms and along chains of molecules. From book to photograph to computer disk, our means of storing and retrieving information has grown. New media technologies rely strongly on visual communication, requiring users to be visually literate. We must be knowledgeable about both the *production* and the *consumption* of images. Because media technologies are constantly evolving, we need to be prepared to renew our knowledge base constantly throughout our careers.

Digital Focus

An integral member of the creative design partnership is the tool itself. The precursors of today's computers were number crunchers developed in the 1940s, during and after World War II. In the early 1950s scientists at MIT (the Massachusetts Institute of Technology) developed a computer system that could show the position of a flying aircraft as a moving dot on a vector display. This was a forerunner of computer graphics. Today computer-generated graphics are revolutionizing the way we communicate with one another around the globe. New technology and new ways of seeing are inseparable. Research that led to the development of the Web dates back to the 1960s at MIT and the U.S. Department of Defense (DoD). In 1969 the DoD commissioned a research project aimed at linking the separate computer networks of the military contractors and universities performing military research. This project led to the establishment of TCP/IP, the protocols now used to allow computers to communicate with each other throughout the Internet. Currently Yahoo! alone has more than 300 million users around the world. The Web is a nonlinear, interactive medium with few geographic boundaries. It allows ease of international exchange, as our communication and design media become a shared worldwide experience.

The Web-based medium is very different from print, because it is nonlinear and interactive. DVDs can also be burned with nonlinear, interactive information, using programs such as Macromedia Director, but the Web is the most powerful of the interactive media. Web data can be delivered simultaneously around the world, freed from the physical constraints of traditional media. Time and space are easily traveled via the Web.

When you type an address into a Web browser such as Netscape Navigator or Internet Explorer, your computer sends a request over the Internet for a specific URL address. The file at that address is then downloaded over the Internet to your computer. Finally, the browser displays the file. The *URL* (Uniform Resource Locator) is the address entered to access a particular Web site. This URL consists of 3 parts:

- **Protocol** = http://
- **Domain name** = www.server.com
- **Pathname** = folder/filename.ext

The *protocol* is the communications language the URL uses. The *domain name* is the server where the desired file is located. The *pathname* is a particular file at a site. For example, **http://www.portfolio.com** takes you to a site for viewing artists' and designers' portfolios (**Figure 12-1**), and **http://www.portfolio.com/search/search_quickfinder.html** takes you to a particular page at that site for a quick search of their offerings. (See the accompanying Web site.)

There are many similarities and differences between print-based and Web-based design. Let's begin by examining the similarities and then look at the differences.

COMMON METHODOLOGY

- Begin any publication by defining the message and the audience.
- Familiarize yourself with the competition.
- Research and analyze the available resources.

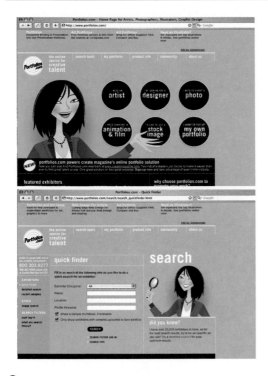

12-1 *Web pages viewed with Netscape Navigator.*
Copyright 2004 Portfolios.com.

- Organize the content. In Web design that means developing a flow chart for content. **Figure 12-2** shows a typical student flow chart for a portfolio site.
- Design the visuals, developing a look and feel tied by a common visual and conceptual theme.
- Produce the Web site or print piece.

DESIGN SIMILARITIES

A book or magazine presents information in a sequence of pages, as does a Web site. All pages should be tied together with a similar visual treatment, such as a uniform grid, a consistent choice of font, and alignment of typography.

In addition, a successful publication, whether online or in print, typically uses a visual and conceptual theme to unite the publication. Consistency in placement and treatment of items such as page numbers and navigation bars or buttons is important.

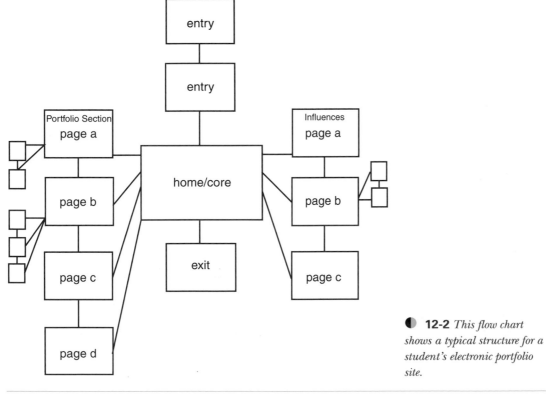

12-2 *This flow chart shows a typical structure for a student's electronic portfolio site.*

In **Figure 12-3a**, a pebble functions as a navigation button, generating animated water-like waves. The color for this site was carefully chosen to set an overall tone. Remember, color sets a mood and communicates a message, whatever your method of output. Each section of a Web site or a print publication can be color coded.

The 20th century produced wonderful examples of graphic design. A study of basic design principles applied to the field of graphic design/communication shows a number of visual principles that seem to cross cultures and decades. The gestalt unit-forming principles of visual perception form a basis for design of Web graphics as well as print media. Repetition and variation, rhythm, continuation, and figure/ground treatment are fundamental to the design of any publication. Although various cultures have devised unique design solutions using these visual components, all cultures deal with these visual founda-

tions. **Figure 12-3b** shows a design integration of ceramics, graphics, and Web site.

PRODUCTION SIMILARITIES

A bottom-line production similarity between print publication and online publication is that when a Web site is mounted online or a print piece is sent to press, all elements must be prepared correctly in order to function properly.

DESIGN DIFFERENCES

A book or magazine presents linear information. The pages follow each other sequentially from front to back. The structure of the information flow is one-directional and relatively simple to create. Information on the Web is nonlinear and interactive. **Figure 12-4a** shows a student Web portfolio with multiple choices on its home/core page. **Figure 12-4b** shows a direction pursued.

● **12-3a** *These four sequential pages from* **Leah Shea's** *Web portfolio display her use of a consistent, unifying style as well as highly interactive buttons and links.*

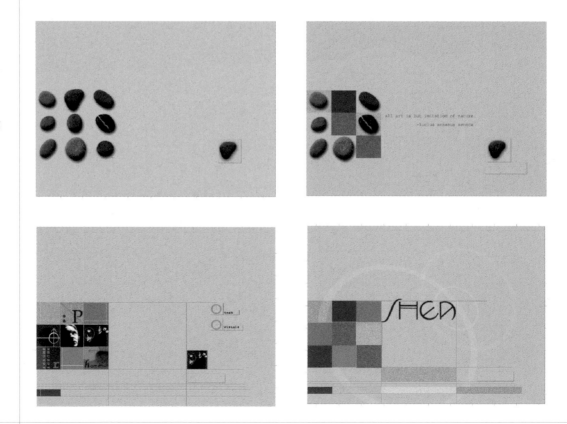

12-3b *Breayn Park created this Web site portfolio that showcases her work as a double major with a BFA in ceramics and graphics. The quiet, subtle Web pages echo the shapes and colors in her ceramic sculpture, while the graphic design work also shows her preference for subtle color.*

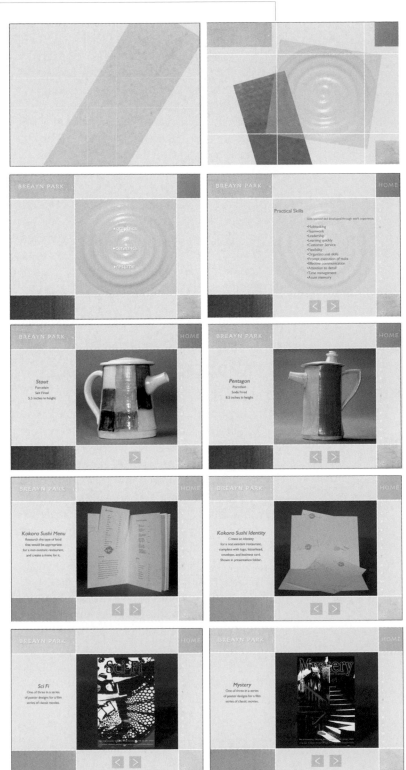

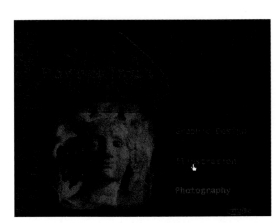

12-4a *This home page offers a choice of three directions. One direction leads to the portfolio section, which offers three subcategories.*

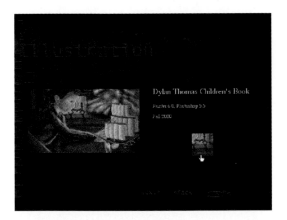

12-4b *Following the Illustration subcategory in the portfolio section takes the viewer to a page with interactive show/hide behaviors on the buttons.*

The buttons on this portfolio site have interactive show/hide behaviors.

The structure of Web-site information flow tends to be complex and should be diagrammed before the site is created. It is possible to get stuck out on a limb on a Web site, with no links back into the information flow, causing a viewer to end the session. A successful flow leaves the viewer only a click or two from the home/core page.

Time, motion, and sound are important components of Web design. You will want to learn the design sensibilities and the production skills necessary to create animation and sound files that communicate the intended message. All design communicates a message, but it may not have the desired effect if the designer lacks skill.

PRODUCTION DIFFERENCES

In terms of production, online publication differs from print publication in many ways. The dpi of image scans, availability of fonts, appropriateness of file formats and sizes, and color gamuts of RGB versus CMYK must all be learned anew for their application to Web graphics. Consider the ephemeral quality of the online environment, with the variable characteristics of its users and their equipment, versus the concrete reality of the printed page. This is a very important difference. Download time is also a crucial issue in Web design that does not exist in print graphics. What's more, in Web graphics, naming conventions must be understood and rigidly adhered to.

The Web is a picky medium, and it is vital to understand its rules in order to reach the audience with the intended message.

WHAT ARE THE RULES?

Naming Your Files

Filenames use different conventions and restrictions, depending on the operating system (Windows, Mac OS X, UNIX).

Because the server computer mounting your site may run an operating system different from yours, name your files so that they can be used on the server computer. Use filenames that are no longer than eight characters, followed by a three- or four-character extension. Do not use spaces or other special symbols; use only lowercase letters and numbers. For example, a Web page would have an html extension. Name your first page index.html, and your image and GIF animation assets with recognizable names of no more than eight characters, followed by the extension .JPEG or .GIF (**Figure 12-5**).

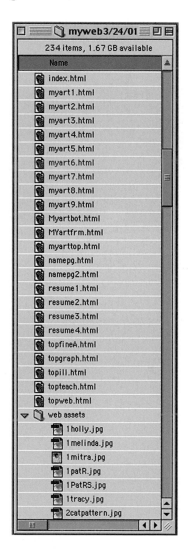

12-5 *Web-site directories follow strict naming conventions.*

Graphic Design Basics

Keep all files related to your site in one folder, with sections grouped together either by folders or naming conventions.

Resolution

Prepare final Web files at 72 dpi. Keep in mind, though, that the best results often come from scanning or otherwise preparing images at a higher resolution and reducing the file later. Keep an unflattened high-resolution version of your image files, so you can go back and make all changes on the original.

Print graphics at a resolution of 72 dpi look terrible. However, Web graphics are displayed on monitors. The Mac monitor has a resolution of about 72 pixels per inch (ppi), while the default on a PC is slightly higher. The bigger the monitor is, the more pixels it can display on-screen. A larger monitor simply displays a larger image, not a higher-resolution image.

File Size

File size, measured in bytes, is the amount of disk space required to store a file. The larger the images, and the more complex and numerous the elements added to a page, the longer that page will take to view in the browser window.

Keep graphics as small and concise as possible to avoid long download times and frustrated users. Reuse graphics on your site. Once a graphic is used, it is downloaded. Downloaded graphics are cached in memory, eliminating the need to download the graphics again.

Flat, solid areas of color reduce a file's size considerably. Top-to-bottom gradations create a smaller file size than right-to-left gradations.

Monitor Size

For the most conservative size, guaranteed to reach all users, keep important elements of text and graphics of your Web page within a 640 × 480 pixel area. Reserve the rest of the window for decorative ele-

ments. Although most people have a larger monitor, they often surf the Web with more than one window open. If that size is too restrictive for you as a designer, an 800 × 600 display is usually safe. To get an approximate idea of how your file will look on various monitors, go to Chooser>Monitors>Resolutions and change the default, or use the size pop-up at the bottom of the Dreamweaver page. As shown in **Figure 12-6a**, the bottom of the window contains information on the file's download speed, based on the Internet connection. It also contains screen size viewing options. **Figure 12-6b** shows a linked page of artwork.

12-6a, b *Tracy Landowski created this section of her student portfolio Web site to indicate her personal design influences. This site, created in Dreamweaver, is unified throughout by its visual treatment.*
Copyright Macromedia Dreamweaver.

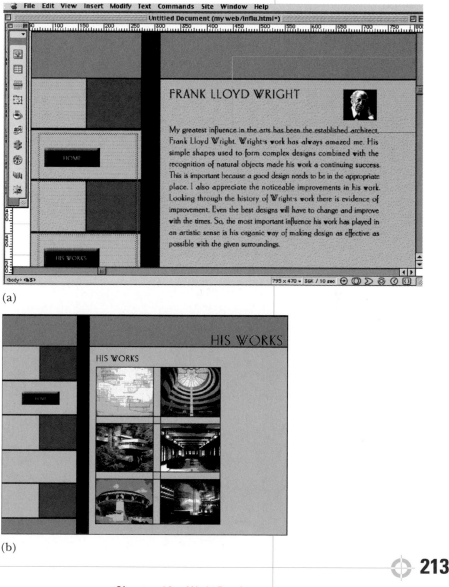

(a)

(b)

If your monitor is 640 × 480, and you change its default resolution to 800 × 600, you'll have more pixels, but they'll be smaller. A setting of 1024 × 768 will give even more pixels, showing more image. The converse is also true. A Web file you create to fill a 1024 × 768 screen will be too large to view on someone else's 640 × 480 screen.

File Formats

A file format tells a computer what kind of file it is dealing with. The Web accepts *GIF* (graphics interchange format) and *JPEG* (Joint Photographic Experts Group). Both of these are compressed file formats, producing graphics with reduced file sizes. The GIF is used for images featuring type and flat-color images. It is a *lossless* file format, which means that it compresses graphics without eliminating detail and is designed for 8-bit (256 colors or fewer) graphics. You can reduce file size and improve loading time by saving solid-color graphics as a GIF.

Use *JPEG* for graduations or photographic images. Complex graphics with photo-based imagery reproduce better as JPEG. It is a *lossy* file format, which removes data from an image when it compresses a file. Designed for displaying 24-

bit true color, it can describe a larger, more photograph-like image with less data, making for a smaller file and a faster download.

PNG (portable network graphics) is another compressed, lossless file format. Not all browsers support PNGs, but one of their advantages is 256 levels of transparency.

Color

Converting files to the RGB color palette is the final image production step. Rendering an image with a limited number of colors produces a pixilated effect called *dithering*, in which pixels of two colors will be juxtaposed to create the illusion that three colors are present. To avoid dithering of solid-color GIF files, use Web-safe colors from a 216 Web-safe color table. (This produces an 8-bit file.) Current versions of Photoshop let you "save for Web" and help you through a pop-up window of choices to specify the format and color table (**Figure 12-7** shows JPEG and GIF options). You can also create a GIF with a reduced color palette by choosing Image>Mode>Indexed Color. Then choose Web from the Palette menu and save as CompuServe GIF.

Changing an image from RGB to *Indexed Color* reduces an image's color usage from RGB's 16.8 million colors to a smaller

● **12-7a, b** *The Photoshop Save for Web pop-up allows the user to specify JPEG or GIF, as well as transparency and color palette.*

Adobe Product screenshots reprinted with permission from Adobe Systems Incorporated.

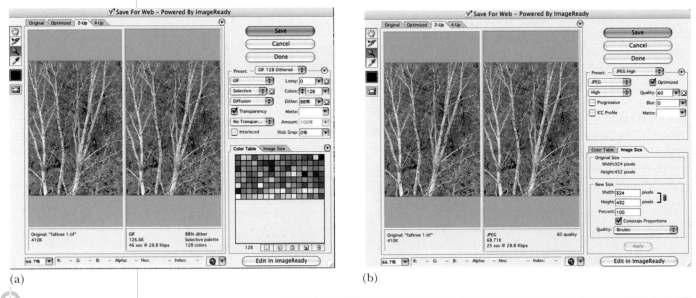

(a)   (b)

palette. You can choose from a number of standard color palettes, including the 216 Web-safe colors, the 256-color Mac and Windows system palettes, or custom palettes such as adaptive.

When preparing a GIF image, the two palettes to consider are the Web-safe and the adaptive. Both are accessible from the Photoshop Mode/Indexed color command from the Image menu. If the graphic contains photographic imagery and some flat-color elements filled with Web-safe colors, choose an adaptive palette. It is made up of colors most appropriate for the particular image. Dithering is most noticeable in solid flat-color areas. Choosing colors from the reduced Web-safe palette as often as possible when creating flat-color graphics helps reduce dithering. When composing background colors in Photoshop that need to match the background of your Web site, it is advisable to use Web-safe color. Increasingly, software has been updated to make such choices for you.

WEB COMPONENTS

Pages and Sites

A Web site is composed of separate, linked pages. The site must be mounted on a server if it is to be viewed anywhere but from a disk.

Links

A link (also known as a *hyperlink*) is an active part of a document.

Clicking a link can take you to another part of the same Web page, to other Web pages on your hard disk, or to a location on a remote computer. Every link contains the Web address for the page that the link refers to. This Web address is called the page's URL.

Tables and Frames

Tables allow you to precisely align online layout elements into columns and rows.

They also keep data from jumping around when a window is resized. Think of tables as similar to the underlying grid that provides structure to a print publication design.

Frames are very different from tables, although they look similar. A frame splits a Web page into sections. Typically one stationary frameset on the left side has links that call varying content into the frame on the right side. Each frame is actually a separate Web page. Frames are excellent devices for controlling the presentation and flow of information.

Animation and Sound

GIF files can be used to create animations. Adobe ImageReady, which comes packaged with Photoshop, is an excellent program for creating small animations. Flash is the top program on the Web for generating sophisticated motion that downloads quickly, as well as for designing interactive sites. Interactivity means that something happens in response to a viewer action. For example, clicking an image or button can cause a sound file or animation to run. There are many forms of interactivity on Web sites. The simplest one is a button link to another page. **Figure 12-8** is a Flash interactive file that shows a new image and a connected song as each of three buttons is clicked.

Web Software

All Web sites are actually created with HTML (hypertext markup language). Designers do not necessarily need to know this language, but a little background is advisable. Many software packages write the HTML for you invisibly. Third-semester graphics students produced several examples in this chapter by using Dreamweaver. It is an excellent professional design and production tool for the Web from Macromedia, although several other programs on the market also do a good job. Simpler programs include PageMill and FrontPage. Netscape Navigator comes packaged with

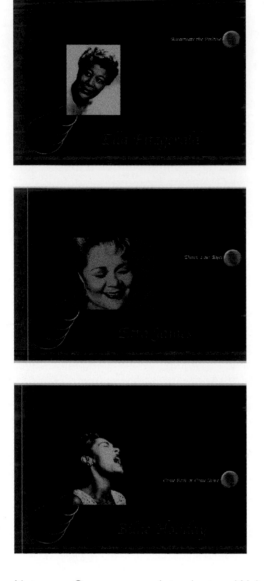

12-8 *Dawn Disch created this interactive sound animation in Flash as a tribute to women who sing the blues. Clicking a button presents an image and plays a corresponding music clip.*

Netscape Composer, an introductory Web program that many people already have on their computers.

Web Publishing

A great variety of online services for Web publishing are available. America Online and CompuServe are familiar to most. Many local Internet service providers offer access to the Web, e-mail, and free space for a Web site.

The location **http://www.geocities.com** also offers free space for publishing your Web site. Like commercial television, it runs advertisements to turn a profit, so be prepared to have ads running along with your pages. It gives excellent practice in troubleshooting and mounting a site.

SUMMARY

Characteristics of Good Web-Site Design

- Appealing entry page or sequence that attracts viewers
- Clearly marked navigational devices
- All elements (links and assets) functional
- Integrated design with possible use of metaphor or symbol
- Good use of design basics
- Acceptable download time
- Communication of an appropriate message to an identified audience

In the way it presents information the Web combines modernist and postmodernist values. It reflects both modernism's emphasis on rational organization and postmodernism's emphasis on eclecticism and layering.

Critique

The critique of a print-based or Web-based design should center on issues specific to the design medium. The critique should also consider the larger issues of medium and message and cultural impact.

- Consider the overall complexity of the site. How many elements such as JPEG files, GIF files, animations, and links are there?
- How complete is the research on the site's topic?
- How successfully is the visual and conceptual theme communicated?
- Is there a clear logic to the navigational structure?
- Are the files error free?
- How well does each image fit the intended screen size?

216

How is the computer a tool like any other throughout history? How does it present ways of seeing and shaping reality that make it significantly different from tools of the past?

What are the constants we bring to the use of new technology?

What is truly new about the new media that cannot be duplicated by any other media?

PROJECTS

These three assignments take the designer from Web-page design to Web-site production. Begin with the first assignment, and ask your instructor about continuing.

Web-Site Review

Choose a Web site to evaluate. Use the terms found throughout the chapter to identify elements. Refer to the list Characteristics of Good Site Design to help you in your evaluation. Refer to the Critique section for additional ideas. You'll also want to use these references to plan and evaluate your own design work and that of your classmates if you continue to the next two assignments.

Beginning Web-Page Design

Refer to the methodology discussed earlier in this chapter to plan and design a small Web site of about six pages. These will be prepared as print pages. Research and prepare a short presentation on a graphic designer mentioned in Chapter 2. Gather and prepare several images for your topic. The Internet is a good research tool. Prepare a sample flow chart to show the instructor. Then construct the pages in Photoshop, writing a brief amount of copy to include. Be sure to design button icons intended to act as links between pages.

Print these pages for presentation and critique. Discuss their intended navigational structure and overall design theme.

If you have time, either now or in a later class, "slice" the Photoshop pages in ImageReady and insert them into a Web program. **Figure 12-9** shows a Web page that uses words and photographs as links.

Beginning Web-Site Design

Assemble your buttons, images, and text in a program such as Netscape Composer to prepare your Web site to mount online. Include active links and tables. View this site on the monitor for final critique. Consider using GeoCities or another Web site to actually post your design on the Internet. Both Composer and GeoCities are free and come with tutorials.

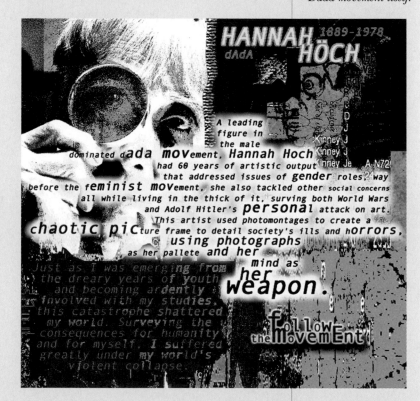

● **12-9** *Adam McKee's Web site for his student portfolio includes research on Dada artist Hannah Höch, as well as a highly individual surface treatment of type and image. Clicking on various words leads to pages that discuss Höch's life and the Dada movement and show a gallery of her artwork. This site is creative and unpredictable, mirroring characteristics of the Dada movement itself.*

GLOSSARY

Abstraction   Simplification of existing shapes.

Acetate Overlay   Clear plastic overlay that permits the positioning of units on a pasteup that cannot be put together on a single sheet.

Additive Primaries   Red, blue, and green, which combine to produce white light.

Advertising   The activity of attracting public attention to a product or business. Advertising appears in paid announcements in print, broadcast, or electronic media.

Advertising Illustrations   Images created for the purpose of selling a product or a service.

Aerial Perspective   Creation of a sense of depth and distance through softening edges and decreasing value contrast.

Aliasing   Visual effect that occurs on a computer's visual display screen whenever the detail in the image exceeds the resolution available. It looks like a "stair stepping."

Alternating Rhythm   A regular variation on a repeated visual theme.

Analog   Signal that may be varied continuously. Computers cannot process this kind of signal, so their information must be converted to digital. Analog refers to everything in the real, noncomputerized world.

Analogous Colors   Hues that lie next to one another on the color wheel.

Animation and Motion Graphics
Animation is a moving image created by moving quickly through a series of still images. Motion Graphics involves the change of an object's position in space but does not necessarily use still images, It may be video based.

Applied Art and Design   Disciplines that use the principles and elements of design to create functional pieces for commercial use.

Arbitrary Color   Assigns whatever color seems artistically desirable to artwork, rather than photo-real colors.

Ascender   Section of a lowercase letter that extends above the x-height.

Asymmetrical Layout   See definitions for *Asymmetry* and *Layout*.

Asymmetry   Distribution of shapes of different visual weights over a picture plane to create an overall impression of balance.

Balance   Distribution of the visual weight of design elements.

Bit   Abbreviation of Binary Digit. The most basic unit of digital information. A bit can be expressed in only one of two states, 0 or 1, meaning on or off, yes or no. This is actually the only information that a computer can process. Eight bits are required to store one alphabet character.

Bitmap   Text character or image comprised of dots. A bitmap is the set of bits representing the position of items forming an image on the display screen.

Bitmapped   Font or image comprised of dots (pixels), as distinct from an object-oriented graphic. Characterized by jagged edges. Also known as a raster image.

Bitplane   A single bitmap is a bitplane and is only one bit deep, storing a zero or one in each pixel location to represent black or white.

Bleed   Part of an image that extends beyond the edge of a page and is trimmed off.

Body Type   Type smaller than 14 point, generally used for the main body of text. Also called text type.

Boldface   Heavy version of a typeface.

Byte   Unit of information made up of eight bits. Bytes are commonly used to represent alphanumeric characters or the integers from 0 to 255.

CAD/CAM Stands for computer-aided design/computer-aided manufacturing.

Camera-Ready Art Artwork that has been assembled and prepared for reproduction on a process camera.

Cartesian Coordinates Numerically represent a two-dimensional area. The horizontal axis is the X axis, while the vertical axis is the Y axis.

CD-ROM Compact disk-read only memory. A storage system of large capacity.

Centered Type Lines of type of varying length that have been centered over one another.

Central Processing Unit (CPU) Part of a computer system that contains the circuits that control and execute all data.

Character Count Number of characters in a piece of copy. This number is used in copyfitting calculations.

Choke Method of altering the thickness of a letter or solid shape, used in trapping to ensure peoper registration of colors.

Clip Art Libraries of copyright-free imagery available in print or electronic form.

Closure When the eye completes a line or curve in order to form a familiar shape.

CMYK Process colors of cyan, magenta, yellow, and black inks used in four-color printing.

Color The way an object absorbs or reflects light.

Color Scheme Categories of color combinations based on position on the color wheel. (See *Analogous, Complementary, Monochromatic*.)

Color Wheel Part of color theory that demonstrates color relationships on a circle.

Combination Mark Trademark that combines symbol and logo.

Complementary Hues Colors that are opposite one another on the color wheel.

Comprehensive (COMP) Highly finished layout for presentation.

Computer Graphics Branch of computer science that deals with creating and modifying pictorial data.

Continuation When the eye is carried smoothly into the line or curve of an adjoining object.

Continuous Tone Illustration that contains continuous shades between the lightest and darkest tones without being broken up by the dots of a halftone screen or a digital file.

Continuous Tone Art Art, such as illustrations or photographs, with a range of values. Must be reproduced with a halftone screen.

Copyfitting Process of determining the amount of space it will take to set copy in a specific type size and style.

Corporate Identity Elements of design by which an organization establishes a consistent identity through various forms of printed materials and promotions.

Corporate Photography Photography created for a variety of corporate publications including annual reports.

Counters White shapes inside a letterform.

Cropmarks Short, fine lines drawn on the image to indicate a cropped area, or at the corners of a pasteup to indicate where a printed sheet will be trimmed. When used to indicate trim size, they can be called trim marks.

Cropping To eliminate the unwanted sections of image area.

Digital Signal that can only be in one of two states, on or off. Information, such as sound or image, that is in a form that can be electronically manipulated.

DIMM Dual In-line Memory Module.

Direct Advertising Any form of advertising issued directly to the prospect through any means that does not involve the traditional mass media.

Direct Mail   Advertising in which the advertiser acts as the publisher.

Direct Marketing   Sale of goods and services direct to the consumer without intermediaries. Can include door-to-door sales.

Disk   Off-system data storage device for computers, consisting of one or more flat circular plates coated with magnetized material.

Display Type   Any type larger than 14 point.

Dithering   Technique used to add extra pixels to an image to smooth it, or to reduce the number of colors or grays in an image by replacing them with average values. It smooths the jagged effects of pixellation.

Domain Name   A series of alphanumeric strings separated by periods, such as *www.server.com,* that is an address of a computer network connection and that identifies the owner of the address.

Dot Gain   Aberration that can occur in a printed image, caused by the tendency of halftone dots to grow in size. This can lead to inaccurate and coarsely printed results.

DPI   Dots per inch. This refers to the number of dots (resolution) a device is capable of producing.

Dropout   Copy that is reversed out of a halftone or a tint screen background.

Duotone   Two-color halftone reproduction made from one-color, continuous tone artwork.

Editorial Content Theme   A repeated theme based on a conceptual, word-based idea.

Egyptian   A slab-serif type category.

E-Mail   Electronic mail sent between computers either over a network or with a modem over phone lines.

EPS   Encapsulated PostScript. A standard graphics file format based on vectors, or object-oriented information.

Figure/Ground   Relationship between the figure and the background of an image.

File Format   A type of format for encoding the information in a data file. Some common image file formats include TIFF, JPG, and BMP.

Flush Left and Flush Right   Formats for typography that give an aligned left or right edge.

Focal Point   Area of a design toward which the viewer's eye is primarily drawn.

Font   Complete set of type of one size and one variation of a typeface.

Four-Color Process   Printing process that reproduces full-color images by using cyan, magenta, and yellow plus black for added density.

Frames   On the Web, frames give a method of displaying more than one page at a time within the same window. Frames are the separate viewable areas.

Gestalt   Unified configuration having properties that cannot be derived from simple addition of its parts.

GIF   Graphic Interchange Format. A file format used for transferring graphics files between different computer systems via the internet. It creates very small data files.

Gigabyte   Unit of measure to describe 1,024 megabytes.

Golden Section   A mathematical proportion in which the ratio between a small section and a larger section is equal to the ratio between the larger section and smaller sections put together. Shapes defined by the golden ratio have long been considered aesthetically pleasing in Western cultures. The ratio is about 8:13.

Graphics Standard Manual   A master corporate identity plan.

Grid Layout   An arrangement of horizontal and vertical lines that produce a network of squares and rectangles giving underlying structure to elements in page layout.

Gripper Edge   Leading edge of paper as it feeds into a press. Usually it calls for an unprinted margin of about 3/8″ (1cm).

Gutter   Inner section of a page caught in the center binding.

Halftone   Reproduction of continuous-tone art, such as a photograph, through a screen that converts it into dots of various sizes.

Hard Copy   Printed copy of an image produced on a computer screen.

Hardware   Physical components of a computer graphics system, including all mechanical, magnetic, and electronic parts.

HLS   Hue, lightness, and saturation. A color model.

Horizontal Balance   Visual balancing of the left and right sides of a composition.

Hot Type   Typesetting in which the type is cast in molten metal.

HTML   Hyper Text Markup Language. A page description language used to format documents on the Web.

Hue   Name of a given color. Hue is one of the three properties of color.

Hyperlink   A Web link to other documents that is embedded within the original document. Clicking on the link will take users to another Web site or document.

Icon   In the study of semiotics, an icon is a sign that bears a direct relationship to the object described, such as realistic drawings and photographs.

Illustration   A specialized area of art that uses images to make an applied, visual statement, usually accompanying text.

Index   In Semiotics, a sign that bears a direct relationship to the object it represents without simply showing the object. For example, a shadow or a footprint of an animal.

Indexed Color   An image mode of a maximum of 256 colors that can reduce the file size of RGB images for use in Web pages.

Intellectual Unity   An idea-generated and word-dominated method of unifying a publication.

Intensity   Saturation or brightness of a color. Intensity is decreased by the addition of a gray or a complement.

Internet   Electronic network that spans the globe.

Interpolation   A computer process used to add or delete approximate pixel data when resizing an image.

Italics   The slanted version of a Roman type design originally derived from cursive handwriting.

JPEG   Joint Photographic Experts Group. A lossy data compression file format that creates small compressed files by discarding part of the data before compressing. The reconstructed file usually looks quite good on photographic images.

Justify   To align lines of type that are equal in length so both edges of the column are straight.

Kerning   Selectively altering the spaces between letter combinations for a better fit.

Keylining   Drawing an outline on a finished pasteup to indicate the exact position for art that will be stripped in by the printer. Used when hairline registration is important.

Kinesthetic Projection   A sensory experience stimulated by bodily movements and projected onto the images we view.

Layout   Page design for a piece to be printed or published electronically.

Leading   Amount of space placed vertically between lines of type.

Letterspacing   The adjustment of space between type characters by kerning or tracking.

Light Waves   The part of the electro-magnetic spectrum that contains visible light. The colors, from longest wavelength to shortest, are red, orange, yellow, green, blue, indigo, and violet.

Line Art   Black and white copy with no variations in value. Suitable for reproduction without a halftone screen.

Line Length   The length of a typeset line, traditionally measured in picas and points, but now measured in inches as well.

Link   A pointer in an HTML document that takes the user to another location by clicking on it.

Local Color   Retains the photo-realistic color of objects.

Logo   Tademark of unique type or letter-ing, spelling out the name of a company or product.

Lossless   A method of compression in which no data is discarded.

Lossy   A lossy image is one in which the image after compression has lost informa-tion. A lossy conversion process does not retain all the original information. JPEG is an example of a lossy compression method.

Lowercase   Small letters of an alphabet.

LPI   Lines per inch. Printing term refer-ring to the resolution of an image.

Market Research   A study of consumer groups and business competition used to define a projected market.

Master Page   Page to which certain attributes can be given, which can then be applied to any other page in a docu-ment.

Mechanical   Camera-ready pasteup, which contains all copy pasted in position for printing.

Memory   The recall of digital data on a computer. Usually referring to RAM or ROM.

Menu-Driven   Computer graphics system that operates when a user selects options from those displayed on the monitor.

Modern   Type category that has great variation between thick and thin strokes and thin, un-bracketed serifs.

Moiré   An unwanted pattern caused by the overlapping of multiple halftones or tint screens in incorrect positioning.

Monochromatic Color   Use of a single hue in varying values.

Network   Connection of two or more computers. This assemblage of computer hardware and software allows computers to share data, software, and other resources.

Nonobjective Shapes   Shapes that are pure design elements, not related to any pictorial source.

Object-Oriented   Graphics applications that allow the selection and manipulation of individual portions of an illustration or design. This is a characteristic of a vector graphic file and is the opposite of bitmapped graphics.

Old Style Type   Type category character-ized by mild contrast between thicks and thins, and by bracketed serifs.

Orphan   A short line that falls at the bot-tom of a column of text.

Pasteup   Assemblage of the elements of a layout, prepared for reproduction.

Path Layout   The harmonious arrange-ment of elements that assume no under-lying grid structure.

Path Name   The name of a file or folder listed with all parent folders. This is the full name that the computer uses for a folder or a file.

Phosphor   Material coating the inside of a picture tube. When an electron beam hits this coating, the phosphor emits light in proportion to the voltage of the beam.

Photo Illustration   Photography that illustrates an accompanying story.

Photo Journalism   Candid photography that captures a news event on location.

Pica   Typographic measurement of 1/16 inch (0.4 cm).

Pictogram   Symbol used to cross language barriers for international signage.

Picture Plane   Flat surface of a two-dimensional design, possessing height and width, but no depth.

Pixel   Individual picture element. It is the smallest element of a computer image that can be separately addressed.

Point   Typographic measurement of 1/72 inch, or 1/12 pica.

Postscript   Page-description language used to describe how a page is built up of copy, lines, images, and so on, for output to laser printers and high-resolution imagesetters.

Prepress Production   The reproduction processes that occur between design and printing.

Preseparated Art   Art that has been separated onto acetate overlays by the pasteup artist before being sent to the printer.

Primary Colors   Three basic pigment colors of light—red, blue, and green—from which all other colors can be made are called "additive" primaries because when added together they produce white light. "Subtractive" primaries are the magenta, cyan, and yellow of process printing.

Printer Font   High-resolution bitmaps or font outline masters used for the actual laying down of the characters on the printed page, as opposed to displaying on the screen.

Process Camera   Large graphic arts camera used to make film negatives and positives for platemaking.

Product Photography   The intent to promote or sell a product using photography.

Progressive Rhythm   When a repeated element changes in a regular fashion in layout design.

Proportion   The relationship in size of one component of a work of art to another. The size relationship of parts to a whole and to one another.

Protocol   A set of rules that hardware and software must observe in order to communicate with one another.

Proximity   Visually grouping by similarity in spatial location.

Radial Symmetry   Equal proportion around a central point like spokes radiating out from the center of a wheel.

Ragged Right (or Left)   Unjustified column of type in which lines of varying length are aligned on either the right or left side.

RAM   Random Access Memory.

Raster Graphics   Computer graphics comprised of bitmaps that create a grid of individual picture elements (pixels).

Rebuild Desktop   Rebuilding the desktop gets rid of obsolete material that builds up as a computer is used. Doing this on a regular basis improves the operation of the computer. The desktop is rebuilt by holding down Option-Command while restarting the system.

Registration   Fitting two or more printing images on the same paper in exact alignment.

Resizing   Changing the size of an image with an understanding of cropping and the retaining of correct proportions.

Resolution   Ability of a computer graphics system to make distinguishable the individual parts of an image.

Retail Advertising   Advertising sponsored by a retail establishment such as a clothing or motorcycle store.

Reversal   Change to opposite tonal values, as when black type is altered to white.

Reversible Figure/Ground   Relationship in which it is likely that figure and ground can be focused on equally.

RGB   Red, green, and blue are the primary colors of the additive color model used on the Web.

RIP   Raster Image Processing. Converting data into a form that can be output by a high-resolution imagesetter for use in commercial printing.

ROM   Read-Only Memory. ROM resides in a chip on the motherboard. This memory can be read from, but cannot be written to.

Roman   The standard characters of a font in which the characters are upright and not boldface.

Rough   Layout plan that comes after preliminary thumbnails and is usually executed in half or full size.

Runaround   Type fitted around a piece of artwork.

Sans Serif   Letterforms without serifs. *See* Serif.

Saturation   Intensity or brightness of a color. Saturation is decreased by the addition of gray or a complementary color.

Scan Line   On a raster-scan computer monitor, one traversal of an electronic beam across the picture.

Screen font   Low-resolution bitmaps of type characters that show the positioning and size of characters on a computer screen.

Secondary Colors   Hues obtained by mixing two primary colors.

Semiotics   The study of signs and symbols, what they mean and how they are used.

Serif   Stroke that projects off the main stroke of a letter at the bottom or the top.

Service Bureau   Company used by designers for high-resolution imagesetting. It provides an array of computer services from file conversions to scanning. Service bureaus RIP the information from disk onto film, for offset reproduction. Some printing companies do this work in house.

Shade   Darker value of a hue, created by adding black.

Shading Film   Commercially available textured screens of line art on a transfer sheet.

Shape   Figure that has visually definable edges.

Similarity   Visual grouping of images with similar shape, size, and color.

SIMM   Single In-line Memory Module. This plug-in board contains the chips some computers use for RAM.

Simultaneous Contrast   Colors, side by side, interact with one another, changing our perception of color accordingly.

Software   Computer programs.

Spec   Short for "to specify." To write type specifications (line length, size, style, leading) on copy.

Split Complementary   A color scheme based on one hue and the hues on either side of its complement on the color wheel.

Stable Figure/Ground   The unambiguous relationship of an object to background.

Stet   Latin word used when marking up copy to signify "let it stand."

Story Board   A series of sketches showing each shot of a scene or film in order.

Stress   The distribution of weight through the thinnest part of a letterform.

Subtractive Primaries   Magenta, cyan, and yellow—the colors left after subtracting one additive primary from white light.

Surprint   Line art superimposed over a screened area of the same color.

Symbol   Type of trademark to identify a company or product. It is abstract or pictorial but does not include letterforms.

Symmetrical Layout   See definitions for *Symmetry* and *Layout.*

Symmetry   Formal placement of design elements to create a mirror image on either side. A less common form of symmetrical balance also creates the mirror image vertically.

Tables   Boxes made up of rows and columns in which data, such as images and text, can be organized for placement on a Web page.

Technical Illlustration   The creation of scientific or technological ojects to illustrate a subject.

Tertiary Colors   Hues obtained by mixing a primary color with a secondary color.

Text Type   Book-size type, set in paragraphs, as opposed to headlines.

Thumbnail   First-stage miniature plan for a layout.

TIFF   Tagged Image File Format. This widely used file format is used for saving scanned, bitmapped images.

Tint   Light value of a hue, created by adding white.

Tint Screen   Flat, unmodulated light value made of evenly dispersed dots, usually achieved by stripping a piece of halftone film into the area on the negative that the artist has masked out.

Tone Hue that has been decreased in intensity by the addition of black or a complement.

Tracking   Adjustment of space between characters throughout a range of text.

Trademark   Any unique name or symbol used by a corporation or manufacturer to identify a product and to distinguish it from other products.

Transitional Type   Category of type that blends old style and modern, with emphasis on thick and thin contrast and gracefully bracketed serifs.

Trapping   Slight overlap of two colors to eliminate gaps that can occur due to normal registration problems during printing.

Tritone   An image that is printed using three colors. Typically, a black-and-white image is enhanced using the addition of two additional colors.

Trompe L'Oeil   French for "fool the eye." A two-dimensional representation that is so naturalistic that it looks actual or real (three-dimensional).

Type Categories   Typefaces grouped into categories such as Old Style, Transitional, Modern, Egyptian, and Sans Serif.

Type Family   Complete range of sizes and variations of a typeface.

Typeface   Style of lettering. Each family of typefaces may contain variations on that typeface, like "italic."

Typesetting   Composition of type by any method.

Unjustified Type   Lines of type set with equal word spacing and uneven length.

Uppercase   Capital letters.

URL   Uniform Resource Locator. This is the address of a resource on the Internet. World Wide Web URLs begin with "http://".

Value   Lightness or darkness of a color or a tone of gray.

Variety   Variations on a visual theme causing contrast in a design.

VDT   Visual Display Terrminal.

Vector Graphics   Type of computer graphics in which graphic data is represented by lines drawn from coordinate point to coordinate point.

Vertical Balance   Visual balancing of the upper and lower portions of a composition.

Visual Design Theme   A visual content that unites the pages of a layout.

Visual Direction   When the eye is directed in a particular direction across a composition.

Visual Rhythm   The repetition of shapes, values, color, and textures to set up a visual or intellectual pattern.

Visual Texture   Visual creation of an implied tactile texture.

Visual Unity   The placement of design elements to achieve a harmonious whole.

Visual Weight   Lightness or heaviness of a visual image.

Widow   Short line at the end of a paragraph that falls at the top or bottom of a column page, or a single word on a line by itself at the end of a paragraph. Also called an *orphan*.

Windows   Solid black or red areas of the pasteup that will convert into clear areas on the negative for a screen to be stripped onto.

Word Spacing   The varying space between words, often adjusted to create a justified line of copy.

X-Height   Height of the body of a lowercase letter like an *a*, with no ascenders or descenders.

BIBLIOGRAPHY

See the Webliography Links on the Accompanying Web Site.

CHAPTER 1

Applying the Art of Design

Albers, Josef, *Interaction of Color*. New Haven, Conn.: Yale University Press, 1972.

Baumgartner, Victor, *Graphic Games*. Englewood Cliffs, N.J.: Prentice-Hall, 1983.

Behrens, Roy, *Design in the Visual Arts*. Englewood Cliffs, N.J.: Prentice-Hall, 1984.

Bevlin, Marjorie, *Design Through Discovery*. New York: Holt, Rinehart and Winston, 1985.

Buchanan, Margolin, *Discovering Design*. University of Chicago Press, 1995.

Gomez, Edward, *New Design: Tokyo*. Gloucester, Mass.: Rockport Publishers, 1999.

Itten, Johannes, *The Art of Color*. New York: Van Nostrand Reinhold, 1974.

Kepes, Gyorgy, *Language of Vision*. Chicago: Paul Theobald, 1969.

Lauer, David, *Design Basics*. Harcourt Brace, 1995.

McKim, Robert H., *Experiences in Visual Thinking*. Monterey, Calif.: Brooks, Cole, 1980.

Rand, Paul, *Design Form and Chaos*. New Haven and London: Yale University Press, 1993.

Supon Design Group, *International Women in Design*. New York: Madison Square Press, Distributed by Van Nostrand Reinhart, 1993.

CHAPTER 2

Graphic Design History

Aynsley, Jeremy, *A Century of Graphic Design*. Hauppauge, N.Y.: Barrons, 2001

Bayer, Herbert, et al., eds., *Bauhaus 1919–1928*. New York: Museum of Modern Art, 1938.

Berryman, Gregg, *Notes on Graphic Design and Visual Communication*. Los Altos, Calif.: William Kaufmann, 1990.

Cirker, Hayward, and Blanche Cirker, *Golden Age of the Poster*. New York: Dover, 1971.

Craig, James, *Graphic Design Career Guide*. New York: Watson-Guptill Publications, 1983.

Friedman, Mildred, and Joseph Giovannini, eds., *Graphic Design in America: A Visual Language History*. New York: Harry Abrams, 1989.

Garner, Philippe, *Sixties Design*. Taschen, 1996.

Glaser, Milton, *Milton Glaser: Graphic Design*. Woodstock, N.Y.: The Overlook Press, Walker Art Center, 1983.

Green, Oliver, *Underground Art*. London, England: Studio Vista, 1990.

Greiman, April, *Hybrid Imagery: The Fusion of Technology and Graphic Design*. New York: Watson Guptil, 1990.

Heller, Steven, and Elinor Pettit, *Graphic Design Timeline*. New York: Allworth Press, 2000.

Hoch, Hannah, et al., *The Photomontages of Hannah Höch*. Minneapolis, Minn.: Walker Art Center, 1997.

Hoffman, Armin, *Graphic Design Manual*. New York: Van Nostrand Reinhold, 1965.

Hurlburt, Allen, *Layout: The Design of the Printed Page*. New York: Watson-Guptill Publications, 1977.

Jackson, Lesley, *The New Look and Design in the Fifties*. New York: Thames and Hudson, 1991.

Meggs, Philip, *A History of Graphic Design*. New York: Van Nostrand Reinhold, 1998.

Motherwell, Robert, *Dada Painters and Poets*. New York: Wittenborn, Schultz, 1951.

Müller-Brockmann, Josef, *The Graphic Artist and His Design Problems*. New York: Hastings House, 1961.

Müller-Brockmann, Josef, *A History of Visual Communication*. New York: Hastings House, 1971.

Nelson, Roy Paul, *Publication Design*. Dubuque, Iowa: William C. Brown, 1991.

Pesch and Weisbeck, *Technostyle*. Zurich: Olms, 1995.

Rand, Paul, *A Designer's Art*. New Haven, Conn.: Yale University Press, 1985.

Rand, Paul, *Thoughts on Design*. New York: Van Nostrand Reinhold, 1971.

Scheidig, Walter, *Crafts of the Weimar Bauhaus 1919–1924*. New York: Reinhold Publishing, 1967.

Schwartz, Lillian, *The Computer Artist's Handbook, Concepts, Techniques and Applications*. New York: W.W. Norton & Co., 1992.

Snyder, Peckolick, *Herb Lubalin*. New York: American Showcase, 1985.

Varnedoe, Gapnik, *High & Low: Modern Art and Popular Culture*. New York: Museum of Modern Art, 1991.

Velthoven, Willem, and Jorinde Seijdel, *Multimedia Graphics, The Best of Global Hyperdesign*. Chronicle Books, 1997.

Wheeler, Daniel, *Art Since Mid-Century, 1945 to the Present*. New York: Vendome Press, 1991.

Wrede, Stuart, *The Modern Poster*. New York: The Museum of Modern Art, 1988.

CHAPTERS 3–5

Perception

Arnheim, Rudolf, *Art and Visual Perception*. Berkeley, Calif.: University of California Press, 1974.

Behrens, Roy, *False Colors: Art, Design and Modern Camouflage*. Dysart, Iowa: Bobolink Books, 2002.

Bloomer, Carolyn M., *Principles of Visual Perception*. New York: Van Nostrand Reinhold, 1976.

Gombrich, E. H., *Art and Illusion: A Study in the Psychology of Pictorial Representation*. New York: Pantheon Books, 1960.

Gombrich, E. H., Julian Hochberg, and Max Black, *Art, Perception, and Reality*. Baltimore: Johns Hopkins University Press, 1972.

Goodman, Nelson, *Languages of Art*. Indianapolis: Bobbs-Merrill, 1968.

Graphis Letterhead: An International Compilation of Letterhead Design. Zurich, Switzerland: Graphis Press, 1996.

Graphis Logo: An International Compilation of Logos. Zurich, Switzerland: Graphis Press, 1996.

Gregory, R. L., *Eye and Brain*. New York: McGraw-Hill, 1966.

Gregory, R. L., *The Intelligent Eye*. New York: McGraw-Hill, 1970.

Letterhead and Logo Design: Creating the Corporate Image. Rockport, Mass.: Rockport Publishers, Distributed by North Light Books, 1996.

Meggs, Philip and Rob Carter, *Typographic Specimens and the Great Typefaces*. New York: Van Nostrand Reinhold, 1993.

Steuer, Sharon, *The Illustrator Wow! Book*. Berkeley, Calif.: Peachpit Press, 1995.

Zakia, Richard, *Perception and Photography*. Rochester, N.Y.: Light Impressions Corporation, 1979.

CHAPTERS 6–7

Text Type

Blackwell, Lewis, and David Carson, *The End of Print: The Grafik Design of David Carson*. San Francisco: Chronicle Books, 2000.

Carter, Rob, et al., *Typographic Design: Form and Communication*. New York: Van Nostrand Reinhold, 1985.

Craig, James, *Designing with Type*. New York: Watson-Guptill Publications, 1992.

Dair, Carl, *Design with Type*. Toronto: University of Toronto Press, 1982.

Dürer, Albrecht, *On the Just Shaping of Letters*. Mineola, N.Y.: Dover, 1965.

Giordin, Daniel (ed.), et al, *The Whole Mac: Solutions for the Creative Professional*. Indianapolis, Indiana: Hayden Books, 1996.

Graphis Book Design II. Zurich, Switzerland: Graphis Press, 1995.

Graphis Brochures, *An International Compilation of Brochure Design*. Zurich, Switzerland: Graphis Press, 1996.

McLean, Ruari, *Jan Tschichold: Typographer*. Boston: David R. Godine, 1975.

Massin, *Letter and Image*. New York: Van Nostrand Reinhold, 1970.

Ruder, Emil, *Typography*. New York: Hastings House, 1981.

Tschichold, Jan, *Asymmetric Typography*. New York: Van Nostrand Reinhold, 1980.

CHAPTERS 8–10

Color, Illustration, Advertising

Cabarga, Leslie, *Dynamic Black & White Illustration*. Glenbrook, Conn.: Art Direction Book Co, 1997.

Cassandre, A. M., *A. M. Cassandre*. St. Gall, Switzerland: Zollikoffer & Company, 1948.

The Creative Illustration Book #7. New York: The Black Book, 1996.

Delamare, Francois, and Bernard Guineau. *Colors: The Story of Dyes and Pigments*. New York: Abrams, 2000.

Douglas, Torin, *The Complete Guide to Advertising*. New York: Chartwell Books, Inc., 1984.

Dover Pictorial Archives. Mineola, N.Y.: Dover, 1979.

Graphis Advertising: The International Annual of Advertising. Zurich, Switzerland: Graphis Press, 1996.

Graphis Poster Design: The International Annual of Poster Art. Zurich, Switzerland: Graphis Press, 1996.

Haller, Lynn, *Fresh Ideas in Promotion*. Cincinnati, Ohio: North Light Books, 1994.

Heller, Steven, and Marshall Arisman, *The Education of an Illustrator*. New York: Allworth Press, 2000

Hurley, Gerald D., and Angus McDougall, *Visual Impact in Print*. Chicago: Visual Impact, Inc., 1971.

Itten, Johannes, *The Art of Color*. New York: Van Nostrand Reinhold, 1974.

Kerlow, Isaac V., and Judson Rosebush, *Computer Graphics for Artists and Designers*. New York: Van Nostrand Reinhold, 1994.

Koehler, Nancy, *Vietnam, The Battle Comes Home: Photos by Gordon Baer*. Dobbs Ferry, N.Y.: Morgan & Morgan, 1984.

Leland, Karyn, *Licensing Art & Design*. Cincinnati, Ohio: North Light Books, 1990.

Nyman, Mattias, *Four Colors/One Image*. Berkeley, Calif.: Peachpit Press, 1993.

Pitz, Henry, *200 Years of American Illustration*. New York: Random House, 1977.

Pring, Roger, and Alastair Campbell, *www .color*. New York: Watson-Guptill, 2000.

Steuer, Sharon, *The Illustrator Wow! Book*. Berkeley, Calif.: Peachpit Press, 1995.

Vaizey, Marina, *The Artist as Photographer*. New York: Holt, Rinehart and Winston, 1982.

Whelan, Richard, *Double Take*. New York: Clarkson N. Potter, 1981.

Wilson, Stephen, *Using Computers to Create Art*. Englewood Cliffs, N.J.: Prentice-Hall, 1986.

Zelanski, Paul, and Mary Pat Fisher. *Color*. Englewood Cliffs, N.J.: Prentice Hall, 1989.

Ziegler, Kathleen, *Digitaline Digital Design and Advertising*. Southhampton, Pa.: Dimensionals Illustrators, Inc., Distributed by North Light Books, 1996.

CHAPTERS 11–12

Production, Web Design

Bennett, James Gordon, *Design Fundamentals for New Media*. Clifton Park, N.Y.: Thomson Delmar Learning, 2005.

Blatner, David, and Steve Roth, *Real World Scanning and Halftones*. Berkeley, Calif.: Peachpit Press, 1993.

Chartier, Lee, and Scott Mason, *Creating Great Designs on a Limited Budget*. Cincinnati, OH: North Light Books, 1995.

Dennis, Ervin, Olusegun Odesina, and Daniel Wilson, *Lithographic Technology in Transition*. Thomson Delmar Learning, 1997.

Evans, Poppy, *The Graphic Designer's Source Book . . . An Indispensable Treasury of Suppliers*. Cincinnati, Ohio: North Light Books, 1996.

Giordin, Daniel (ed.), et al., *The Whole Mac: Solutions for the Creative Professional*. Indianapolis, Ind.: Hayden Books, 1996.

Gordon, Bob and Maggie Gordon. *The Complete Guide to Digital Graphic Design*. New York: Watson-Guptill, 2002.

Graphic Artists Guild Handbook: Pricing and Ethical Guidelines. New York: Graphic Artists Guild, 2002.

Hillman Curtis, *Flash Web Design*. Indianapolis, Ind.: New Riders, 2000.

Niederst, Jennifer, *Web Design in a Nutshell*. Sebastopol, Calif.: O'Reilly & Associates, 1999.

Pocket Pal. New York: International Paper Company, 2002.

Siegel, David, *Creating Killer Web Sites*. Indianapolis, Ind.: Hayden Books, 1997.

Towers, J. Tarin, *Dreamweaver for Windows & Macintosh: Visual Quickstart Guide*. Berkeley, Calif.: Peachpit Press, 2002.

Ulrich, Katherine, *Flash for Windows & Macintosh: Visual Quickstart Guide*. Berkeley, Calif.: Peachpit Press, 1999.

Ziegler, Kathleen, Nick Greco, and Tamye Riggs, *MotionGraphics Film and TV*. New York: Watson-Guptill, 2002.

Ziegler, Kathleen, Nick Greco, and Tamye Riggs, *MotionGraphics Web*. New York: Watson-Guptill, 2002.

Periodicals and Annuals

AIGA Graphic Design, USA. New York: Watson-Guptill Publications, annual, 1980–present.

Artists' Market: Where and How to Sell Your Artwork. Cincinnati, Ohio: Writers Digest Books.

Artnews. New York.

AV Video. Torrance, Calif.: Montage Publishing, Inc.

Ballast. Roy Behrens, ed., Dysart, Iowa: Boblink Books.

Communication Arts. Palo Alto, Calif.: Coyne & Blanchard, Inc.

Fine Print. San Francisco, Calif.

Graphic Artists' Guild, *Handbook of Pricing & Ethical Guidelines*. Cincinnati, Ohio: Writers Digest Books.

Graphis. Zurich, Switzerland: Walter Herdig.

How. New York: RC Publications.

Print. Washington, D.C.: RC Publications.

Print Casebooks. Washington, D.C.: RC Publications, six annual volumes, 1975–present.

Step-by-Step Graphics. Peoria, Ill.: Dynamic Graphics Educational Foundation (DGEF).

Women in the Arts. Washington, D.C.: National Museum of Women in the Arts.

INDEX